Politics, shipping and the repeal
of the navigation laws

Politics, shipping and the repeal of the navigation laws

Sarah Palmer

Manchester University Press
Manchester and New York
Distributed exclusively in the USA and Canada *by St. Martin's Press*

Copyright © Sarah Palmer 1990

Published by Manchester University Press
Oxford Road, Manchester M13 9LP, UK
and Room 400, 175 Fifth Avenue,
New York, NY 10010, USA

Distributed exclusively in the USA and Canada
by St. Martin's Press, Inc.,
175 Fifth Avenue, New York, NY 10010, USA

British Library cataloguing in publication data

Palmer, Sarah
    Politics, shipping and the repeal of navigation laws.
    1. Great Britain. Shipping, history
    I. Title
    387.510941

Library of Congress cataloging in publication data
Palmer, Sarah,1943-
    Politics, shipping, and the repeal of the navigation laws/Sarah Palmer.
        p.cm
    Includes bibliographical references and index.
    ISBN 0–7190–2399–8
    1. Shipping—Government policy—Great Britain—History.
2. Maritime law—Great Britain—History.   3. Great Britain—
Commercial policy—History.   I. Title.
HE823.P34   1990
387.5′ 1—dc20   90–6273

ISBN 0 7190 2399 8 *hardback*

Typset by Megaron, Cardiff, Wales
Printed in Great Britain
by Biddles Ltd., Guildford and King's Lynn

Contents

Tables

Figure

Abbreviations

Add. MS.	Additional Manuscripts
BL	British Library
GSS	General Shipowners' Society
GUA	Glasgow University Archives
KAO	Kent Archives Office
IHR	Institute of Historical Research
LCL	Liverpool City Libraries
LSE	London School of Economics and Political Science
MCC	Manchester Chamber of Commerce
MRO	Manchester Record Office
NMM	National Maritime Museum
PD	Hansard's Parliamentary Debates
PP	Parliamentary Papers
PRO	Public Record Office
S. C.	Select Committee
SS	Shipowners' Society
SUL	Southampton University Library

To Glyn
Jessica and Matthew

The navigation laws

Hail! Chiefs of Albion's mercantile marine!
Ye who have waked the patriotic voice
That heaves, and swells, and murmurs like the sea
And rings with loud acclaim through all the isle,
From shore to shore re-echoing; a voice
Of direful warning and prophetic truth,
To those, whose blind, erratic and misguided zeal,
Would alter or annul our maritime decrees,
Laws wisely framed to nourish, and uphold
What Englishmen in England's wooden walls have won,
The empire of the seas – a proud supremacy!
Outstripping far the fleets of all contending nations.

Patriots awake! Ye mariners arouse!
Rally round the flag your leaders hoist
Nail your unsullied colours to the mast;
With dauntless valour and unshaken front,
Your rights as free-born Englishmen defend!
And ye shall yet victoriously ride out
The battle and the storm, and England still
Shall lead the mighty commerce of the world.
Then be your watchwords in the sacred cause
'Ships, England and the Navigation Laws!'

Anon.; published in the *Shipping Gazette*, 16 February 1849.

Preface

The repeal of the Navigation Laws in 1849 brought to an end two centuries of legislative protection for British shipping, setting a pattern in the maritime sphere which has lasted until the present day. Repeal represented a major change in Britain's commercial policy, yet it has been largely neglected by both political and economic historians. The end of the Laws has proved a less compelling political event than the abolition of the Corn Laws, to which it has sometimes been seen as a mere postscript; and confusion as to how much protection the Navigation Laws provided in the 1840s has led some to conclude that repeal had little practical significance. Two historians must be excluded from this criticism. In *The Fall of the Old Colonial System*, R. L. Schuyler sets repeal within an imperial context and J.H. Clapham's two articles of 1910 in the *Economic History Review* must form the starting point for any understanding of the issues involved. Essentially, then, this book, which bestrides the conventional gulf between political and economic history, is an attempt to give the Navigation Laws and their repeal the attention they deserve as an important aspect of nineteenth-century British history. I hope also that it may go some way to support the growing claim of maritime history to be considered a field of historical study in its own right.

Numerous people have contributed in some way or other to the making of this study. My debt to the help I have received from archivists and librarians is reflected in the list of manuscript sources in the bibliography, but I particularly want to acknowledge the assistance of another maritime historian, Mr Michael Moss, of the Glasgow University Archives. The General Shipowners' Society features a great deal in these pages, and I am very grateful to the current Secretary, Mr Kenneth Hallpike, for allowing me access to its historical records. I owe a great debt to Professor Glyn Williams, who read through all the chapters and made many helpful comments. Finally, I should also like to express my gratitude to the British Academy for a grant which financed several research trips outside London.

S.P.

Queen Mary and Westfield College

September 1989

Chapter One

British shipping in the last decades
of protection

It is possible to understand the call for repeal of the Navigation Laws in the late 1840s and know nothing of the shipping and shipbuilding industries. The drive to pursue free trade into the port and shipyard was political; it owed little to demands outside Whitehall and Westminster. But to understand the reaction of shipowners and shipbuilders to this threat, the duration and scope of the ensuing debate and the impact of the final decision, requires some wider knowledge of the British shipping industry in the last decades of protection.

In 1815 Britain possessed almost 2.5 million tons of merchant shipping. By 1850 a further 1 million tons, virtually all built in British shipyards or those of its colonies, had been added to the United Kingdom register (Table 1). This was a reflection of growth after 1835, rather than over the period as a whole, since the immediate post-war years saw some decline in the size of the merchant fleet, though not to the extent suggested by the relevant register statistics, which were updated in 1827.[1] Nevertheless, at mid-century the fleet belonging to

Table 1. *British registered tonnage 1815/19–1845/49 (five-yearly averages, million tons)*

Years	Tons	Years	Tons
1815/19	2.461	1835/39	2.407
1820/24	2.352	1840/44	2.959
1825/29	2.262	1845/49	3.306
1830/34	2.254		

Source: Based on B. R. Mitchell, *British Historical Statistics*, Cambridge, 1988, pp. 535–6.

Britain was still more than twice the size of the seagoing fleet of the United States of America, its nearest maritime rival.[2]

In terms of tonnage the British merchant fleet grew by 40 per cent between 1820 and 1850, but the volume of goods it carried increased considerably more. British vessels in overseas trades entering and clearing United Kingdom ports with cargoes totalled an average 7.3 million tons annually in the late 1840s, almost twice the amount twenty years previously. Annual entries of shipping in the coasting trade, which had averaged 8.7 million tons in the years 1825 to 1830, had reached 12.7 million tons by the later 1840s.[3] A number of factors, by no means confined to this period, contributed to this greater productivity, including increases in vessel size and investment in port facilities. Steam also made an impact, though as much indirectly as directly. Contemporaries conventionally valued 1 ton of steam shipping at 3 tons of sail in terms of its potential for repeated voyages, but in 1850 registered steam tonnage still amounted to only 168,000 tons, much of this not seagoing. As important, though difficult to measure, was the effect of steam tugs in improving turnround times in port, by reducing the importance of tides, and by enabling vessels, as in the north east's rivers, to reach the open sea in the face of contrary winds. 'Steam', as one shipowner put it in 1844, 'has been the spur to everything'.[4]

Comparing the levels of port entries and clearances in the 1820s with those achieved in the later 1840s cannot, however, be taken as evidence of a generally favourable economic climate for shipping and ship-building over the period as a whole. Both industries necessarily danced to the tune of trade, but with a rhythm complicated by other themes. Demand for cargo space was sluggish in the first ten years following the end of the war, when export volumes grew slowly at a yearly average of only 2 per cent. Such circumstances encouraged shipowners to postpone ordering new tonnage, while at the same time the ending of the war meant a glut in second-hand tonnage which continued to depress shipbuilding until the mid-1830s. Following the repeal of the Bubble Act in 1825, some shipyards benefited from a short-lived boom in demand for steamships in the ensuing company mania.

For shipowners the upward movement in foreign trade which began to make itself felt at this time briefly boosted freight levels. By 1827, however, a sufficiently severe downturn had set in to provoke Huskisson into a major speech defending himself against the charge that this was due to the intrusion of foreign shipping following his reciprocity measures. Six years later, with freight rates still depressed, the shipping interest persuaded the government to agree to the appointment of a Select Committee, which heard evidence of a ten-year fall in freight rates: 40 per cent in the Mediterranean, a quarter to a third in the Baltic and by almost a half in the North American trade.[5]

By the later 1830s the prospects for both industries were much brighter. The Committee of the General Shipowners' Society rejoiced 'to be able to congratulate the shipping interest on some revival from the depression under which it for many years laboured'.[6] Revival fuelled demand for additional vessels. Between 1837 and 1841 British yards built 840,000 tons of shipping, – almost twice the output of the previous five years. North American colonial yards also benefited from the boom in demand.[7] By 1841 the inevitable reaction had set in. The demands of trade could not sustain the supply of tonnage; freights and values fell and orders for new vessels faded. At Sunderland the number of shipbuilding firms was halved in the space of three years.[8] The year 1844 saw yet another Select Committee appointed to examine the state of the industry, though in fact for shipowners the nadir proved to be 1843; trade in guano and corn improved prospects thereafter. Shipbuilders suffered more acutely and longer. Not until 1848 did capacity absorption permit resumption of an upward trend.[9]

There was nothing unique to the period 1820–50 in the fluctuating fortunes of shipping and shipbuilding. The problem of relating the supply of shipping space to the needs of commerce was perpetual in an industry where cheap second-hand vessels made entry relatively easy and demand ebbed and flowed. Undoubtedly, for individual investors in shipping, expectations of levels of return had been formed by wartime conditions and had to be adjusted to the realities of the post-war years, but there is little sign that this, or downturns in the market, discouraged shipowning. In any case, if freight rates were falling, so also were wages and operating costs. As G. R. Porter of the Board of Trade commented, 'although shipowners have certainly been very loud in their complaints as to their conditions and prospects, they have gone on adding, from year to year, to the amount of their tonnage'.[10] What was exceptional about these years was the degree and intensity of concern voiced by those in the shipping business. Its root was an assumption that the difficulties facing shipping must be abnormal because they coincided with new conditions – the changes in the protective system, instigated by Huskisson, which had, in the view of

3

shipowners, made certain British trades more attractive to foreign shipping. Depression was blamed on foreign competition.

But to set aside for the present the question of how much trade in these last years of protection was carried by vessels belonging to other nations, let us look in general terms at how Britain's shipping was deployed. In 1824 the nation's registered tonnage stood at 2.349 million tons. In which trades, and in which regions, did this shipping find work? It is impossible for the most part to answer these questions directly. The shipping registers themselves, even if they could be analysed on the scale required, would provide little assistance. In the East Indies trade the size of vessel proclaimed its vocation but this was the exception. Some owners specialised in particular trades, but it cannot be assumed that ships did so also. The typical deep and narrow ocean-going merchant vessel averaged only 200–250 tons even by the 1840s and the life cycle of a vessel might take it through several existences, moving from distant to nearer trades as time and the sea took its toll on hull and rigging. But even the space of a few years could see a vessel used on voyages to the Baltic, South America and the West Indies as her owners responded to opportunities for cargo.[11]

If the non-specialised nature of much shipping means that no ready connection can be made between build and a particular trade, the details of entries and clearances collected by the local Customs, and collated to provide the national figures to which we have already referred, do provide a means of approach. In shipping it is volume and distance that matter most; trade values are of lesser significance. Bulk commodities, like timber and coal, contributed much more to the earnings of shipping than they did to the value of trade. Thanks to the work of Imlah, trade values have been translated into volume indices so it is now possible to trace the movement of trade volume over time, but such published data relates to total trade; it is not disaggregated.[12] The entry and clearance statistics have their limitations: until 1827 they do not distinguish between vessels in ballast or with cargo, they relate to the last and first ports of call and increasingly important by the 1840s fail to reflect accurately the movement of passenger-carrying steamers.[13] But, by counting repeated voyages, they provide the best indication we have of which trades employed the most tonnage and hence were of the greatest significance to the British shipping industry.

Table 2 shows the percentage share of various regions in the tonnage of British-owned shipping entering United Kingdom ports in 1824 and 1841. It is clear from the totals for foreign and coasting entries that the routine business of transporting goods along Britain's coastline, into her rivers and across the Irish Channel employed the greatest amount of tonnage, though comparatively less so by the later date. By far the most important overseas trade, accounting for almost a quarter of the total in both years, was the softwood timber trade with British North America. Timber, a veritable devourer of shipping space, also contributed to the demand for shipping in the Baltic trades. But discriminatory duties and the role of foreign shipping meant that timber accounts only in part for the volume of northern European business handled by British vessels. Other bulk commodities – hemp, flax, tallow and, in the case of 1841, grain – were also important here. Cotton and sugar were more distant trades requiring plenty of tonnage, and the share of vessels coming from the United States of America and from the West Indies reflects this.

The composition of British overseas trade in the post-war years was such that the shipping space needed for the export of cargoes from Britain fell well short of that for imports. The volume of cotton goods sold overseas continued to grow, but coal, Britain's truly bulk product, had not yet assumed the central role in demand for foreign-going

Table 2. *Regional deployment of British shipping 1824, 1841: voyages ('000 tons)*

	1824		1841	
	Tonnage		Tonnage	
From	*Entered*	%	*Entered*	%
North Europe	369	22	399	13
Near Europe	218	13	788	25
Mediterranean	184	11	275	9
Africa	23	1	77	2
United States of America	44	3	121	4
British N. America	427	25	841	27
West Indies	254	15	217	7
South America	46	3	119	4
Asia	80	5	245	8
Australasia	4	0	29	1
Fisheries	45	3	13	0
Total Overseas	1,694	100	3,124	100
Coastal & Channel Islands	8,320		11,036	

Sources: Calculations based on 'Statement of the Tonnage Entered Inwards . . .', *S. C. British Shipping*, PP 1844 VIII, pp. 217–20 and *Accounts Relating to Shipping from 1815 to 1852*, PP 1852 XLIX, p. 22.

shipping which it was later to play. Re-exports to some extent compensated, but even so 27 per cent of outward bound vessels British and foreign in 1827 sailed in ballast. By the 1840s the situation was changing. In 1842 for the first time the tonnage of vessels with cargo cleared through British ports exceeded that of those entering.[14]

Two points should be kept in mind in connection with the information in Table 2. First, it deals only with British shipping, not with all shipping coming into and leaving British ports; the important question of the part played by foreign owned shipping has still to be considered. Second, it is concerned only with the United Kingdom, so tells us nothing of the role of British ships as carriers in trades which did not touch on the home country. On this there are no comprehensive records, although a Board of Trade return for 1846, which shows that 16 per cent of ships entering and clearing major European ports were not in direct trade with Britain, is suggestive.[15]

The tally of repeated voyages shows where British vessels found most work but not how much actual shipping was involved. There is no easily discernible relationship between the entry statistics shown in Table 2 and the information on the size of the mercantile marine which appears in Table 1. Yet it is clearly desirable to have some impression of the distribution of shipping investment between the various types of business. Fortunately, with the aid of contemporary estimates of the number of voyages which vessels in particular trades would be likely to make on average over a year, it is possible to use the entry statistics to arrive at a rough breakdown of the merchant fleet to show the actual amount of tonnage each trade employed. For example, on the assumption that vessels in the Russian trade would undertake two voyages a year, with the recorded tonnage of entries amounting to 294,000 tons in 1841, the actual tonnage of shipping employed was 147,000 tons.[16] The results of this fairly crude analysis appear in Table 3. What emerges here is the dominant proportion of Britain's total merchant fleet employed in the more distant, oceanic, trades. This is hardly a surprising conclusion, given the fact that distance alone meant that a vessel could be used much more intensively in trade with the Continent than in trade across the Atlantic. But it deserves emphasis in the context of the present study, where the importance of particular trades to the shipping interest is a central issue. In 1841 4,399 vessels entering British ports came from the colonies, amounting to 1.3 million tons of shipping, rather less than half the total of all entries from overseas. But perhaps almost 1 million tons of shipping was involved in this protected trade; 60 per cent of Britain's overseas fleet. If in the early nineteenth century Britain's ports were busy with coasters and with vessels completing short voyages to and from European ports, the real focus of the industry's capital was more distant, and lucrative, business.

Table 3. *Estimated regional deployment of British shipping 1824, 1841: vessels (% share of total tonnage in overseas trade)*

Trade	1824	1841
Northern Europe	16	11
Near Europe	3	7
Mediterranean	7	7
Africa	2	4
United States of America	2	4
British N. America	25	30
West Indies	17	9
South America	4	6
Asia	10	19
Australasia	1	3
Fisheries	13	2

Source: Based on 'Statement of the Tonnage entered Inwards . . . with a Calculation of the Real Tonnage upon the average number of voyages', *S. C. British Shipping*, PP 1844 VIII, pp. 218–20.

In 1815 the British shipping industry remained in its organisation and technology substantially as it had been a hundred years earlier. It was a much larger industry, for the impetus given to trade by industrialisation and population growth had increased the fleet by 1 million tons after 1790. Shipping and shipbuilding, long-established industries, capitalist before capitalism, had responded to the new opportunities without much disturbance to the existing framework. A revolution had taken place in cargo-handling for this is how the progress of dock-building in Bristol, Hull, London and Liverpool should properly be viewed, which had implications for efficiency. Yet set within the context of overwhelming traditional practice, the impact of dock development, like the improvement in ship design which led to the merchant schooner or the enhancement of performance in the coal trade, was hardly profound.[17] Despite some claims to the contrary, any revolution in shipping still lay in the future. The settled features of the industry were much more in evidence than any tendency to alteration. But in the years between the coming of peace and the ending of protection for British shipping and shipbuilding at mid-century, this stability began to give way to change, with the application of steam power the most visible development.

The first steamboat to be put to commercial use went into service on the Clyde in 1812. Thereafter the technical feasibility of steam in most contexts was established fairly rapidly but the subsequent spread of the new marine technology was uneven, moving in stages from rivers, to cross-channel, Irish Sea and coastal trades in the 1820s, to the near sea business in the 1830s and across the Atlantic only in the 1840s.[18] Engine efficiency was the key element governing the introduction of steam on increasingly longer routes. As this improved, and bunkers gave way to cargoes, so the financial prospects for steam vessels were progressively transformed. However, not until the 1850s, with the adoption of screw propulsion and iron hulls, did the steamship begin to present a genuine economic alternative to sail, and even then the older technology was to prove resilient.[19] For this reason, the transition from wooden paddle steamer to iron screw steamship is often seen as merely the infantile prelude to the coming of age of marine steam power in the second half of the century. But if the test is not the extent to which steam replaced sail, but the growth of a distinct branch of the shipping and shipbuilding industries, then the impact of steam in this period can be seen as of different significance.

High capital and running costs for these early steamers, as much as the speed and regularity of service which they could provide, dictated frequent operation over defined advertised routes. These conditions encouraged restriction of competition as well as in some, though not all, ports a type of investment previously unknown in shipping; the joint stock company.[20] From the late 1830s, steamship services were artificially nurtured on the oceans by government mail contracts. The Peninsular & Oriental, Royal Mail and Cunard companies were all beneficiaries here.[21] Elsewhere, in the absence of government subsidy, the most important determinant of commercial success in steamship enterprise was the availability of a sufficient volume of business, able to bear higher freight rates, which would permit frequent voyages to be undertaken. For this reason, steam proved particularly suited to the carriage of passengers, livestock and perishable goods. But these were new shipping markets to a large extent created by the availability of swift, and for the most part reliable, steam services. Sail and steam were not rivals here. As Brodie McGhie Willcox, a founder of the Peninsular and Oriental Steam Ship Company, explained in 1844:

With regard to the coasting trade, I do not think that steam navigation has at all materially interfered with that trade; much of the conveyance now by coasting in steam vessels has taken existence from steam navigation, such as whole cargoes of cattle and dead meat, which never came by sailing vessels. All the main articles conveyed coastwise are still left untouched to the sailing coasting vessels, such as iron, copper, lead, stone, lime, coals, timber.[22]

A similar division between sail and steam also emerged in ship-building, though more gradually. The first steamboats consisted of wooden hulls built in yards by the same firms which built sailing vessels, to which were added boilers and engines usually constructed elsewhere. These early vessels were a combination of the traditional skills of the wooden shipbuilder with the new, still experimental skills of the engineer; hermaphrodites rather than hybrids. The reshaping and strengthening of established hull forms was the only concession possible to the demands of the new power. As boiler pressures increased and the screw propeller gained adherents among steamship operators, so the limitations of wood in terms of strength and rigidity became apparent. By the early 1840s the way was open for iron shipbuilding, dominated by engineers who had little connection with the traditional ship-wrights' skills.[23]

The consequence, then, of the intrusion of steam into maritime enterprise up to mid-century was the creation of a separate sector; a new industry existing alongside the old. This duality, rather than the relatively small share of steamship tonnage in Britain's merchant fleet, helps to explain one puzzling feature of discussion in the 1840s on the repeal of the Navigation Acts – a remarkable absence of reference to the potential of steam in ensuring the future general competitiveness of British shipping. For most observers, both within and outside the industry, sail and steam were different spheres. Later commentators, their view distorted by the role of steam in the subsequent success of British shipping and shipbuilding, have sometimes seen Britain's abandonment of protection as evidence of confidence in the new technology, or even of British duplicity in encouraging other powers to follow its lead. There is no historical basis for this suggestion.

Britain's merchant fleet was the product of a great commitment of capital, labour and skill. The ships themselves represented in 1830 perhaps 2.6 per cent of the nation's gross capital stock. But any assessment of activity directly associated with the industry, besides that connected with docks and harbours, must also take into account investment in the yards where vessels were built and repaired, and in the variety of ancillary businesses associated with their equipment. One contemporary estimate assessed the industry's capital in 1846 at 56 million, of which over a third was accounted for by the shipyard industries.[24]

In terms of its workforce, the shipping industry involved a variety of skills. In 1847 G. F. Young listed the following trades as part of the shipbuilding branch: shipwrights, shipping ropemakers, sailmakers, mast and block makers, coopers, ship joiners, ship blacksmiths, ship sawyers, ship painters, riggers, ship chandlers, ship coppersmiths, ship brassworkers, ship plumbers and glaziers.[25] Had Young paid due attention to steam shipping, he would also have identified marine boilermakers and engineers. A similarly all-embracing definition on the carrying side would have included not only seafarers but also ship and insurance brokers, underwriters, surveyors, agents, victuallers, pilots and harbour masters, lodging-house keepers, slopsellers and crimps. Unfortunately it is not possible to distinguish all these trades in the occupational information supplied for the 1841 Census of Great Britain. Ropemakers, for example, did not only meet the demands of shipping, and the job of boatman might have more to do with cross-river ferrying than with the shipping industry. Even the indisputably maritime category of shipowner cannot be treated as representing the true number of those deriving income from shipping, for reasons to be considered shortly. Nevertheless, provided it is treated with due caution, the Census evidence, summarised in Table 4, provides some guide to the numbers of those involved and leaves no doubt as to the importance of the industry in a total labour force of about 8 million.[26]

Among all those who made their living directly from shipping the key figure was the shipowner: the provider of capital and the employer of labour. In the first half of the nineteenth century most ships were owned by individuals, though some steamships were owned by companies, and the basic unit of investment was the vessel herself. An interest in a ship was established through the ownership of shares, typically denominated as fractions of sixty-four. Legally, shipping investors were tenants-in-common, rather than partners. They could freely sell, subdivide or mortgage their share irrespective of the wishes of the other shareholders. Lord Liverpool's Act of 1786, which required the registration of all vessels over 15 tons, meant that in

Table 4. *Maritime-related occupations in Great Britain, 1841*

Occupation	Number
Shipbuilder, carpenter, shipwright	20,242
Boat and barge builder	2,924
Anchorsmith and chainmaker	1,852
Block, oar and mastmaker	1,488
Sail, sailcloth and tarpaulin maker	3,883
Caulker	614
Rigger	727
Shipsmith	180
Chandler	211
Ropemaker, cordspinner and maker	11,319
Nautical instrument maker	25
Shipbreaker	10
Ship and smack owner	1,153
Boat owner	187
Shipping agent and broker	782
Boatman	24,192
Harbourmaster	145
Pilot	2,157
Seaman – ashore	45,915
Seaman – at sea	138,156
TOTAL	256,162

Source: *1841 Census of Population*, PP 1844 (587)(588) XXVII.

addition to details of a ship, the names of all shareholders together with their occupations and addresses were officially recorded in each port of registration's 'Registry of Shipping'. A large number of these registers have survived and enough have been the subject of study by local historians to make it possible to write with some confidence about the major features of shipowning. The summary which follows draws upon this work.[27]

The first point which needs to be made is that throughout the period with which we are concerned it is more accurate to speak of 'investors in shipping' than 'shipowners', when dealing with the industry as a whole. There is some debate between maritime historians as to when shipowning as a specialised occupation first emerged. Certainly by the beginning of our period there were men who depended sufficiently for their living on ships for this term to appear in directories, in the ship registers and to be encountered by the Census enumerators. Nevertheless, the most common type of investor in shipping in the largest ports, London and Liverpool, was not properly described as a shipowner. 'I do not know where to find a legitimate shipowner: I mean a man that depends on it entirely', commented the Liverpool shipowner Henry Chapman in 1844. Rather, the person who put money into ships tended to be someone who had broader maritime or commercial connections, perhaps as a merchant, shipbuilder or master. Only 26 per cent of those holders of shipping shares recorded in the London registers for 1824 chose to describe themselves as 'shipowner'. In 1848 they made up 37 per cent; a marked increase but still not the majority.[28]

If an association with some sea-related activity characterised investors in shipping over the country as a whole, so also did the local nature of their investment. Not all ships operated out of the port where they were registered, but the overwhelming majority of shareholders, including those who were specialist shipowners, recorded in the registers for any particular port came from that place or the surrounding region. Subsequent transfers of shares also tended to involve individuals living in a common geographical area.

In the coal trade and whaling, both highly organised integrated businesses, vessel and cargo normally had the same owners. 'The shipowner is the merchant buying and selling coals', explained Biddle to the Lords' Select Committee on the Coal Trade in 1829, 'coal owners only resort to freighting when prices are so low that they cannot get shipowners to buy.'[29] But evidence to the two parliamentary committees which investigated the shipping industry in the 1830s and 1840s suggests that such integration was the exception in the industry as a whole. Merchants who invested in ships might do so as a venture totally independent of their trading concerns, or combine the two interests as particular circumstances dictated. The mesh of personal contact in port communities, together with informed mercantile interest in the prospects for certain cargoes, as well as the practice of repaying shipbuilders and rewarding masters were among the factors encouraging ownership of shares in vessels.[30]

No doubt some of those who put money into shipping knew little of the industry and were pure speculators, but this seems to have been the exception to judge from the relatively small number of investors who appear in the London and Liverpool registers with no evident maritime occupational connection. This supports G. F. Young's impression 'that ships are much more extensively owned by those who have pursued maritime commerce practically, than by capitalists who simply embark their money in it as an advantageous investment'.[31] Specialist shipowners routinely complained when high freights brought a surge of investment in vessels intended for speculative voyages. But an element of sensitivity to new opportunities was always present in trading and maritime circles, and these, rather than groups totally ignorant of the business, were the main source of the additional capital which tended to flow fairly readily into the industry when prospects seemed promising.

Nevertheless, although specialist shipowners were at mid-century still outnumbered by other investors, the evidence of the shipping registers shows, first, that they were a larger presence in terms of tonnage held than fifty years earlier; and second, that this was associated with an increasing separation of the functions of merchant and shipowner. The interests of carriage and commerce were always potentially in conflict, with the profits of one the costs of the other. Now the two were becoming increasingly identified with separate occupational categories. It was a development with political as much as economic implications.

This trend towards specialisation revealed by analysis of the registers was also noted by some contemporaries. In a letter of 1826, Swinton C. Holland, a partner in Baring Brothers, reported:

Within the last thirty years, the shipowners of London have entirely changed character; the increase of population, and extent of the Metropolis, has given a natural division of labour, and except in some peculiar trades, either that enjoy a monopoly from charter, or a monopoly from the mortgage of the West India Planters' land, the merchant and the shipowner are becoming two distinct classes.

Holland detected a similar tendency in Liverpool, and to some extent in Bristol, but not yet in the east-coast ports. His explanation, that the widening of the market was a factor encouraging greater functional specialisation, is convincing.[32]

Another development discernible through the shipping registers, a movement away from shared ownership by several individuals towards only one or two, suggests that investing in shipping was less of a financial risk than was the case in the past. In the light of the often depressed state of shipping in the post-war decades, it seems unlikely that shipping was perceived as a more settled, safer business, though in contrast with the war years this may have been to some extent true. Rather the key element was perhaps the availability of cheap tonnage, which meant that the necessity to divide the ownership of a vessel, with all the implications for management and division of profit, was less pressing.

It might be expected that increasing specialisation in shipowning would have been accompanied by greater concentration of ownership. Some individuals certainly owned large quantities of tonnage. In 1847, for example, Duncan Dunbar had interests in twenty-four ships totalling 15,000 tons, while the government transport contractor, Joseph Somes, who on his death in 1845 left an estate valued at £434,000, was commonly identified as one of the greatest shipowners in the country. The largest investor in shipping at this time was, however, probably the less publicly prominent Baltic merchant and insurance broker, Richard Thornton, who left over 2 million when he died in 1865. Studies of some smaller ports have also revealed the local dominance of certain individuals or families, as in the case of the Whites at Sunderland and the Chapmans at Whitby.[33] But when set against the millions of tons owned nationally the share of such men was miniscule and there is nothing to suggest any progressive movement of tonnage into fewer hands. Indeed, if the evidence of the representatives of the shipping interests to various parliamentary committees is to be believed, the tendency was rather the other way. In any case entry to the industry in terms of capital required was too easy, the unit of ownership – the ship – too small in relation to total tonnage, the industry too geographically dispersed and the trades too distinct, for such concentration to seem likely. Conditions favoured oligopoly only when merchanting and shipowning were closely identified throughout a particular trade, where access to cargo might perhaps not be open to all, or for commercial reasons, as in the case of steam shipping, but such instances were not typical of the industry as a whole.

Although the registers of shipping do allow us to identify certain characteristic features of the investing group, it is impossible to draw any firm conclusion about social status or economic motive merely from the fact that a certain individual owned shares in ships. The investment might represent a rare speculative venture, an established sideline to a main occupation or the main source of income. If the last, the individual concerned might be a shipowner on a large scale, a wealthy man of clear upper middle-class status. Alternatively, while no less justified in calling himself a shipowner, he could be of much more humble means; perhaps a former master who had fulfilled a lifetime's ambition to call a vessel his own. In his study of nineteenth-century wealth, W. D. Rubinstein has identified shipping as an industry with an exceptionally high rate of upward mobility for the individual capitalist.[34] Certainly, as far as the first half of the century is concerned, there is no shortage of examples of men who began in a small way with only one vessel, but who from this modest start were able to move to ownership of a substantial fleet, though more often making their money from broking or agency than directly from freight. In an industry with so many participants it is hardly surprising that some with exceptional enterprise, or luck, were able to make their fortune, but it would be wrong to see their experience as typical. For the majority, investment in shipping was the means not of changing social and economic status but of confirming it.

A similar diversity characterised shipbuilding. Vessels were built in ports, major and minor, and in small harbours and creeks all along the British coastline, but in the 1820s the major southern concentrations were in London, and between the Thames and the Bristol Channel. At this time Scotland was relatively unimportant; in the north, the Mersey and the north-east's rivers had the greatest output. By the early 1840s, however, the geographical location of the industry was beginning to change. In terms of shipbuilding employment, the north-east had overtaken London, with the growth of Sunderland's output regarded by contemporaries as a particularly noteworthy development. Scotland's share of total output had also increased, with the Clyde already established as a steamship-producing river. Specialisation in different standards of vessels muted direct competition between these centres. In any one year London prices per ton could be a third higher than those in the north-east. Thus the Thames and Wear, to take the two extremes in terms of quality and cost, were not rivals. There was in any case a tendency to produce for local demand, and one effect of the LLoyd's Registry classification system, whereby vessels built in certain ports were automatically assigned a certain rating, was to reinforce this established pattern of production.[35]

Large, family-dominated, shipbuilding establishments existed on the Thames, Tyne and Clyde, but these were the aristocracy of the business; they were not representative of the industry as a whole. The fine ships built by Wigram & Green at Blackwall had little in common with those produced at Sunderland; neither did the shipbuilders. At the lower end of the market, working men employed each other, and co-operative ventures, sometimes created in the wake of trade disputes, were not unusual. Capital requirements for building the 200 ton timber sailing vessels typically required by shipowners were not high;

in the north-east yards timber merchants were a major source of
finance. Working shipwrights commonly made the transition to
master, and back again; but not always without loss. As the shipowner
Joshua Wilson commented in 1848, 'working men with ordinary
management may make a very fair living at the trade, but they have
not the capital to stand against the sudden times of depression to which
shipbuilders are liable sometimes and to the large bad debts from
trusting so much money in one hand'.[36] Shipbuilding was a risky
business, but, like shipowning, exerted a powerful attraction to men of
relatively small means.

Finally, if the vessels which sailed regularly from individual ports
were usually owned, and had often also been built, in the surrounding
region, local interest was confirmed by trade specialisation. Geography
determined each port's pattern of activity: the Thames, Humber and
Forth handled European trade; transatlantic traffic entered the
Mersey, Clyde and the Severn; and coal was still shipped primarily out
of the Tyne, Wear and Tees. In fact, as Table 5 shows, in the first half of
the nineteenth century just four ports, London, Liverpool, Newcastle
and Hull, together handled two-thirds of the nation's traffic, with
London and Liverpool, respectively accounting for 27 per cent and 22
per cent of the tonnage of shipping entering Britain from overseas in
the early 1840s. But these statistics reflect the concentration of trade,

Table 5. *Foreign-going vessels entering the principal UK ports, cargo and ballast, 1820/
24 and 1840/44 (five-yearly averages, '000 tons)*

	1820–24		1840–44	
Entries	Tons	%	Tons	%
UK total	2,225.2		4,741.4	
London	779.2	35.0	1,313.6	27.7
Liverpool	444.2	20.0	1,053.0	22.2
Hull	160.8	7.2	335.0	7.1
Bristol	63.2	2.8	82.8	1.7
Newcastle	56.6	2.5	326.0	6.9
Leith	47.7	2.1	83.0	1.8
Southampton	26.4	1.2	119.4	2.5
Greenock	44.8	2.0	72.0	1.5
Glasgow	4.4	0.2	50.8	1.1

Source: Gordon Jackson, 'The ports', in Michael J. Freeman and Derek H.
Aldcroft, *Transport in Victorian Britain*, Manchester, 1988, p. 220.

not any limitation on the geographical extent of maritime activity. The official returns for 1841 identify no fewer than 110 foreign trade ports, although this might mean entries and clearances of less than 1,000 tons of shipping over the year.[37] If coastwise business were also to be included, the number of places which served in some sense as a port would be even greater. The British shipping industry as it existed in the early nineteenth century was not a truly national entity, but rather a collection of localities.

Notes

1 On the registration system see the evidence of W. H. Noss, Registrar of Shipping, to the *Select Committee of the House of Lords on the Policy and Operation of the Navigation Laws*, PP 1847–48 (340)(431)(754) XX Pt. II, Q. 7651–763.

2 *Comparative Trade Statistics*, PP 1903 [C. 1761] LXVII, pp. 688–9. On the general history of the nineteenth-century British shipping industry see G. Jackson, 'The shipping industry' and P. S. Bagwell and J. Armstrong, 'Coastal shipping', in Michael J. Freeman and Derek H. Aldcroft, *Transport in Victorian Britain*, Manchester, 1988, pp. 171–217, 253–83.

3 *Accounts and Papers*, PP 1852–53 LVII, p. 200; 1852 XLIX, p. 376.

4 *Report from the Select Committee appointed to inquire into the state and condition of the Commercial Marine of the Country, and to take into consideration and report on the best mode of encouraging and extending the employment of British Shipping*, 1844 (545) VIII, Q. 609.

5 *Report from the Select Committee on the present state of Manufactures, Commerce and Shipping in the United Kingdom*, 1833 (690) VI, Q. 519, Q. 802–5.

6 General Shipowners' Society, (GSS) *Report of the Committee to the Annual General Meeting of Subscribers*, 16 April 1839.

7 Mitchell, *Historical Statistics*, p. 420; *Return of the Number of Colonial Built Ships registered at each Port of the United Kingdom 1841–1846*, PP 1847 (309) LX, p. 309.

8 *Lords S. C. Navigation Laws*, PP 1847–48, XX Pt. II, Q. 4075.

9 On cyclical fluctuation in shipping and shipbuilding see Arthur D. Sayer, W. W. Rostow and Anna Jacobson Schwartz, *The Growth and Fluctuation of the British Economy 1790 – 1850*, 2 vols, Oxford, 1953; R. C. O. Matthews, *A Study in Trade Cycle History*, Cambridge, 1954, pp. 118–20; A. Slaven, 'The shipbuilding industry', in Roy Church (ed.), *The Dynamics of Victorian Business: Problems and Perspectives to the 1870s*, London, 1980; A. H. Imlah, *Economic Elements in the Pax Britannica*, Cambridge, Mass., 1958.

10 *Reports from the Select Committee of the House of Commons to Inquire into the Operation and Policy of the Navigation Laws*, 1847 (232)(246)(392)(556) (678) X, Q. 6118.

11 On the characteristics of shipping in this period see Basil Greenhill, *The Ship: the Life and Death of the Merchant Sailing Ship 1815–1965*, London, 1980, pp. 5–19. For examples of varied deployment of vessels see Sarah Palmer,

'John Long: a London shipowner', *Mariner's Mirror*, LXXII, 1986, pp. 43–61.

12 Imlah, *Economic Elements*, Table 8, pp. 94–8.

13 See the discussion of the entry and clearance statistics by G. R. Porter, *Lords S. C. Navigation Laws*, PP 1847–48 XX Pt. II, Q. 128–152.

14 Imlah, *Economic Elements*, p. 135n; *Account of the Amount of Tonnage employed in the Foreign and Coasting Trade stated exclusive of vessels in ballast*, PP 1852 (376) XLIX, p. 17.

15 *Lords S. C. Navigation Laws*, PP 1847–48 XX Pt. II, Q. 5161.

16 Estimates of the average annual number of voyages were supplied by the General Shipowners' Society to the *S. C. British Shipping*, PP 1844 VIII, Appendix 2, pp. 217–20.

17 See R. Davis, 'Maritime history: progress and problems', in S. Marriner (ed.), *Business and Businessmen*, Liverpool, 1978, pp. 167–87. On productivity in the coal trade, see S. Ville, 'Total factor productivity in the English shipping industry: the north east coal trade, 1700–1850', *Economic History* Review, 2nd ser., XXXIX, 1986, pp. 355–70 and William J. Hausman 'The English coastal coal trade, 1691–1910: how rapid was productivity growth?', *Economic History Review*, 2nd ser., XL, 1987, pp. 588–96. On the technical developments in sail during the early years of industrialisation, see Alan McGowan, *The Ship: the Century Before Steam: the Development of the Sailing Ship 1700–1820*, London, 1980.

18 For the early technical history of steam shipping see K. T. Rowland, *Steam at Sea: a History of Steam Navigation*, Newton Abbott, 1970; Sarah R. Palmer, 'Experiment, experience and economics: some factors in the development of the early merchant steamship', in Keith Matthews and Gerald Panting (eds), *Ships and Shipbuilding in the North Atlantic Region*, St John's, Newfoundland, 1977, pp. 231–47. Early commercial aspects are covered in P. Bagwell, 'The Post Office steam packets 1821–1836 and the development of shipping on the Irish Sea', *Maritime History*, I, 1971, pp. 4–28; C. H. Lee, 'Some aspects of the coastal shipping trade: The Aberdeen Steam Navigation Company , 1835–1880', *Journal of Transport History*, new ser., VIII, 1975, pp. 94–107; Sarah Palmer, 'The most indefatigable activity – the General Steam Navigation Company 1824–1850', *Journal of Transport History*, 3rd ser., III, 1982, pp. 1–22.

19 Gerald S. Graham, 'The ascendancy of the sailing ship 1855–1885', *Economic History Review*, 2nd ser., IX, 1956, pp. 74–88; Charles K. Harley, 'The shift from sailing ships to steamships 1850–1890', in Donald N. Mccloskey (ed.), *Essays on a Mature Economy: Britain after 1840*, Harvard, 1971, pp. 215–34.

20 The connection between joint stock investment and steam shipping was strong in the case of London, less so in the case of Liverpool. See Sarah Palmer, 'Investors in London shipping 1820 – 1850', *Maritime History*, II, 1972, p. 52 and P. L. Cottrell, 'The steamship on the Mersey 1815–1880: investment and ownership', in P. L. Cottrell and D. H. Aldcroft (eds), *Shipping, Trade and Commerce: Essays in Memory of Ralph Davis*, Leicester, 1981, p. 143.

21 See P. N. Davies, 'The development of the liner trades', in Keith Matthews

and Gerald Panting, *Ships and Shipbuilding in the North Atlantic Region*, St John's, Newfoundland, 1978, pp. 173–206; Freda Harcourt, ' British oceanic mail contracts in the age of steam 1838–1914', *Journal of Transport History*, 3rd ser., IX, 1988, pp. 1–18.

22 *S. C. British Shipping*, PP 1844 VIII, Q. 1134.

23 Slaven, 'Shipbuilding industry', p. 123; Sydney Pollard and Paul Robertson, *The British Shipbuilding Industry 1870–1914*, Cambridge, Mass., 1979.

24 C. H. Feinstein, 'Capital formation in Great Britain', in P. Mathias and M. M. Postan (eds), *Cambridge Economic History of Europe, VII Part I*, Cambridge, 1977, pp. 42, 63–5; *Commons S. C. Navigation Laws*, PP 1847 X, Q. 6101–6118. On the problems of measuring capital investment in shipping, see also R. Craig, 'Capital formation in shipping', in J. P. P. Higgins and Sidney Pollard (eds), *Aspects of Capital Investment in Great Britain 1750 – 1850: a Preliminary Survey*, London, 1971, pp. 131–48.

25 *Commons S. C. Navigation Laws*, PP 1847 X, Q. 6108.

26 *Census of Population 1841, Great Britain – Occupation*, PP 1844 (587)(588) XXVII, p. 587 (England), p. 588 (Scotland).

27 R. C. Jarvis, 'Fractional shareholding in British merchant shipping', *Mariner's Mirror*, XLV, 1959, p. 301; R. S. Craig, 'The ports and shipping, c.1750–1914', in Arthur John and G. Williams (eds), *Glamorgan County History V: Industrial Glamorgan 1700–1970*, Cardiff, 1980; F. Neal, 'Liverpool shipping in the early nineteenth century', in J. R. Harris (ed.), *Liverpool and Merseyside: Essays in the Economic and Social History of the Port and its Hinterland*, Liverpool, 1969; Cottrell, 'Steamship on the Mersey'; Sarah Palmer, 'Investors in London shipping 1820–1850', *Maritime History*, II, 1972, pp. 46–57; Stephanie Jones, 'A Maritime History of the Port of Whitby 1700–1914', unpublished Ph.D. thesis, University of London, 1982; S. Jones, 'Shipowning in Boston, Lincs.' *Mariner's Mirror*, LXV, 1979 pp. 339–48.

28 *S. C. on Shipping*, PP 1844 VIII, Q. 952; Palmer, 'Investors in London shipping'.

29 See Simon P. Ville, *English Shipowning during the Industrial Revolution, Michael Henley and Son, London Shipowners 1770–1830*, Manchester, 1987; Gordon Jackson, *The British Whaling Trade*, London, 1978; *Report from the Select Committee of the House of Lords on the State of the Coal Trade*, PP 1830 (663) VIII, Q. 69.

30 *S. C. Manufactures, Commerce and Shipping*, PP 1833 VI; *S. C. on Shipping*, PP 1844 VIII.

31 *Commons S. C. Navigation Laws*, PP 1847 X, Q. 6093.

32 BL, Huskisson Papers, Add. MS. 38748 ff. 217–28, Holland to George Lyall, 17 December 1826.

33 *Lords S. C. Navigation Laws*, PP 1847–48 XX Pt II, Q. 7756–7; *Report from the Select Committee on the Dartmouth Election Petition*, PP 1845 (164) XII, Q. 1386; KAO, Colyer Fergusson Papers, U295, f14; W. D. Rubinstein, 'British millionaires – 1809–1949', *Bulletin of the Institute of Historical Research*, XLVII, 1974, p. 207; Simon Ville, 'Rise to pre-eminence: the development and growth of the Sunderland shipbuilding industry, 1800–

50', *International Journal of Maritime History*, I, 1989, p. 81.
34 W. D. Rubinstein, *Men of Property: the Very Wealthy in Britain Since the Industrial Revolution*, London, 1981, p. 98.
35 Slaven, 'Shipbuilding'; Anthony Slaven, 'Shipbuilding', in John Langton and R. J. Morris (eds), *Atlas of Industrialising Britain 1780–1914*, 1986, p. 132; C. H. Lee, *British Regional Employment Statistics*, Cambridge, 1979; Ville, 'Sunderland shipbuilding', *International Journal of Maritime History*, I, 1989, pp. 65–86; Jones, 'Whitby'.
36 *Lords S. C. Navigation Laws*, PP 1847–48 XX Pt II , Q. 4011–14, 4043–91.
37 PP 1842 (259) XXXIX, p. 626. On nineteenth-century port development, see Gordon Jackson, 'The ports', in Freeman and Aldcroft, *Transport in Victorian Britain*, pp. 218–52.

Chapter Two

The shipping interest

By any measure shipping and shipbuilding constituted a substantial economic presence in early nineteenth-century Britain. The industry also occupied a recognised position in the political sphere; it was an 'interest'. Shipping ranked in political mythology among those forces in the realm which would always intuitively resist with vigour any attack on their established privileges.

When contemporaries referred to an 'interest', what did they mean? Its foundation was a common economic bond; the sum of the parts of an industry. 'When I speak of the shipping interest', William Buckle told the Select Committee on Foreign Trade in 1820, 'I do not mean to confine myself to the individual interest of the shipowners, but to the many interests that are connected with it. The revenue, as respects the duty upon hemp, upon foreign iron upon, upon flax; the home interest, as it is connected with the timber, with copper, the iron, the labour, the manufacture of the cordage and of sailcloth.'[1] An interest as defined in this broad fashion might be deemed worthy of government attention simply because its size identified it as an important species of property. On this basis those identified with shipping argued that their industry could bear comparison with cotton.

As more precisely understood, interest also implied parliamentary representation. The fate of straw-bonnet makers and ribbon weavers was closely tied to import duties, and no doubt they had strong opinions about these, but this did not make them an interest; they were without political presence. In its narrower sense the term implied simply the existence at Westminster of men with identifiable economic associations. Both the old-established East and West India interests and the newer railway interest conformed closely to this definition. They might strengthen their hand by organising extra-parliamentary

21

support, but fundamentally they consisted of individuals, in the Lords as well as in the Commons, with a direct financial stake.[2]

But parliamentary interest also possessed a constituency dimension. Local needs created local lobbies, as the large number of private bills which came forward every year eloquently testified. MPs were expected to serve as the channel for such local business, overseeing the passage of private bills, presenting petitions and accompanying deputations. More than that, faced with questions of national policy, they were expected to show sensitivity to local needs and conditions. Where the question at issue was perceived to have an impact on the inhabitants of a particular area, particularly on their livelihood, this could be reflected in constituency politics. In such circumstances political prudence dictated that the MP take account of local opinion in his public stance, though the degree to which he saw himself obligated to carry constituency commitment into the division lobby against his own inclination depended on the degree of electoral risk. Many MPs in the post-reform parliaments still owed their seats to patronage, and influence pervaded the ballot. Nevertheless, the Reform Bill had confirmed and extended the concept of representation of propertied interest in the state and convention dictated that MPs behaved with due decorum when faced with conflict between their views and those of the electors. Absence from the House on the night of the key division could prove the better part of valour for the member mindful of constituency sensitivities.[3]

These are general considerations, but it is worth noting that they had particular force in respect of shipping because of the kind of industry it was. Maritime related activities were necessarily confined to particular geographical areas, and hence constituencies, where in this period the concentration of capital frequently went beyond that implied by the word 'port' to include shipbuilding. Furthermore, the characteristics of the coasting trade, particularly the importance of the carriage of coal from the north-east to London, in some places produced relatively settled populations of seafarers. The limited franchise even after 1832 meant that such men, and also port workers and shipwrights, were typically denied participation in the formal political system. But this did not mean that they were totally without influence.

When looking, then, at the shipping interest within its Westminster context, two aspects have to be considered: personal stake and constituency representation. A related central issue, which leads to consideration of the role of shipowners' societies and associations as extra-parliamentary lobbies, is how far those associated with shipping, both within and outside Parliament, felt a sufficient sense of common identity to encourage them to act in concert, as a group.

Table 6. *Number and political affiliation of MPs with interests in shipping and transport in each Parliament 1832–47*

Parliament	1832	1835	1837	1841	1847
Whig/Liberal	9	8	7	6	15
Tory/Cons.	1	–	2	5	5
TOTAL	10	8	9	13	20

Source: J. A. Thomas, *The House of Commons 1832–1901*, Cardiff, 1939, pp. 4–5.

In June 1848 Joseph Warner Henley MP, himself the son of a former prominent London shipowner, told the Commons that 'if there was one interest in the country which was now and had at all times been, weakly represented in the House, it was the shipping interest'.[4] This judgement seems to be confirmed by J. A. Thomas's, now rather elderly, study of the composition of the House of Commons after 1832 (Table 6). According to Thomas's estimates, only twenty members of the 1847 Parliament had interests in 'shipping and transport' (excluding railways). This number was greater than that in the previous four Parliaments, but less than the representation of other commercial groups. In addition, Thomas identified fifty-six MPs in the same Parliament as having mercantile connections, some of whom would also come under his 'shipping and transport' heading.[5] Thomas provides only his statistics; he does not identify MPs by name. Table 7 is a list of MPs with shipping interests, which is based on biographical information compiled by Boase, supplemented by miscellaneous other sources.[6] Unfortunately it has proved impossible to reconcile this information on individuals with Thomas's numerical estimates. For example, for the Parliament 1847–52, the available biographical information suggests a total of only eleven as against Thomas's figure of twenty.

Four of these men (George Lyall, Joseph Somes, George Frederick Young and Aaron Chapman) were active in the industry's extra-parliamentary organisation, the General Shipowners' Society, but there is no evidence that their candidatures originated with that

Table 7. *Members of the Parliaments between 1832 and 1852 identified as having interests in shipping*

A. Anderson	Steamship proprietor	Orkney & Shetland 1847–52 Lib.	
M. W. Attwood	Steamship proprietor	Greenwich	1837–41 Cons.
A. Bannerman	Merchant, shipowner	Aberdeen	1832–47 Lib.
G. Barnard	London shipbuilder	Greenwich	1832–51 Lib.
J.S. Brownrigg	Shipowner	Boston	1825–41 Cons.
A. Chapman	Shipowner	Whitby	1832–47 Cons.
Sir William Clay	Shipowner, merchant	Tower Hamlets	1832–57 Lib.
J. Collier	Shipowner, merchant	Plymouth	1832–41 Lib.
G. Duncan	Steamship proprietor	Dundee	1841–57 Lib.
J. Humphery	Wharfinger	Southwark	1832–52 Lib.
G. Lyall	Shipowner, merchant	City of London	1833–35 Cons.
J. Mangles	Shipowner, shipchandler	Guildford	1831–37 Whig
J. Marryat	Shipowner	Sandwich	1826–35 Lib.
T.A. Mitchell	Merchant, shipowner	Bridport	1841–75 Lib.
G. R. Robinson	Shipowner, merchant	Worcester	1826–37 Cons.
		Poole	1847–50
Visc. Seaham	Dock proprietor	Durham N.	1847–54 Cons.
J. Somes	Shipowner, shipbuilder	Dartmouth	1844–45 Cons.
W. Thompson	Shipowner, ironfounder	Sunderland	1833–44 Cons.
		Westmorland	1841–54
J. T. Wawn	Shipowner	South Shields	1841–52 Lib.
B. M. Willcox	Steamship proprietor	Southampton	1847–62 Lib.
G. F. Young	Shipowner, shipbuilder	Tynemouth	1831–38 Whig

connection. Men of wealth and position commonly saw election to Parliament as the crowning achievement of their career and ship-owners were no exception. Indeed, Somes's candidature necessitated the legal transfer of many of his vessels to his nephews because of his position as a contractor for government transports.[7] Furthermore, for most of them the fact that they held public office had no connection with their business endeavours; they were not seeking to gain direct economic benefit through being elected to Parliament. Certainly there were few contexts where that would be possible. Steam shipping can perhaps be identified as one exception. With government mail contracts subsidising private oceanic steam companies, there were advantages from a presence at the political centre and this motive may have inspired the candidacies in 1847 of Arthur Anderson and Brodie McGhie Willcox, founders of the Peninsular and Oriental Steamship Company. Dock and port development was of particular concern to such enterprises, encouraging them to cultivate local influence. The comment of the Thames shipbuilder Thomas Mare on his parliamentary candidacy in 1852 is illuminating:

My first thoughts of going down to Plymouth were in consequence of my connection with the General Screw Steam Shipping Company of which I am a large proprietor. The screw vessels of that company it was intended should leave from Plymouth , and the Managing Director had declined standing for Plymouth.[8]

Some of those having personal connections with shipping sat for seaports, where such a background was undoubtedly an asset, though few were in the position to make the kind of election promise contained in a squib put out in Dartmouth in 1844: 'Somes with ships will fill our harbour, And the town with constant labour.'[9] But most such constituencies sent to Westminster men who had no direct experience of shipping or shipbuilding. Nevertheless, the maritime dimension had an impact on parliamentary representation. Even before the 1832 Reform Act, those seaports which returned members had a reputation for proving politically troublesome. In a comment which is also informative about the nature of the shipping interest, Swinton C. Holland warned of the likely reaction to Huskisson's reciprocity proposals:

I think you will concur that the shipowners generally are a class of persons with very limited views, looking solely to their own local interests, or what they conceive from habit to be such, and that any idea of placing foreign ships on the same footing with respects to imports into this country will be met by them with decided hostility, and all their borough and county interests will be united against it . . . [10]

One effect of the 1832 Act was to increase the number of seaport constituencies. Its impact was particularly marked in the north-east, where previously only Berwick and Newcastle had been enfranchised. Here Gateshead, Tynemouth and South Shields became single-member, and Sunderland two-member, constituencies. In Yorkshire, Whitby also gained an MP. Elsewhere in England, the most significant change occurred in the representation of naval ports, with Chatham, Devonport and Falmouth joining Portsmouth, Plymouth and Harwich as 'government boroughs'.[11]

The new constituencies represented a considerable increase in potential shipping influence at Westminster. Whereas London and Liverpool were great cities where economic interests vied with one another, these smaller ports were maritime through and through. 'Almost every man of means in Sunderland is more or less a shipowner', commented the shipowner W. S. Lindsay, 'The grocer when he has spare money invests it in a vessel. The sail maker does the same thing to increase his regular trade. The blockmaker and the rope maker and even the shoe maker acts upon the same principle, for if he has a ship, he must get meat and flour, rope and tar and the sellers of these articles all require shoes.'[12]

Only a minority of those who got their living directly or indirectly from the sea were likely to be also electors, and the grip of traditional landed influence continued to be felt, but shipping proved a powerful political force in some constituencies, new and old, after 1832. The new constituency of Whitehaven merely extended the patronage of the Lowther dynasty. Patronage played a similar role at Whitby, but here it brought shipping to the fore. With the Chomeleys of Whitby Abbey the only other influence in the town, a prominent local shipowning family, the Chapmans, provided the town's first MP. A director of the Hudson's Bay Company, the London Dock Company and the London Assurance, Aaron Chapman was an active campaigner on shipping issues. When Chapman stood down in 1847, the family's choice as his successor, the railway engineer Robert Stephenson, fitted into the same protectionist mould.[13]

G. F. Young, later to achieve prominence as a Tory Protectionist, gained his first experience of Parliament as the member for Tynemouth, which he represented between 1832 and 1838 in the Whig interest.[14] The Tory Duke of Northumberland owned land in the borough, but, in Dod's words 'chief weight resides with the shipowners'. The Whig Ralph Grey wisely espoused the popular cause of emancipation from Newcastle and was unopposed in 1847. Less acceptable were his free trade views, and anger against repeal of the Navigation Laws proved to be a factor in his defeat by the Tory shipowner Hugh Taylor in 1852. (This election, a particularly corrupt contest even by the standards of the day, was declared void.) On the opposite bank, South Shields was equally dominated by shipping. Its member between 1841 and 1852, the Liberal James Twizzell Wawn, was a member of a local shipowning family. Shields politics was marked by a distinctive collaboration between radical and capitalist interests, and Wawn's local brand of liberalism encompassed traditional reform elements, plus an equally traditional commitment to the Navigation Laws. Another, more advanced Liberal, William Hutt, formerly MP for

Hull, represented Gateshead after 1841. Gateshead, which had an exceptionally middle-class electorate, was entirely under Whig coal-trade influence; in effect, a company town.[15]

The constituencies of Tynemouth and South Shields had been created by the Whigs to provide a counterpoint to Newcastle, where Corporation, coal trade and shipping traditionally provided Tory support. The relative impact of these groups diminished, however, as Newcastle increased in size and its economy became more diverse. Nossiter's occupational analysis of its electorate in 1852 shows a large 'shopocracy' against a tiny presence for shipping. This changing social composition no doubt contributed to increased support for the Whigs; in 1847 they won both seats for the first time. But, as we shall see, many constituencies where shipping was a sizeable presence saw nothing incompatable between this interest and Whig/Liberal representation; not least because treating and rounds of drinks, rather than gradations of political conviction, determined the outcome of many electoral contests.

Sunderland, where shipping interests accounted for as much as a fifth of the electorate at mid-century, proved supportive of Tories in a town dominated by the landowning Whig interests of the Greys and Williamsons. A Grey nominee, first Andrew White and then Viscount Howick, sat as one of the two members between 1837 and 1845, and the London merchant David Barclay held the seat for Williamson in 1835, 1841 and 1847, but the only election in which the Whigs managed to take both seats was that of 1841. The Williamson family were the promoters of the Sunderland North Docks, a costly and ill-conceived venture, indicative of more business ambition than business sense. In contrast, Sunderland's first Tory member was the extra-ordinarily able Alderman William Thompson, ironfounder, shipowner and Director of the Bank of England. Thompson's successor as Tory candidate in 1841 was another businessman with shipping connections, Wolverley Attwood, the Chairman of the General Steam Navigation Company. Attwood's defeat was avenged in 1845, when railway entrepreneur George Hudson, replete with offers to purchase local railway shares and to promote new docks, became the town's new member.[16]

Hull's politics were notoriously venal and representation swung between factions, according to what their candidates could offer. Maritime issues were important, and shipping sympathies broadly protectionist and Tory, but the fortunes of neither party were guaranteed.[17] In the 1820s the Hull Shipowners Association believed that their interests had suffered from the absence of effective representation at Westminster. What was needed according to Stanhope, the peer who had handled some of their petitions, was 'an active and zealous advocate'. In 1831 he advised them to use their influence appropriately:

Whenever a General Election takes place, the shipowners and those interested for them should refuse their votes for any candidate who will not pledge himself to bring their case before Parliament and to support it by all the means in his power and no other considerations should induce them to to give to him their suffrage.[18]

Hull shipowners tended to back the Tories. In 1835, for example, they enlisted the help of the London-based General Shipowners' Society, which distributed a handbill urging support for the Tory candidate. But it was a Liberal, William Hutt, a member for the city between 1832 and 1841, who proved their most industrious representative. Hutt's work in pressing for negotiations to abolish the Stadt Duties, which particularly affected Hull shipping, was valued, but appreciation did not extend to ensuring his return, hence his departure to a safer seat in the family sinecure of Gateshead in 1841.[19]

In the south of England, by the 1840s shipping had its own company town – Southampton. Here the Peninsular & Oriental Company held sway, ensuring the return to Parliament of its Liberal nominees. The naval boroughs were in general similarly dominated by patronage. At Chatham, for example, the government candidate always succeeded, whether Whig or Tory.[20] At Bristol commercial, rather than purely shipping interests, determined that port's elitist style of establishment politics. Just two men, the Tory banker P. W. S. Miles and the Liberal F. H. Berkeley, sat for Bristol between 1837 and 1852. London returned in all sixteen members; four for the City and two each for Westminster, Finsbury, Marylebone, Tower Hamlets, Lambeth and Southwark. Although the riverside wards were the site of much port activity, this was not translated into electoral influence and, faced with the multitude of conflicting interests which the capital threw up, London MPs typically found themselves freer to follow their, generally Whig or Liberal, inclinations than men in more economically specialised constituencies. Liverpool was a city of equally conflicting mercantile groups, but the sum of their parts tended to ensure not only that the Tories dominated the parliamentary seats but also that there was a preference for members seemingly independent of particular economic interests. Thus an aristocrat, Viscount Sandon, served as one of its representatives between 1831 and 1847.[21]

Glasgow was another port in which the shipowners vied with other groups, but here mercantile, free trade, interests dominated. Elsewhere, the thick strand of sectarianism which ran through Scotland's politics in the early Victorian period makes it particularly difficult to separate shipping from other influences. For example, the Dundee politician, George Duncan, was closely associated with the London & Dundee Steam Shipping Company, but the basis of his support owed more to Non-Intrusionism than to business connection.[22]

In conclusion, it is clear that, irrespective of the exercise of influence at election time, seaports varied considerably in the extent to which shipping constituted an important part of the electorate. Only in a handful of places, virtually all in the north-east apart from Southampton, were shipping elites sufficiently dominant to have a direct impact on local parliamentary representation. The rarity of shipping as a business interest among MPs was thus only to a slight degree compensated for by constituency maritime interest.

Measured in terms of numbers at Westminster, then, the shipping interest, whether defined in terms of individual financial interest or constituency obligation, was hardly formidable. It is difficult to reconcile this relatively insignificant presence with the long-standing reputation of the shipping interest as a political force to be reckoned with. In part, such an assessment reflected the extent to which shipping was connected with wider commercial or regional concerns. Measures affecting the timber or West Indian trades also involved shipowners and resulted in the forging of effective parliamentary alliances. In 1831, for example, these groups together brought about the rejection of Althorp's Budget over the question of alteration of the timber duties.[23] (Less remarked was the outcome if only maritime interests were challenged; in 1827 the Liverpool member, General Gascoigne, got little support in his attempt to raise the issue of shipping depression in the House.)[24].

Another factor was that in every Parliament there were a few MPs who saw themselves, and were seen by others, as the representatives of the shipping industry. George Lyall, G. F. Young, Alderman William Thompson, William Hutt and the North Durham member, Henry Liddell, all fell into the category of 'experts', who could be relied upon to participate in any debates in which shipping featured. But what gave some of these men their authority was the perception that they spoke not on their own behalf but on behalf of a mighty constituency composed of shipowners in all the major seaports of the kingdom. 'There is a society of shipowners', G. F. Young told a Committee of the Corporation of the City of London in 1833, 'and we have correspondents in all parts of the Kingdom; when speaking the sentiments of the shipowners I do so through the medium of the General Shipowners' Society.'[25]

Seemingly, what the shipping interest lacked in direct parliamentary representation was more than compensated for by the existence of the unique permanent organisation, of which few who moved in official circles could remain unaware. In most years after 1833 the Board of Trade was reminded of the General Shipowners' Society's existence by receipt of its annual report and its committee claimed a special right to be consulted by government on matters affecting shipowners.[26] The society played a central role in the two Select Committees which investigated the shipping industry in 1833 and 1844. It encouraged George Lyall MP to promote the first and nominated witnesses to both, briefing them on the points they should be raising. In the case of the 1844 Select Committee (proposed by Lyall on his own initiative), it prepared a list of leading questions to be put by the Chairman.[27] When, writing in 1847, the free trader J. L. Ricardo paid this hostile tribute to the success of protected trades as parliamentary lobbyists, it was the General Shipowners' Society which he had in mind:

The truth is, that all protected trades make it part of their business to remind parliament of their existence. They have a committee constantly on the look out for fresh privileges and to resist invasions of the old; to give note of any pause in their progress and diminution of their profits; and whenever the trade looks down, or the like trade looks up, anywhere else, to run to the ministry of the day, and get a parliamentary committee appointed to hunt up some fresh means of help. Unprotected trades work their way manfully out of embarrassments and periods of distress. The protected leave on record great blue books of unreal grievances and prophecies of ruin never fulfilled.[28]

The General Shipowners' Society, dating from December 1831, was the successor to an earlier national body, the Shipowners' Society of Great Britain, set up in 1816 and itself based on a former body, the Ship Owners of the Port of London. No formal permanent association of London shipowners seems to have existed before 1811, but group involvement in the publication of a registry of shipping in the late eighteenth century suggests that such combination was not a new development.[29] Payment of a fee based on tonnage (raised from ½*d* per to 1*d* in 1817) gave membership of the first society, while its national character came from contact with similar associations in Liverpool, Sunderland, Scarborough, Leith, Dundee and Greenock. From the beginning expenses tended to outstrip income and by 1822 the Committee reported financial difficulties, warning that 'unless Ship Owners contribute more generally than they have hitherto done . . . the Committee must terminate their labours with the expiration of the present year'.[30] Attendance at the Annual Meeting in 1822 was seventy-four but three years later this had fallen to thirty-three and by 1828 the Shipowners' Society was effectively defunct.[31]

The lack of interest which dwindling numbers indicated was not, however, felt by all and in 1831 the association was reconstituted under the new name of the General Shipowners' Society, with a foundation capital of £1,500. Membership continued to be on an individual or district basis, with business conducted by an elected committee of twelve, plus outports' representatives. Voting strength varied according to the level of annual subscription, which included a substantial initial donation intended as the means of providing the society with the sound financial base lacking before. Thus payment of £25 plus 5 guineas per annum gave a member three votes, while payment of £50 by an outport association entitled it one place on the Committee, £200 to three places.[32] Despite this, the General Shipowners' Society was not to be free of financial difficulties. In 1841 diminishing outport representation necessitated a tour by the Secretary to rally support and in 1854 Committee members had to discharge debts of £280 out of their own pockets.[33]

What were the objectives of the General Shipowners' Society and its predecessor? The original society seems at first to have seen its role as being that of a promoter of measures to benefit the shipping industry. A formidable list of matters 'deserving of attention' were reported to its general meeting in 1816, including customs reform, pilotage, apprenticeship, tonnage measurement, stamp duties, charges in the Port of London and warehousing regulations.[34] Undoubtedly the subjects chosen for investigation by the 1820 Select Committee on Foreign Trade owed much to lobbying from this source, led by George Lyall, as did the choice of witnesses. In the event, the shipowners found that they had got more than they had bargained for in encouraging government to take an interest in such issues and the society moved to an increasingly defensive position when faced with changes in timber duties and proposals for reciprocity treaties.[35]

The successful reconstitution of the Shipowners' Society in the early 1830s was in part the result of new threats from government to reduce the colonial timber preference, so it is not surprising to find the first report of the new body emphasising its role as a guardian of the industry:

The activity of modern legislation, and the necessity for providing some vigilant check on the continual liability to the invasion of the general interests in British shipping, in the bills which from time to time are submitted to Parliament, were among the most prominent reasons for the establishment of the Society.[36]

The General Shipowners' Society did not confine itself to being a Westminster watchdog, although employment of a parliamentary agent was probably its major regular expense. Through annual reports and the evidence of its witnesses to Select Committees, as well as through those members who sat at Westminster, it sought to alert government to the state of the industry more generally. Outside the parliamentary sphere it concerned itself with such questions as the development of victualling scales, the organisation of the Port of London, and (at the prompting of members in the north-east) in the early 1840s drew up an ingenious relative freight scale for the Baltic trade.

To all appearances the General Shipowners' Society was an formidable organisation, indicative of a considerable degree of cohesion within the shipping interest on a national scale. The reality was rather different. Despite its grand title, and impressive outward show of activity, the General Shipowners' Society consisted at any one time of perhaps four or five men who met together once or twice a month at the society's offices in Cornhill and who in some years reported to a general meeting, itself indifferently attended. Both this society and its predecessor were the product of the enthusiasm and support of a relatively small group of larger shipowners, most owning London-registered ships. The Committee elected in 1831 included three men (William Tindall, J. W. Buckle and Jonathan Chapman) who had served on the earlier body.[37] Both George Lyall MP, who had been Chairman between 1823 and 1825, and Duncan Dunbar were active in the General Shipowners' Society. But the single most committed member was the G. F. Young, five times its Chairman between 1834 and 1852. Young was a partner in the Thames shipbuilding firm of Curling & Young, and also a shipowner, with a particular interest in whaling.[38]

As an association concerned with questions of interest to those operating out of the Port of London the General Shipowners' Society had a clear function, similar to that of similar associations in other ports. However, those who formed and sustained the society saw its central role as political. For this it had to be a national body, supported by shipowners in other ports. But here lay a problem. In Liverpool, as also in Glasgow, shipowners looked first to their local associations to voice their concerns. They saw benefits from acting in concert with the General Shipowners' Society and its predecessor when great national issues were at stake, but regarded the latter as essentially a London organisation, pursuing London interests and issues. The outports in general could gain little from the short-lived experiment which the society began in 1818 to set up a an office for registry of Merchant Seamen for the purpose of giving 'to good men, facilities hitherto unknown in obtaining employment; and to shipowners, the means of procuring complete crews at an hour's notice', or from the continuing attention the Committee paid to the question of facilities and charges in the Port of London.[39]

In fact, relations between the Liverpool Shipowners' Association and the General Shipowners' Society were not altogether friendly. The General Shipowners' Society had an influential part in the establishment of Lloyd's Register of British and Foreign Shipping in 1833, and under its constitution was responsible for nominating half of the Comittee members. Liverpool shipowners and shipbuilders alleged that the Lloyd's classification system discriminated against Liverpool shipping, unfairly favouring London-built vessels, and they responded by setting up an alternative register.[40] This failed to gain subscribers and in 1841 the Liverpool Association was persuaded to agree to send a representative to serve on the General Shipowners' Society, but only, as it pointedly maintained, in order to secure some representation on the Lloyd's Register Committee and 'for no other object'.[41]

But in general apathy rather than hostility explained the difficulty the General Shipowners' Society encountered in maintaining connections with other ports. Its constitution assumed the existence of local shipowners' associations throughout Britain which might be persuaded to see the benefit of participating in a national body. It was a false assumption. In many ports no such society existed and even where a formal organisation had been set up, it often proved to have a fragile, ephemeral existence. In the autumn of 1840 Oviatt, the paid Secretary of the General Shipowners' Society, toured the outports on its behalf. His report allows us a rare insight into the organisation of the shipping interest outside London.[42]

Oviatt's trip started in Hull, where he met Ward, the one-time Chairman of the Hull Shipowners' Association, a body which no longer existed, not having met for four or five years. Scarborough continued to send a delegate, so he thanked their Committee for its past support, moving on to Whitby, where he found the association 'in abeyance but not actually dissolved'. A meeting was arranged, but only five attended, and it was agreed to try again at the end of January when more shipowners would be in port and the mutual insurance club settlements were made. At Stockton and Middlesborough no association existed and Oviatt could arouse no enthusiasm, but in Hartlepool a Committee of Shipowners agreed in principle to fund a representative through a levy of 1*d* per ton. Sunderland had two representatives on the General Shipowners' Committee, but according to information provided by its MP, Hudson, was considering reducing this to one. Oviatt appealed to local pride, pointing out to the Committee that this would mean that the Tyne ports would be contributing more and it was agreed to withdraw the proposal. At Shields Oviatt enjoyed hospitality from Robert Anderson, a long-term supporter of the society, who accompanied him to Newcastle. Here there was no Shipowners' Society as such, but shipowners were grouped in five mutual insurance clubs. Oviatt was introduced to the leading members of the largest of these, 'the Liberal', who agreed to recommend to their association the appointment of two representatives at the cost of £100.

Moving on to Scotland, Oviatt found shipowners in Leith dis-enchanted with their existing society following a costly legal dispute with Edinburgh, but prepared to form a new association which would send representatives if it could get sufficient support. Neither Dundee nor Greenock had an association but both were prepared to try to set one up. At Glasgow the Directors of the Shipping Association agreed to join the General Shipowners' Society.

As already described, the Liverpool Shipowners' Association agreed to support the General Shipowners' Society, but Whitehaven, with allegedly only five shipowners concerned with foreign trades, proved unresponsive. At Bristol the Chamber of Commerce, having somewhat unwillingly agreed to call a special meeting of shipowners, proved resistant to the formation of a new society, instead suggesting an expansion of its existing shipping sub-committee as a means of sending a representative. Oviatt's efforts in Ireland met with a mixed reception. Dublin proved a 'signal disappointment'; he could not get anyone even to attend a meeting. Wexford and Waterford showed little enthusiasm, but Belfast and Limerick shipowners agreed to establish an association. Cork already had a society and agreed to donate £40 a year.

Thus, in a majority of cases, Oviatt found himself confronted not with the problem of persuading local associations to join the General Shipowners but of bringing them into existence as a first step towards this. It is perhaps not surprising that permanent associations seem to have been rare. Shipowners might be persuaded to band together for a specific local purpose; for example, to defeat a seamen's combination or to campaign for a reduction in port charges. But there was little to encourage long-term mutual commitment in an industry where shipowners found themselves in daily competition. Apathy and local loyalty were not, however, the only difficulties the General Shipowners' Society encountered in establishing and maintaining support. Behind these lurked a fundamental question – whether there existed sufficient community of purpose, the sense of a common identity, to permit the extra-parliamentary shipping interest to speak with one voice.

The General Shipowners' Society itself represented an elite. Given the nature of the industry, with the range of trades and pattern of investment, the specialist, mainly London-based, shipowners with large tonnages who were active in the General Shipowners' Society were hardly typical. Their experience of the industry was different from that of those operating on a smaller scale, whether in London or elsewhere. They looked to their long-term profits and questions such as the Light Dues and the Stamp Duties on marine insurance policies, which they saw as a permanent surcharge on earnings, attracted their attention to a much greater extent than would be the case for the more short-term investor, who tended to accept such things as a fact of life. Furthermore, the perennial charge of the larger shipowners that falling profits resulted from an unwarranted influx of new shipping can be seen as typical of the established sector of any industry facing competition from smaller enterprises, the 'cowboys'.

But the question went deeper than this. One possible explanation of the apparent fragility of a general shipowners' association is that its appeal was felt most strongly when the direction of national policy seemed most threatening. Thus the scope of the investigations of the Select Committee on Foreign Trade and Huskisson's reciprocity proposals provided ample justification for a concerted approach to government in the immediate post-war years, as did the timber duty issue and unprofitability a few years later. Once depression gave way to greater prosperity, and when the attention of the legislature wandered away from issues affecting shipping, as happened in the later 1820s and later 1830s, both the membership and income of the society shrank.

This is a convincing interpretation of the ebb and flow of support, but it obscures a factor of enormous significance for the functioning of the extra-parliamentary shipping interest. If the justification for the General Shipowners' Society as a national rather than a London association was defence of 'the general interests' in British shipping, there had to be agreement as to what those interests were. This presented a problem, as the response to some of the society's initiatives shows. In 1838 a bill promoted by G. F. Young to restrict shipping mortgages had to be withdrawn in response to opposition from 'many of the friends of the society in the North of England'. Three years later, the Committee's decision to unite with North American colonial interests over timber duty proposals led to resignations by members with Baltic interests. In turn, Young's advocacy of a duty on North American-built shipping brought protests from those in the colonial timber trade. But within the context of the present study the most important area of dispute was over the principle of trade liberalisation. 'There are shipowners who look to the extension of the carrying trade by the free introduction of foreign corn', noted the General Shipowners' Society Annual Report for 1841.[43]

For an industry itself so dependent on protection, this was a significant admission. But it should not be regarded as surprising. Personal economic interest, not political principle, dictated shipowners' attitudes to issues of public policy. They would support anything which promised more business; a fact which put them on the side of the commercial liberalisers, leading to Derby's judgement of the early 1850s, that 'the shipowners were always free traders at heart'.[44] By the same token, they resisted any change which might assist their competitors, hence the opposition to reciprocity treaties and, in the North American colonial trade, to anything which might favour either British or foreign operators in the Baltic timber trade. Moreover, while the prosperity of British shipping was seen by many shipowners to be dependent on the protective support provided by the state, the same men argued for a less-restrictive regime as it affected their own commercial freedom. If Britain's protective code was extraordinarily complicated, so also was the response it evoked, both outside and within Parliament. As the varied political affiliations of those who made up the shipping interest at Westminster suggests, this meant that there was no predictable association between shipping and party. Moreover, this remained true even in the later 1840s, when protection for shipping arguably became for the first time a clear party issue.

These were among the reasons why, when faced with the repeal of the Navigation Laws, undoubtedly the greatest issue of public policy ever to confront British shipping, the General Shipowners' Society found itself in difficulties. In theory, it was an issue on which its members might be expected to agree. In practice it proved surprisingly divisive.

Notes

1 *Report from the Select Committee on Foreign Trade*, PP 1820 (300) II, p. 63.
2 On the concept of interests, see Geoffrey Alderman, *The Railway Interest*, Leicester, 1973, pp. 12–13. Alderman is, however, mistaken in suggesting that an organised shipowning interest did not emerge until the late nineteenth century.
3 On the post–1832 electoral system, see N. Gash, *Politics in the Age of Peel*, London, 1953; Derek Fraser, *Urban Politics in Victorian England: the Structure of Politics in Victorian Cities*, Leicester, 1976; J. R. Vincent, *Poll Books*, London, 1967; D. C. Moore, 'The other face of reform', *Victorian Studies*, V, 1961–62; D.C. Moore, *The Politics of Deference*, London, 1976.
4 PD, Third Series, XCVIX, 1 June 1848, c.227.
5 J. A. Thomas, *The House of Commons 1832–1901, a Study of its Economic and Functional Character*, Cardiff, 1939.
6 Frederic Boase, *Modern English Biography*, 6 vols, 1892–1921, reprinted 1965 ; Charles R. Dod, Electoral Facts from 1832–1853, *Impartially Stated*, 2nd edition 1852, reprinted with an introduction by H. J. Hanham, Brighton, 1972.
7 *S. C. Dartmouth Election Petition*, PP 1845 XII, Q. 50–93.
8. *S. C. on the Plymouth Election Petitions*, PP 1852–53 XVIII, Q. 1244.
9. KAO, Colyer-Fergusson MS, U295, f. 12–13.
10 BL, Huskisson Papers, Add. MS. 38748, ff. 217–28, Holland to Lyall, 17 December 1826.
11 Michael Brock, *The Great Reform Act*, London, 1973, pp. 19–22, 310–13.
12 National Maritime Museum (NMM), Lindsay Papers, Journal, II, p. 16.
13 See W. W. Bean, *Parliamentary Representation of the Six Northern Counties of England*, Hull, 1890; Dod, *Electoral Facts*; C. F. O'Neil, 'The contest for dominion: political conflict and the decline of the Lowther interest in Whitehaven, 1820–1900', *Northern History*, XVII, 1981, pp. 133–52; Gash, *Politics in the Age of Peel*, pp. 209–11.

14 Much of the following discussion of political representation in the North East relies on T. J. Nossiter, *Influence, Opinion and Political Idioms in Reformed England: Case Studies from the North East 1832–1874*, Brighton, 1975. See also N. McCord and A. E. Carrick, 'Northumberland in the General Election of 1852', Northern History, I, 1966, pp. 92–108.

15 See N. McCord, 'Gateshead politics in the age of reform', *Northern History*, IV, 1969, pp. 167–83; John Foster, *Class Struggle and the Industrial Revolution: Early Industrial Capitalism in Three English Towns*, London, 1974, pp. 120–3.

16 Nossiter, *Influence*, pp. 124–5.

17 K. J. Allison (ed.), *A History of the County of Yorkshire, East Riding: I, The City of Kingston-upon-Hull, Victoria History of the Counties of England*, Oxford, 1969, p. 216.

18 KAO, Stanhope Papers, U1590 C203, Stanhope to Cooper, 15 March 1831.

19 Lucy Brown, *The Board of Trade and the Free Trade Movement 1830–1842*, Oxford, 1958, p. 175, n.3; James Sheahan, *History of Hull*, Hull, 1866, pp. 322–3.

20 Gash, *Politics in the Age of Peel*, pp. 444–59.

21 Brock, *Great Reform Act*, p. 329.

22 See I. C. G. Hutchison, *A Political History of Scotland 1832–1924: Parties, Elections and Issues*, Edinburgh, 1986, pp. 59–89.

23 Brock, *Great Reform Act*, pp. 173–4.

24 *Blackwoods Edinburgh Magazine*, XXII, July 1827, p. 2.

25 Corporation of the City of London, *Report of an Inquiry into the Port of London*, 1 March 1833, Q. 381.

26 Brown, *Board of Trade*, pp. 175–6.

27 General Shipowners' Society (GSS), Committee Minutes, III, 24 June 1833; IV, 21 May 1844.

28 J. Lewis Ricardo, *Anatomy of the Navigation Laws*, London, 1847, p. 46.

29 On the Society see Leonard Harris, *London General Shipowners' Society, 1811–1961*, London, 1961. Its role in the creation of LLoyd's Registry of Shipping is dealt with in Sarah Rosalind Palmer, 'The Character and Organisation of the Shipping Industry of the Port of London, 1815–1849', unpublished Ph.D thesis, University of London, 1979, pp. 220–32.

30 GSS, General Meeting Minutes, 12 December 1822.

31 *Ibid.*; 15 December 1825; GSS, General Meeting of Shipowners of London specially convened by Public Advertisement, Committee Minutes, III.

32 GSS, General Meeting Minutes, III, 13 December 1831; Rules as Adopted 9 June 1831, III.

33 GSS, III, 30 July 1840, 5 January 1841; V, 14 November 1854.

34 Shipowners' Society (SS), General Meeting Report, 11 September 1816.

35 See below p. 00 – p. 00.

36 GSS, Report of First Annual Meeting, 22 January 1833.

37 Members of the Committee elected in 1831: George Palmer, Robert Carter, William Tindall, Nathanial Gould, J. W. Buckle, Henry Blanshard, John Pirie, J. D. Powles, John Chapman, Nathanial Domett, Jonathan Chapman, Henry Nelson; GSS, General Meeting Minutes, III, 13 December 1831; Harris, *General Shipowners' Society* gives a list of chairmen.

38 *Illustrated London News*, LVI, 12 March 1870; See Young's evidence to the *Commons S. C Navigation Laws*, PP 1847 X.
39 SS, Committee Minutes, Report of the Sub-Committee on the Proposal for a Registry of British Seamen, I, 16 December 1817.
40 GSS, Committee Minutes, III, 2 October 1833, 19 August 1833, 4 December 1833; Anon., *Annals of Lloyd's Register: Being a Sketch of Origin, Constitution and Progress of LLoyd's Register of British and Foreign Shipping*, London, 1884, pp. 48, 67–8.
41 GSS, Committee Minutes, III, 5 January 1841.
42 *Ibid*.
43 GSS, Report of the Annual Meeting, 22 May 1838; Committee Minutes, III, 8 June 1841; 5 August 1844; Report of the Annual Meeting, 18 June 1841.
44 BL, Young Papers, Add.MS 46712, ff. 147–50, Derby to Young, 13 January 1852.

Chapter Three

Ships, colonies and commerce

If the British shipping industry of the 1840s retained many of its traditional characteristics of organisation and technology, another legacy of the past was the protectionist framework, at once supportive and restrictive, within which it still operated. At its centre were the Navigation Laws, which were far from being, as is sometimes suggested, merely a vestigial formal code, easily abandoned because largely symbolic. About two-fifths of British shipping tonnage entering United Kingdom ports at this time was employed in trades from which foreign owned-ships were totally barred. Furthermore, ship-building served a totally protected market, and legal requirements as much as employers' preferences put limits on the employment of foreign seamen on British vessels. The shipowners, shipbuilders and seafarers who petitioned and demonstrated in 1848 and 1849 against repeal were not defending an abstraction. For them protection was a reality.

Originally devised in the seventeenth century as a weapon directed against England's maritime rivals, the large number of statutes affecting shipping which together constituted the Navigation Laws formed the keystone of an imposing edifice of restriction which still dominated national commercial policy in the first years of peace. Discrimination against foreign shipping was not confined to this legislation. Duties affecting the carriage of such important cargoes as timber, sugar and coal gave a preference to British shipowners, as did the host of local taxes, dues and payments which afflicted every vessel which frequented a British port. Behind the thicket of regulations, duties and artificial monopolies which hedged Britain's trade sheltered a number of interests, including those associated with the West and East Indies and with the North American timber trades. But no measure defined or trammelled the course of commerce to the same extent as did the navigation code.

To stress the survival of the Navigation Laws as a real influence on the conduct of business at the time of their repeal is not to suggest that they had an equal impact on every branch of the industry. Nor, given reciprocity treaties and tariff reforms, can it be supposed that the protective system as it affected shipping had defied all change over the previous thirty years. Indisputably a central question is what role these earlier modifications played, not only in determining the eventual outcome, the abandonment of protection, but also in influencing the attitudes and expectations of those concerned? In short, 1849 has to be placed in a context which includes developments over the previous quarter century.

The remoter origins of, and motives for, the Navigation Laws need not detain us here, nor do we need to be concerned with their application in the seventeenth and eighteenth centuries; both have been extensively and intensively studied.[1] What is relevant are the main features of the protective system as it existed immediately after the close of the Napoleonic Wars. One way to approach this question, as far as it applies to the navigation code, is by considering the categories of import trade (there were no limitations on outward carriage from Britain) as defined in the legislation itself. Five types were recognised: the fisheries; the coasting trade, trade with Africa, Asia and America; colonial trade; and trade with Europe. The first two of these were open only to British ships. Goods produced in Africa, Asia and America had to be brought directly to Britain from those regions' ports, or the usual port of first shipment, and again this business was reserved to British ships. There were some exceptions to the rule requiring direct shipment and foreign vessels were permitted to carry bullion, cochineal, precious stones, ivory and tobacco. Under free port acts, certain ports in the British West Indies could tranship the produce of non-British territories. However, the greatest departure from the general rule affecting distant trades was in respect of United States vessels. These could carry national produce to United Kingdom ports without, after the Reciprocity Treaty of 1815, any discriminatory duties being imposed. British ships had a monopoly of colonial carriage with the exception of the free port cases. Certain enumerated colonially produced goods could be exported only to Britain, while imports into the colonies, with some exceptions, had to come from or via the mother country. As far as Europe was concerned, foreign ships could bring in any article of commerce except for those enumerated, which could be carried only in British ships or ships belonging to the producer country. There was still a prohibition on importation of some goods from certain countries in Europe, in particular Holland.

Clearly, the definition of what constituted a national vessel was central to the practical application of these laws. The Registry Laws therefore formed part of the navigation code. Where a vessel was built, the nationality of the owner, master and crew were all relevant criteria. To qualify as British, a ship had to be British-built and British-owned, with the master and three-quarters of the crew British. British meant also colonial, so colonially owned and built vessels were included. Prizes, ships captured in war, were an exception to this rule.

Such a summary is misleading in suggesting a neat and tidy system. While there was adherence to the general principles of the original acts, a large number of legally permitted exemptions and exceptions, together with the scope for interpretation allowed in practice to the customs, resulted in extraordinary, sometimes baffling, complexity. Moreover, the discrimination against foreign shipping associated with the Navigation Laws was reinforced by other measures, such as the higher customs duties imposed on certain goods when carried in a foreign vessel. In a number of ports, also, it was the practice to charge foreign vessels more in the way of tolls, dues and fees than those paid by their British counterparts. At London, for example, the duty on the export of coal was 2*s* for British vessels, but double that amount for foreign vessels. Dock dues at London and Liverpool were the same for all vessels, irrespective of their origin, though Liverpool charged foreigners more for anchorage; but at Hull foreign vessels paid twice as much as British for the use of the docks, as well as being subject to special corporation tolls. Indeed, among British ports, Bristol seems to have been exceptional in making no distinction between vessels in terms of nationality.[2]

This long-established legal framework under which shipping operated did not entirely survive the re-evaluation of commercial policy associated with the later years of Lord Liverpool's administration. In 1822 a series of five Acts, in substance based on the work undertaken by the 1820 Select Committee on Foreign Trade, modified the Navigation Laws. Repeal of the measures directed against particular states put all European nations on an equal footing. The list of enumerated articles was updated and importation in vessels belonging to the port of shipment was permitted, while cargo from Asia, Africa and America could now come from ports in the region, irrespective of country of origin, provided, of course, it was carried in British ships. Importation into Britain from these distant regions via the continent of Europe was allowed – but only for goods destined for re-export. Goods from former Spanish possessions in the Americas could enter in national vessels, providing British ships had equivalent rights. American, including United States, vessels could trade with colonial free ports on reciprocal terms, and British colonies could export to Europe directly and import enumerated foreign products, but still only in British ships.[3]

These changes amounted to a refashioning and updating of the navigation code. They did not represent any significant alteration in the preference given to British vessels, and protection remained the central principle of state maritime policy. The following summary, provided by G. F. Young, of the state of the law in the early 1840s, indicates the considerable degree of restriction which still remained:

> The great protection we at present enjoy in navigation may be classed under three heads. The first is, the entire restriction of importation from the colonies for consumption in this country to British ships, together with a similar restriction in the coasting trade. The second is, the prohibition on the importation of all articles the produce of distant quarters of the world, Asia, Africa and America, from any of the ports of Europe, in any ships. The third is, the limitation of the produce of foreign countries to British ships, or ships belonging to the countries in which the articles are produced, or ships belonging to a country in Europe in which the produce, if European, may be found.[4]

This categorisation is helpful in that it highlights the fact that the protection provided by the Navigation Laws was not simply a matter of excluding foreign vessels from Britain's coasting and colonial trades; it also involved a distortion of trade by preventing transhipment through Europe, and a limitation on the ability of other national fleets to act as indirect carriers.

Faced with the problem of measuring the degree of protection offered by the Navigation Laws, G. R. Porter of the Board of Trade tackled the subject by looking at the relative share of tonnage employed in the protected and unprotected trades. Using the entry statistics for 1846, Porter calculated that protected trades accounted for 1.7 million tons, or 40 per cent, of total tonnage entering United Kingdom ports, leaving 2.5 million tons as the share of unprotected trades. These statistics excluded the coasting trade, where entries in

1846 totalled almost 12 million tons. In his evidence to the Lords' Select Committee on the Navigation Laws, G. F. Young objected to Porter's analysis, arguing that it understated the degree of protection because it took no account of the limitations on third party carriers. He reorganised Porter's figures into his own three categories. The first of these, 'trade strictly prohibited against all foreign shipping', covered British possessions and was identical to that of Porter. Young then divided foreign trades into two groups. China, Sumatra, Java, Mexico and the South American states he described as 'virtually protected' because they did not possess vessels of their own, and could use only British vessels in the trade with Britain. The remaining trades he listed under the heading 'in competition with ships of the respective countries though protected against the ships of other states', in recognition of the subsidiary elements of the navigation system.[5] A present-day Porter or Young, aware of counter factoral analysis, might approach the problem rather differently, seeking to establish the importance of protection by comparing the performance of British shipping under the protective system with its hypothetical performance under a non-restrictive system. In so far as the protective system was ended in 1849, we have some basis for such a comparison, but, as will be shown when the aftermath of repeal is considered, it is hard to provide clear answers. The British navigation code, taken in its entirety, was remarkably complicated and its context – the world shipping industry – no less so.

Certainly, it would be wrong to assume that all British trades were potentially of interest to foreign carriers. Protection of coastal trade, the single most important sector employing shipping in the first half of the nineteenth century, was total, but contemporary commentators judged that even without legislative interference it would still have been safe from foreign competition. A hazardous business, requiring particular skill and local knowledge, and in the case of its most important branch, the coal trade, monopolistically organised, it held no particular attraction to outsiders. 'There may be here and there a foreigner who is fond of navigating in long dark winter nights on the English coast, but I do not think that there are many foreigners who would undertake that branch of business', commented Captain James Stirling in 1847.[6] The coasting principle, in terms of total exclusion of foreign-owned vessels, not only applied to trade between Britain and her possessions but to inter-colonial routes as well. This meant that a United States vessel could operate between New York and Halifax, but not between Canadian ports; an aspect of the system which came to be a source of complaint for colonial merchants forced to rely on the supply of British-registered vessels for shipment. Given the considerable presence of United States vessels in the trade between Britain and the United States of America, American shipowners and their government had long resented this exclusion from Britain's colonial transatlantic trades. Here was a branch of business which many foreigners were keen to undertake.

Restrictions on the import of non-European products through European ports applied to British and foreign shipping alike, though the British vessels could bring goods in for re-export. This meant that a few products which could not be imported directly in British ships, such as Senegalese gum arabic, came into Britain via the United States of America. But voyages such as that undertaken by the unfortunate bale of wool belonging to the Hamburg merchant Robert Swaine were no doubt rare:

I think it was towards the end of the year 1844 that a large parcel of alpaca wool, which had arrived direct from Peru, was exposed for sale in Hamburg. I purchased it; and being at that time unacquainted with the entire operation of the Navigation Laws, I shipped it in a British ship to Hull, but it was seized on its arrival there as being in contravention of the Navigation Laws. I happened to be in London immediately afterwards and I memorialized the Lords of the Treasury upon the subject and the Lords of the Treasury ordered the wool to be delivered over to me for re-exportation; but I could not obtain their Lordships' permission to send that wool for home use into Yorkshire. That parcel of wool was subsequently shipped from Hull to New York, landed there and re-exported from New York to Liverpool and it was eventually transmitted from Liverpool into the manufacturing districts, where, however it arrived at a season a good deal too late for the purposes for which it had been intended.[7]

Examples such as this, like the illegality of bringing an ostrich feather fan into Britain from the Continent, were readily seized on by free traders anxious to ridicule the Navigation Laws. In so doing, they did their case some disservice because the Laws amounted to a far more substantial barrier to commercial freedom than such anachronisms suggested. And some protectionists had no difficulty in conceding that there was an argument for ending the restrictions on trade through Europe, while at the same time maintaining that the rest of the maritime protection system should remain inviolate.

Revision of the navigation code left shipbuilding untouched. To qualify for the privileges associated with British registry a vessel still had to be built and owned in Britain or the colonies. Apart from the small number of foreign vessels acquired as prizes, or permitted to be naturalised because extensively repaired in Britain, or any sold off by the navy which had been built in Admiralty Dockyards, all vessels coming newly onto the register had been built in British merchant shipyards or in those of Britain's colonies. Shipbuilders were thus totally protected from foreign competition; a fact seldom alluded to by contemporary commentators until the later 1840s and generally unremarked by economic historians. This did not mean, of course, that any individual shipbuilder enjoyed a monopoly position (there were too many yards for that), but production took place within a cost and market framework which excluded the foreigner.

Table 8. *Ships, sail and steam, built in the United Kingdom 1815/19 – 1945/49 (five-yearly averages, '000 tons)*

Years	Tons
1815/19	88.9
1820/24	66.0
1825/29	99.8
1830/34	87.8
1835/9	134.6
1840/44	135.8
1845/9	127.0

Source: Based on Mitchell, *Historical Statistics*, p. 420.

Table 8 shows the British output of sail and steam tonnage in each decade between 1820 and 1850. Colonial builders, predominantly in British North America, themselves contributed significantly to the British fleet. The available statistical series are deficient but Feinstein has estimated that imports per decade of vessels produced in colonial yards rose from 100,000 tons in the 1820s to 400,000 tons in 1840s, which was almost a third of the tonnage produced in British yards.[8] By 1846 colonial-built ships accounted for 13 per cent of ships on the British register. These vessels, costing as little as £7 per ton, compared in quality with the second-class, cheap vessels in which shipbuilding centres like Sunderland specialised. Built not in response to orders from shipowners, but as containers for timber cargoes or in remittance for imports from Britain, they were sold for the best price they could fetch, which was often very low. Most found employment in the timber and cotton trades, with registrations of these Canadian ships particularly high in Liverpool and the north-eastern ports.[9] In 1844 concern about the impact of oversupply of tonnage on freight rates and shipbuilding orders, led the General Shipowners' Society to propose a 'moderate tax' on colonial registrations on the grounds that

the competition of colonial-built shipping has been and is now operating as a direct and powerful discouragement to shipbuilding in this country; a discouragement that may ere long stimulate to increasing production in colonies not destined perhaps to remain permanently possessions of the British crown, which may sooner than many expect prove formidable rivals in naval warfare, as well as in maritime commerce.[10]

Paradoxically, the Navigation Laws not only protected shipbuilders from foreign competition; they also had the effect of protecting foreign yards from British competition. The 'national character' given to British vessels by the registration system had its corollary in the definition of nationality of foreign vessels. In British law, ownership and place of construction taken together defined a ship as French or Prussian as much as it did as British. As the Select Committee on Foreign Trade of 1820 noted, this meant that a British vessel sold to a foreign owner could not trade with Britain either under either her old or new nationality – a strong disincentive against foreigners buying such ships if they intended to trade to Britain.[11] Its recommendation that British-built vessels should be permitted to acquire foreign nationality was not followed in subsequent revisions of the registry regulations. Given that even when other countries permitted vessels built elsewhere to achieve national registration there could be fiscal disincentives (in Sweden, for example, a tax of a quarter of the cost was imposed), it is not surprising that sales of British ships abroad remained low. Nevertheless, here as in much else, steam shipping proved the exception and the right of British-built, but foreign-owned, steamships to a clear national character seems to have escaped challenge by the British customs.[12]

The obverse of protection for British shipbuilders was limitation on the freedom of British shipowners. Here the economic interests of shipowners and shipbuilders were necessarily distinct and opposed. The view expressed by Duncan Dunbar that 'as a shipowner, it would be best for me individually to be able to buy my ships where I could buy them cheapest' was one naturally shared by other shipowners.

Nothing prevented British shipowners from buying foreign vessels, providing local law did not debar them, and some did so. Peter Dickson and Company even built ships in Sweden for the export of naval stores to the colonies, but such vessels could not be used in trade with Britain.[13]

How much were British shipowners disadvantaged by being denied the opportunity to acquire foreign-built vessels? Witnesses to the two Select Committees on the Navigation Laws identified the United States of America, Sweden and the German states as potential suppliers of vessels to British shipowners, because of their relative cheapness in the case of the Europeans, and in the case of the United States, quality. However, the problem of establishing a common standard made it difficult to arrive at reliable international comparisons of the cost of new vessels. At the lowest end of the market, no other country could match what was on offer in Canadian or north-eastern yards. The lowest Sunderland price per ton (£6 15s for an A1. copper-fastened vessel, standing seven years at that classification on LLoyd's Register) was not undercut by any price quoted for a North European vessel. Above that level, the range of possible prices per ton (for example, for a Swedish vessel – £7, for a Norwegian – £8, for a Bremener – £9 to £14 12s and £11–£18 10s for a Hamburg vessel) was broadly similar to those on offer in British shipyards. An 'A1. twelve year' vessel built at London or Liverpool might cost as much as £24 per ton, but this reflected quality in material and craftmanship which was recognised as second to none.[14]

In fact, much of the evidence brought forward on European shipbuilding costs by protectionists was directed towards demonstrating their indirect impact. British shipping, it was argued, could not successfully compete with foreign because of higher costs, including the initial capital outlay. Shipbuilding would suffer, it was alleged, through the continued intrusion of foreign vessels into trades formerly dominated by British-owned vessels and this would in turn reduce the demand for new vessels. But the assumption was that British shipowners would continue to buy from British or colonial yards as far as low or moderate cost vessels were concerned; with such a wide range of prices and types already on offer in these yards there was no particular incentive to go elsewhere. There seems little justification, then, for regarding the limitation on the freedom of British shipowners to buy European-built vessels as of any great economic significance. In the case of United States shipbuilding the position was perhaps rather different. Although Money Wigram, builder of high-quality expensive vessels on the Thames, would publicly admit only that lower costs made similar American-built vessels cheaper, it was the superiority of their design and sailing qualities which impressed shipowners, and had the potential to threaten the hegemony of the prestige British yards.[15] American-owned and -built vessels predominated in Liverpool's export trade with the United States and monopolised the liner trade for reasons described by Henry Chapman: 'the American packet-ships which run from this country are perhaps as fine ships as any in the world, and they cost as much nearly in their equipment as the best built British ships, and they sail punctually to the day whether they have a freight or not'.[16]

The other protective aspect of the registry requirements related to manning. The entire crew of coasting vessels and three-quarters of the crew of a foreign-going vessel had to be British subjects. It was within the discretion of the Customs to determine when a vessel was duly manned and in practice they interpreted the regulation with some flexibility, bearing in mind the problem posed for masters faced with desertion by members of the original crew and the need to find replacements.[17] This was particularly common in the United States trade; in 1847 a third of all men who signed on here 'ran away', and foreigners accounted for approximately a fifth of the number recruited to replace deserters and those who left for other reasons.[18]

Among the ninety-eight instances of ships detained by the Customs between 1841 and 1846 for suspected contraventions of the navigation regulations only eleven concerned manning. Among these was the extreme case of the *Charlotte Laetitia* in 1845. Her crew was found to consist of seven Swedes, two Prussians, two Danes, one American and one Papenberg, but she was allowed clearance 'on the master making the declaration, that having been three years from home, and some of his men leaving, he was obliged to engage the services of the aforesaid persons'. The *Manley*, which entered Plymouth in 1844 with a cargo of barley from Montreal, was not so fortunate. She incurred a fine because the crew was half foreign, but the sum involved – £1 – was hardly draconian.[19]

In fact, where owners and masters were not under such compulsion, it seems to have been rare for even the permitted quarter of a crew to have been foreign. There were no advantages in terms of wages since shipowners judged it impossible to pay different rates based on nationality in a mixed crew and there were some practical cultural disadvantages: 'the men from the Captain downwards, must be accustomed to each other's modes and ways of living and doing'. However, investigation of the manning of coasting vessels undertaken in connection with Sir James Graham's mercantile marine reforms of the mid-1830s revealed a number of non-British seamen, who had been originally recruited when regulations had been relaxed in wartime. Some of these subsequently sought naturalisation in order to continue serving in the coasting trade. Lascar seamen, who were the subject of special legislation, were unique among inhabitants of British possessions in being denied recognition as British. A vessel coming from India could legally enter a British port with a Lascar crew, but could neither discharge these Asian seamen nor use them for the return voyage. In consequence, as one East India merchant put it, 'England, though it is the centre of all commercial operations, must be cast entirely out of the calculation of every Indian shipowner.'[20]

One additional restriction on the freedom of shipowners to operate their vessels as they thought fit was the compulsion to carry a statutory number of apprentices according to tonnage. Although compulsory apprenticeship dated from the early eighteenth century, this particular regulation dated from 1825, when it was pressed on the government by shipowners concerned to expand the supply of seamen at a time of labour unrest. It seems to have been a dead letter until re-enacted in 1835 as part of Sir James Graham's plans to improve the provision of merchant seamen to the navy.[21] No doubt large investors in shipping, whose apprentices normally remained in their service after their indentures were completed, did not require legislation to persuade them to train up boys to seafaring. But those with fewer vessels found the apprenticeship requirement, with the obligation to support the boys when ashore, an economic burden, and by the 1840s it had become a subject of complaint from the shipping interest.[22] In the decade after compulsion ceased, the number of apprentices indentured annually was approximately half the previous level, which suggests that left to themselves shipowners would have taken on fewer apprentices.[23]

Wallace's reform of the Navigation Laws was far less innovative than the Huskisson's Reciprocity of Duties Bill brought forward in 1823. This involved, as its promoter acknowledged, 'an entire departure from the principles which had hitherto governed our foreign commerce', which would allow goods imported in vessels belonging to foreigners to pay the same duties as those carried in British ships, provided reciprocal rights were granted.[24] Authority to equalise or to levy additional duties was to be through Orders in Council, obviating the need for direct parliamentary authorisation in the making of reciprocity treaties. Nevertheless, here the government was acting on past precedent, arrangements made with the United States of America, and seeking an opportunity to deflect retaliatory duties by the Netherlands, Prussia and Portugal. Practical considerations were similarly argued in the extension of reciprocity arrangements to the newly independent states of Colombia and La Plata which was agreed by Parliament in February 1825. Furthermore, in 1825, as part of Huskisson's new colonial system, the trade of the colonies with foreign parts was opened to ships of all countries willing to concede similar privileges in respect of their own possessions, but cargoes had to be nationally produced. Trade between Britain and its colonies, and inter-colonial trade, continued to be reserved for British vessels.[25]

Two points about reciprocity deserve emphasis. First, the treaties meant a reduction of the protection given to national fleets only to the extent represented by the removal, or diminution, of additional charges and duties imposed on a vessel, or its cargo, because it was foreign. Strictly speaking, and this was a point stressed by Huskisson in defending his legislation, they had nothing to do with the Navigation Laws, which remained unaffected. Second, treaties were needed because flag discrimination was not confined to Britain; it was characteristic of all trading nations with national fleets. Whether or not a foreign government responded to the British invitation to conclude a reciprocity treaty, and the particular terms of that treaty, clearly depended on individual circumstances and the perceived balance of advantage. Negotiations with the Netherlands in the 1820s, for example, failed to produce any concessions, despite a British retaliatory tax imposed in 1826 on the shipping of salt in Dutch ships, because the Dutch saw more loss than gain for their shipping from mutual reduction of charges and entry to colonial trades.[26] In the years between the 1823 Reciprocity of Duties Act and the repeal of the Navigation Laws the British government entered into twenty-seven reciprocity treaties affecting shipping (see Table 9). Since such treaties meant a loss of income to the various bodies in those ports which imposed extra charges on foreign vessels, these had to be recompensed. By 1844 the amount that had been paid out of central funds in reciprocity compensation since 1823 totalled the very considerable sum of £503,766.[27]

Table 9. *Reciprocity treaties with Britain, 1844*

Year	Country
1824	Denmark
	Hanse Towns (Bremen, Lubeck, Hamburg)
	Hanover
	Oldenburg
	Prussia
	Sweden and Norway
1825	Buenos Aires
	Colombia
	Rio de La Plata
	Mecklenburg
1826	France
	Mexico
1827	United States of America
	Brazil
1829	Austria
	Venezuela
1832	Frankfurt
1837	Greece
	Netherlands
	Peru
1838	Ottoman Empire
1839	Muscat
1841	Prussia and German Union of Customs
1842	Uruguay
	Portugal
1843	Russia

Source: *S. C. on British Shipping*, PP 1844 (VIII), Appendix 4, p. 231.

Huskisson's recast colonial system meant that trade between foreign countries and British colonies was permitted where granted by Orders in Council, though only into specified free ports. Although the Act specified that such a privilege should be 'limited to the ships of those countries which having Colonial Possessions shall grant the like privileges of trading with those Possessions to British ships', it did not rule out the possibility of allowing entry where no such reciprocity was offered. Thus under the Reciprocity Treaty of 1826 France was allowed to export some produce to British colonies, notwithstanding limitations on British entry to French colonial business, but wine could be carried only in British ships. Trade between the Spanish and British colonies was allowed, but not between the latter and Spain. By the 1840s disputes over American access to the West Indies carrying trade which had marred relations in the 1820s were past history, and United States vessels had over half of their country's trade with the West Indies and British North America.[28] This was, however, an old established connection. In contrast, other direct trades between the colonies and foreign countries represented still relatively new opportunities in the 1840s, the product of the power given to colonists to 'buy the cheapest and sell at the dearest rate' under Huskisson's reforms. British and colonial shipping took the greater share of this business, but not by a large margin. In 1843 their tonnage entering colonial ports from foreign countries amounted to 328,000 tons, as against 239,000 tons of foreign-owned shipping. Nevertheless, for British shipowners it represented an extension of opportunities and few complained that theirs was not a total monopoly.[29]

Shipowners had no objection either to the encouragement provided by the reciprocity treaties signed with the South and Central American states: Brazil, Colombia, Buenos Aires, Peru, Rio, Mexico and Venezuela. With few locally owned vessels able to compete in the trade to Britain, little had been sacrificed and much gained by the mutual element in these treaties giving British ships privileged access to South American ports. Entries into the United Kingdom from this region grew from 46,000 tons in 1824 to 170,000 tons in 1846, with British-registered vessels taking 97 per cent of business in the latter year (Table 10).[30] This was one instance where the shipping interest had no quarrel with reciprocity. Another, but for different reasons, was in respect of the United States of America.

Here reciprocity in the direct trade between the United Kingdom and the United States of America, first established by the 1815 convention, represented an end to damaging discrimination against British vessels in a situation where they were at a competitive disadvantage. Much as British shipowners might regret that shippers preferred United States ships to such an extent that entries by American ships in the 1840s totalled twice the tonnage of British, they recognised that reciprocity could give to the United States shipping no competitive advantage which it did not already possess. Rather, it was seen not only as a means of dividing Anglo-American business between the ships of the two powers to the exclusion of other maritime nations, but as a necessity if British shipowners were to maintain any significant share of this business.[31] However, here, as elsewhere, reciprocity was an

Table 10. *British and foreign tonnage entering UK Ports 1824, 1846 ('000 tons)*

Trade	1824 Brit.	For.	Total	% For.	1846 Brit.	For.	Total	% For.
Russia	239	31	270	11	452	65	517	13
Sweden	17	40	57	70	12	80	92	86
Norway	11	135	146	92	3	113	116	97
Denmark	6	23	29	79	9	105	114	92
Prussia	94	151	245	61	63	270	333	81
Germany	67	46	113	40	206	122	328	37
Holland & Belgium	68	107	175	61	382	230	612	38
France	82	52	134	39	556	262	818	32
Portugal	58	9	67	13	74	8	82	10
Spain	45	5	50	10	65	12	77	16
Italy	40	0	40	0	98	59	157	38
Gibraltar	5	0	5	0	14	0	14	0
Malta	3	0	3	0	8	0	8	0
Ottoman Empire	2	0	2	0	97	7	104	7
China	28	0	28	0	53	0	53	0
East Indies	3	0	3	0	8 2	10	20	
Foreign W. Indies	9	0	9	0	62	18	80	23
United States	44	153	197	78	205	435	640	68
South America	46	0	46	0	170	6	176	3

Source: Based on 'Statement of the Tonnage of British and Foreign Ships that entered the ports of the United Kingdom . . .', *Lords S. C. Navigation Laws*, PP 1847–48 Pt. II, Q. 8256.

adjunct of the navigation code, not its replacement. When MacGregor of the Board of Trade described reciprocity between Britain and the United States of America as 'perfect', he meant 'exact': that rights and limitations on one side precisely mirrored those applied on the other.[32] United States of America vessels were not allowed to carry goods produced in other countries to Britain; they had to come in British ships. Conversely, British vessels could not carry such diverse items as Dutch nutmegs or Swedish iron to the United States because they were not home produced. Such cargoes were reserved to American vessels.[33] How quantitatively significant such restrictions were hard to say, but their existence demonstrates the fallacy of assuming that reciprocity and free trade were synonymous.

When in an unguarded moment, G. F. Young told the House of Commons Select Committee on the Navigation Laws that they had been 'virtually repealed' and shipping 'left virtually unprotected' as a result of reciprocity treaties, – words he was subsequently to retract 'as loose and unconsidered' – the agreements he had in mind were those made with other Northern European powers.[34] Reciprocity treaties had been negotiated with Prussia, Hanover, the Hanse, Oldenburg, Sweden, Norway and Denmark in 1824, with Mecklenburg in 1825 and France in 1826. These treaties, described by Joseph Somes as 'the first great blow which was struck at the shipping interest of this country', were generally regarded by shipowners as the means by which foreign vessels had gained the greater share of much of the carrying trade between Britain and Europe, so creating permanent competitive pressure.[35]

It was certainly the case that most produce entering British ports from Northern Europe in the 1840s came in foreign vessels. As Table 10 shows, only in the trade with Russia, not the subject of a reciprocity treaty until 1843, did British-owned ships predominate. The small contribution of Russian shipping to the carriage of national exports no doubt reflected its own, exceptional maritime incapacity. Ships belonging to all other Baltic powers were the dominant carriers in their trade with Britain, although their share varied, with Norway closest to a total national monopoly. To this situation reciprocity had contributed something, but by no means everything. The timber trade was always subject to considerable fluctuation (tonnage entries, British and foreign, from Norway in 1846 were lower than those recorded for 1824) but trade with Scandinavia was generally sluggish in the period from 1820 to 1850, encouraging British shipowners to move into alternative national trades – an opportunity not open in the same degree to their foreign counterparts. There is plenty of evidence to support the British view that their competitors' costs tended to be lower, and equalisation of port charges and dues under reciprocity removed one countervailing influence, but it seems probable that the balance of advantage was already moving towards the fleets of the exporting countries in the early 1820s. Even before the treaties their vessels accounted for 40 per cent of tonnage.[36]

The belief prevalent amongst British shipowners that the protective system had been substantially undermined by reciprocity provisions was not shared by their European competitors. Britain's willingness to enter into such agreements was less open-handed than might appear at first sight. Their characteristic feature – equalisation of duties on shipping and most favoured nation treatment of imports – made no impact on the navigation regulations which prevented other maritime nations acting as third party carriers or which restricted what they could carry to Britain. Prussian vessels, for example, were until 1841 restricted to carrying goods to Britain only from Prussia, yet there was no similar prohibition on British ships, which could take goods into Prussian ports from anywhere. Most other countries with whom Britain had reciprocity arrangements were similarly willing to permit its ships to come indirectly; a substantial concession to judge from some statistics collected by Porter which show that out of 5,120 British vessels recorded as entering Northern European ports in 1846, 16 per cent had not come directly from Britain.[37] France, whose navigation code equalled Britain's in its rigour, was exceptional among Continental powers in excluding indirect traders.

But while reciprocity treaties were in theory bilateral arrangements involving a limited degree of liberalisation, in practice their separation from the Navigation Laws was to prove, whether by error or intention, difficult to sustain. Orders in Council issued in 1838, allowing Austria to export from the Danube ports to Britain, so obviously contravened the Laws that it necessitated the introduction of a new clause in the navigation code for Europe, 'Her Majesty may allow ports to be used as national ports by the ships of countries, within the dominions of which the ports do not lie, but for the exportation of the produce of which they are convenient outlets.'[38] This set in train, through the most favoured nation clause, a relaxation of the regulations confining export to national ports. The treaty with the *Zollverein* of 1841 permitted the ships of Prussia and the other member states to bring goods to Britain from any Baltic port. This concession, subsequently granted to Hanover, Oldenburg, Mecklenburg and the Hanse Towns, could be claimed by most reciprocity treaty states where similar conditions could be demonstrated.[39] However, the Board of Trade's legal officer, Stafford Northcote, was overstating the case when he told the Lords' Select Committee on the Navigation Laws in 1848: 'if we adhere to the Treaty against the Law the Navigation Act would be repealed with regard to the trade of the Baltic and all the countries of the Baltic', because considerable limitations on their freedom as third parties to carry goods from elsewhere to Britain remained. The degree of continued constraint consistent with reciprocity is well illustrated by MacGregor's description of what total repeal of the Navigation Laws would mean for a country such as Holland: 'you would allow a Dutch ship to come from ports in France, or from ports in Germany, or from ports in Belgium or from ports in any part of the world with a cargo, and bring it to this country without any declaration as to the origin of the cargo.'[40]

Holland, with whom reciprocity was not agreed until 1837, was in fact one country whose export of domestic products was only partly touched by Britain's navigation code. The list of enumerated goods, which in 1845 comprised 'masts, timber, boards, tar, tallow, hemp, flax, currants, raisins, figs, prunes, olive oil, corn or grain, wine, brandy, tobacco, wool, shumac, madders, madder roots, barilla, brimstone, bark of oak, cork, oranges, lemons, linseed, rapeseed, and cloverseed', did not include butter and cheese, which could therefore be brought in freely by vessels of any nationality. That the vessels which regularly plied between Britain and the Dutch ports were British could be attributed to the initiative of British entrepreneurs in investing in fast steamships, not to any protective legislation.[41]

This description of the impact of protection has so far concentrated on Navigation Laws and reciprocity treaties, but other aspects of commercial policy also shaped shipping prospects. Duties affecting such bulk products as corn, sugar, coffee and timber exerted a powerful influence on the pattern and course of trade, distorting it in ways which affected demand for cargo space. The Corn Laws shielded British farmers but reduced business opportunities for their shipowning compatriots, just as the exclusion of 'slave-grown' sugar in favour of the British West Indies until the later 1840s had the effect of confining shipping to what had become a waning trade. Until 1835 West Indian colonial coffee enjoyed such a substantial preference that both East Indian and South American coffee was effectively cut off from the British market. Equalisation of duties on all colonial coffee in 1835 brought an increase in the production of British plantations in the East which to some extent compensated for a decline in West Indian production, while reduced rates on foreign coffee when imported from within East India Company limits brought in the late 1830s the spectacular, if short-lived, development of an indirect trade via the Cape in the later 1830s.[42]

But no trade had so close a connection with public policy as did that in British North American timber, which owed its very creation to colonial preference. The colonial timber industry was a product of the Napoleonic Wars, which exposed the extent of Britain's reliance on Baltic supplies and the vulnerability of these to blockade. Duties first imposed in 1811 on Baltic timber, while the colonial product entered free, guaranteed for the nation a source of supply and for shipowners a source of valuable, long-haul business which (with the exception of the

Baltic merchants) they were reluctant to relinquish with the coming of peace. Wallace's 1821 tariff reforms reduced the duty on foreign timber and imposed one on colonial, but a differential of 45s per load still remained.[43] The timber duties, 'silent partners of the Corn Laws' in Albion's phrase, were nevertheless central in every commercial controversy over the next two decades. They survived Whig attempts at reduction in 1831 and 1841, not least because of the political sensitivity of any attack on 'Great Britain's Woodyard', but could not escape Peel's reforming Budgets of 1842 and 1846, which together brought down rates of duty by 73 per cent, so setting in train a process of abolition finally completed in 1860.[44]

From the point of view of British shipowners the value of the British North American timber trade was twofold: it offered employment to a greater number of vessels than would have been required by the European trade; and, competitive though this business might be, as a colonial trade it was at least safe from intrusion by foreign vessels, such as increasingly dominated the Baltic. In fact, although to the colonial and shipping interests, preferential duties and the fortunes of the timber trade seemed inextricably linked, probably they overestimated the strength of the connection. Falling transatlantic freight rates were also a factor in giving colonial timber a competitive edge over Baltic in the British market, as they were in encouraging a minority of merchants to ship Baltic timber through British North America to Britain until this was made illegal in 1835.[45]

To return by way of conclusion to consideration of the general character of the British shipping industry in the first half of the nineteenth century, it seems clear that this was an industry still very much shaped by protection. Admittedly, outside the colonial and coasting business the ships of other maritime nations had access to British trades, where their share of tonnage testified to their willingness and ability to seize the opportunity this offered, but this access was in general confined to direct trade only. Moreover, the British shipping operating in these more open trades did so under what some shipowners were prepared to argue were distinct handicaps – the compulsion to buy British vessels, to employ a certain proportion of British nationals as seamen and to take on apprentices. It is true that by the 1840s several of the ancillary elements of protection which affected shipping had been reduced, (for example, that associated with the colonial timber preference) and also that the Danube concessions to Austria had opened the door to admission of third party carriers. But in the main, reciprocity notwithstanding, the owner of a British ship, its builder and the men who sailed her operated in a context defined by the traditional principle of national preference.

Notes

1 For a detailed description of the Navigation Laws see Lawrence A. Harper, *The English Navigation Laws, a Seventeenth-Century Experiment in Social Engineering*, New York, 1939. A useful summary appears in *Lords S. C. Navigation Laws*, PP 1847–48 XX Pt. II, Appendix to the Fifth Report, pp. 146–59.
2 PRO, BT 6/237; *Return of all Tolls, Dues, Fees and other charges . . .*, PP 1844 (366) XLV, p. 317.
3 3 Geo. IV. c 41–45; *S. C. Foreign Trade*, PP 1820 II. In all twenty-one acts dealing with aspects of policy towards shipping were passed by parliament between 1822 and 1827.
4 *S. C. British Shipping*, PP 1844 VIII, Q. 669.
5 *Lords S. C. Navigation Laws*, PP 1847–48 XX Pt. II, Appendix E, p. 901; Q. 8256.
6 *Commons S. C. Navigation Laws*, PP 1847 X, Q. 4583. See also *S. C. British Shipping*, PP 1844 VIII, Q. 2960.
7 *Commons S. C. Navigation Laws*, PP 1847 X, Q. 3059.
8 Feinstein, 'Britain: Capital', p. 64; R. S. Craig, 'British shipping and British North American shipbuilding', in H. E. S. Fisher (ed.), *The South West and the Sea, Exeter Papers in Economic History*, 1, Exeter, 1968.
9 *Return of the Number of Colonial Built Ships registered at each port of the United Kingdom*, PP 1847 (309) LX, p. 309.
10 *S. C. British Shipping*, PP 1844 VIII, Appendix I, p. 213; *Letter from the Secretary of the North American Colonial Association and Reply from the Chairman of the General Shipowners' Society*, PP 1846 (83) (97) XLV, p. 347, p. 351; *Lords S. C. Navigation Laws*, PP 1847–8 XX Pt. II, Q. 6215–6.
11 *S. C. Foreign Trade*, PP 1820 II,p. 13.
12 PRO, FO 72/233, Swedish Consul to Palmerston, 15 January 1849; *Commons S. C. Navigation Laws*, PP 1847 X, Q. 3304.
13 *Commons S. C. Navigation Laws*, PP 1847 X, Q. 4438; Q. 1036.
14 See *Lords S. C. Navigation Laws*, PP 1847–48 XX Pt. II, Q. 3742, Q. 7238, Q. 4102, Q. 6018, Q. 6454.
15 *Lords S. C. Navigation Laws*, PP 1847–48 XX Pt. II, Q. 6255.
16 *S. C. British Shipping*, PP 1844 VIII, Q. 8487. On British shipowners' attitudes to American competition, see David M. Williams, 'The rise of United States merchant shipping on the North Atlantic, 1800–1850: the British perception and response', in Clark G. Reynolds (ed.), *Global Crossroads and the American Seas*, Missoula, Montana, 1988.
17 *Commons S. C. Navigation Laws*, PP 1847 X, Q. 2533.
18 *Lords S. C. Navigation Laws*, PP 1847–48 XX Pt. II, Appendix Ee, Return No. 3, p. 1030. This return for 1847 shows that out of 4,611 recorded desertions, only 475 were of men serving outside the United States trade.

19 *Return and further return of Articles Seized, Ships Detained and Penalties Imposed in the United Kingdom for contravention of the Navigation Laws 1841–1846,* PP 1847 (286) LX, pp. 327–31.

20 *Commons S. C. Navigation Laws,* PP 1847 X, Q. 2499–509, Q. 3725–7, Q. 3803.

21 *Lords S. C. Navigation Laws,* PP 1847–48 XX Pt. II, Appendix M, p. 973.

22 *Commons S. C. Navigation Laws,* PP 1847 X, Q. 4997; 5318–21. See also V. C. Burton, 'Apprenticeship regulation and maritime labour in the nineteenth century merchant marine', *International Journal of Maritime History,* I, 1989, pp. 29–49.

23 *Return of the Number of Apprentices 1835–1860,* PP 1861 (849) LVIII, p. 23.

24 4 Geo. IV c. 77; PD. New Series, IX, 6 June 1823, c. 795.

25 6 Geo. IV c. 114; 9 Geo. IV c. 83.

26 See H. R. C. Wright, *Free Trade and Protection in the Netherlands 1816–1830: a Study of the First Benelux,* Cambridge, 1955, pp. 182–4.

27 *Account of the Sums paid out of the Consolidated Duties of Customs,* PP 1844 (551) XLV, p. 367.

28 *Commons S. C. Navigation Laws,* PP 1847 X, Q. 112–24, Q. 6186.

29 *Returns of the number and tonnage of vessels that entered and cleared at each of the ports of each colony, coastwise, to and from the United Kingdom and to and from foreign ports December 1842–December 1843,* PP 1844 (36) XLV, p. 337.

30 *Lords S. C. Navigation Laws,* PP 1847–48 XX Pt. II, Appendix E, Number 4, p. 901.

31 *Commons S. C. Navigation Laws,* PP 1847 X, Q. 389; *S. C. British Shipping,* PP 1844, VII, Q. 265.

32 *Ibid.,* Q. 267; Q. 1590.

33 *Lords S. C. Navigation Laws,* PP 1847–48 XX Pt. II, Q. 8027.

34 *Commons S. C. Navigation Laws,* PP 1847 X, Q. 5524; *Lords S. C. Navigation Laws,* PP 1847–48 XX Pt. II, Q. 8027.

35 *S. C. British Shipping,* 1844 VIII, Q. 258.

36 *Ibid.,* Q. 260. In 1820 tonnage entries of foreign vessels from the Baltic totalled 180,000 tons, as against 449,000 tons of British shipping.

37 *Lords S. C. Navigation Laws,* PP 1847–48 XX Pt. II, Q. 5161.

38 PD, Third Series, 1840, LV, c. 469–87; 3 & 4 Vic. c. 95.

39 *Lords S. C. Navigation Laws,* PP 1847–48 XX Pt. II, Q. 4911.

40 *Ibid.,* Q. 4922.

41 *Commons S. C. Navigation Laws,* PP 1847 X, Q. 549.

42 David M. Williams, 'Customs evasion, colonial preference and the British tariff 1829–42', in Cottrell, P. L. and Aldcroft, D. H. *Shipping, Trade and Commerce, Essays in Memory of Ralph Davis,* Leicester, 1981, pp. 104–10.

43 On timber duties see Arthur R. M. Lower, *Great Britain's Woodyard, British America and the Timber Trade,* 1763–1867, Toronto, 1973; J. Potter, 'The British timber duties, 1815–1860', *Economica,* new ser., XXIII, pp. 122–36.

44 R. G. Albion, *Forests and Seapower,* Harvard, 1926; Lower, *Woodyard,* p. 89.

45 Eric W. Sager and Gerry Panting, 'Staple economies and the rise and decline of the shipping industry in Atlantic Canada, 1820–1914', in

Fischer, Lewis R. and Panting, Gerald E. *Change and Adaptation in Maritime History: the North Atlantic Fleets in the Nineteenth Century*, St John's, Newfoundland, 1984, p. 10; Williams, 'Customs evasion', pp. 100–4.

Chapter Four

'A sense of the great national advantages': the policy of protection

So far this discussion of protection as it influenced the shipping industry in the first half of the nineteenth century has concentrated on measures, not motives. Nothing has yet been said about the issues of public policy involved or how the navigation code was viewed at a time of increasing acceptance of free trade doctrines. Until the Russell administration of the late 1840s, the only government which subjected maritime commercial policy to any evident scrutiny or substantial alteration was that of Lord Liverpool. Huskisson's reciprocity provisions continued to exert an influence on the activities of the Board of Trade throughout the 1830s, as it sought to conclude additional treaties, and other aspects of trade policy such as attempts to alter timber duties touched on shipping interests; but the principle of protection as enshrined in the Navigation Laws remained intact. That further consolidating, updating, measures apparently aroused no debate when they passed through Parliament in 1833 and 1845 is indicative not only of their uncontroversial nature as far the shipping interests were concerned but also of a surprising unwillingness among free traders to confront the issue which clearly requires explanation. Thus although technically the Act repealed in 1849 was that of 1845, the protective system dismantled under the Russell government at mid-century was in essence that refashioned almost three decades earlier by Wallace and Huskisson.[1]

Why did protection for shipping remain so firmly rooted? It might appear that no answer is required other than that offered by Lucy Brown in her convincing study of commercial policy between 1830 and 1842. She points out that for much of this period circumstances were not politically conducive to the progress of free trade measures, despite the fact that the Whigs were more likely on grounds of principle to look for further diminutions of protection than were their opponents. The Whigs' ambitious programme of reform, their wish to respond to popular demands, the parliamentary strength of protective interests and the fact that, the legislation of the 1820s notwithstanding, the Tories when in opposition proved hostile to extensions of free trade – these were all obstacles to further change.[2] But, while these factors had an impact on the timber question, it would be misleading to suggest that they also acted as a brake on progress towards repeal of the Navigation Laws.

They could not do so for two reasons: first, because the Wallace-Huskisson reforms were not intended as an assault on the central principle of protection for shipping; second, because no such confidently unequivocal proposal figured on the free trade agenda. However they have been treated in retrospect, the Navigation Acts were not simply one more example of early nineteenth-century restrictive policy – the equivalent for shipping of the Corn Laws in relation to agricultural interests or of the silk duties for silk weavers and manufacturers. Their position in commercial policy was unique. The essence of the argument against protection was that the needs of the community should not be sacrificed to sectional interest. But protection for shipowners and shipbuilders might be seen as itself serving the widest community interest. Faced with the shipping industry, even convinced free traders faltered.

The Navigation Laws of the seventeenth and eighteenth centuries, for all their complexity in terms of detail, were based on a simple premise: that maritime power, and with it national defence, ultimately depended on the ability to man the navy with skilled men, which in turn relied on the merchant service to supply this need. In the classic phrase, the merchant navy served as the 'nursery' of seamen. What linked the 'nursery of seamen' to the panoply of protection was the assumption that a large merchant navy was necessarily an artificial creation. Left to itself, it was thought, there was no guarantee that the national merchant fleet would be of sufficient size to provide such a pool of labour. It needed the encouragement offered by legislation defining spheres of operation in which the vessels of other maritime powers were either severely disadvantaged, or from which they were completely excluded. From this flowed the main elements of the British navigation system, including manning regulations intended to ensure that protecting shipping did indeed lead to a large pool of native seafarers. There are two concepts here: the need to man the Royal Navy from the merchant marine; and the identification of protection as necessary if this was to be done. By the late 1840s the willingness of certain politicians, such as Sir James Graham, to recognise these as distinct questions enabled them to support abrogation of the Navigation Laws whilst stressing the continued importance of the merchant navy for the country's defence. But for much of the twenty years which preceded repeal the fact that the Royal Navy continued to depend on the merchant marine for its supply of men exerted a powerful influence on attitudes to the shipping industry.

The merchant navy's assigned role as a 'nursery' was a product of the traditional British system of naval manning, which was to continue unchanged in essentials until the early 1850s.[3] The national fleet consisted of vessels manned by crews who served only for the period of the commission, which nominally lasted for five years but was usually in practice three. What happened to the seamen when the commission ended was graphically described by Admiral Cochrane in 1848: 'the ship at last is paid off, when a disruption of their society takes place; the bond that unites them is broken, at the very moment when its effects were becoming most beneficial they are scattered to the winds.'[4] This wasteful and inefficient traditional 'hire and discharge' arrangement was necessarily heavily reliant on recruitment of seamen who had previously served in merchant vessels. According to Admiralty calculations, between 1839 and 1847 68,559 men entered the navy, with the number of men employed in any one year averaging just under 30,000. Of the total recruited in these years 22,543 were merchant seamen, 8,980 had never been to sea before and 37,076 had seen naval service previously. An unknown proportion of these men with naval experience would have also been employed in the past as merchant seamen.[5]

In the competition for labour resources the two services were unequally matched. In wartime, bounties and impressment had shifted the balance away from the mercantile sector; in peace the natural preference of seamen for merchant service reasserted itself, and naval vessels could wait months to achieve their full complement of men. As the Secretary to the Admiralty explained to the Treasury in March 1853:

This desultory mode of proceeding is a cause of great embarrassment and expense in conducting the ordinary duties of naval service. It creates uncertainty as to the period when ships may be expected to be ready for sea; and the evil becomes one of great magnitude and a serious danger when political considerations suddenly demand the rapid equipment of Her Majesty's ships.[6]

Desertion was also a problem. In the period from 1839 to 1847, 26 per cent of men who entered the navy direct from the merchant service, and 16 per cent of those who had previously served, subsequently jumped ship.[7]

There was much within the naval recruitment system to attract the attention of reformers. But few among those who sought to end the right to impress or among the many talented naval officers who offered alternative manning schemes in pamphlets or memoranda appear to have challenged the ultimate role of the mercantile marine in providing naval manpower.[8] As we shall see, this is certainly true of the manning experts who gave evidence to the two Parliamentary Select Committees which examined the Navigation Laws in 1847 and 1848. Even Sir James Stirling, founder of the Swan River colony in Australia, who denied that the merchant service in practice served as a worthwhile nursery for the navy and advocated a permanent standing navy, looked to it for compulsory service in wartime.[9]

Further confirmation that the 'nursery' concept had continuing force in this period is provided by the legislation promoted by Sir James Graham in the mid-1830s. His Merchant Seamen's Act made written engagements compulsory, reaffirmed the right of seamen to break their contracts in order to enlist in the navy and re-enacted earlier legislation which compelled ships to carry apprentices in proportion to tonnage.[10] It also established a registry of seamen, with powers to supervise the apprenticeship scheme. Arguably, encouragement of apprenticeship owed something to concern about paupers, since it compelled masters to take such boys on if they were offered or otherwise incur a fine.[11] But the terms in which Graham commended his proposals to the House of Commons indicated wider concerns. They were

connected with the manning of His Majesty's Navy: for as the merchant service of the country was the nursery from which the King's navy was to be supplied; it was necessary to protect the merchant seaman: otherwise the numbers to which the state would look in time of necessity would be greatly reduced.[12]

If at this time there was still widespread adherence to the 'nursery' concept in political circles, as well as in the country at large, this was certainly even more the case twenty years previously. The years of war which had drained the shipping industry of British labour had revealed the full extent of national dependence on the merchant seaman, and the coming of peace in no way altered this. But peace did, however, have an impact on commercial prospects and hence on commercial policy, including that affecting shipping. With peace seemingly there came also a new willingness in political circles to embrace the liberal economic ideas associated with Adam Smith. The question which needs to be asked in the present context is whether the changes in the system of protection for shipping introduced by Wallace and Huskisson represented a point of departure in policy towards shipping: the first stage in repeal. To answer it requires more detailed scrutiny of the background to these measures.

The commercial reforms of the 1820s, together with the government which implemented them, have attracted considerable scholarly attention in recent years.[13] The traditional view, that these reforms were initiated by a petition of 1820 from the capital's merchant community which complained of 'the impolicy and injustice of the restrictive system', has been shown to be mistaken. Rather, it seems that the London Merchants' Petition was in substance a conventional appeal on behalf of an interest, in this instance the Baltic timber merchants, which had been given a wider free trade gloss by its promoter Thomas Tooke, in response to some encouragement from government. But recognition of the Liverpool administration's part in rallying mercantile support for liberal measures does not imply any doctrinaire adherence to political economy in government circles. The political activity of economic liberals, including David Ricardo's role as an MP from 1819 until his death in 1823, cannot be taken as indicative of the power of economic theory to influence policy. Members of the Ministry may well have been, in Tooke's words, 'far more sincere and resolute Free Traders than the Merchants of London', but practical considerations, not theoretical dogma, determined their approach.[14] A fall in export values in the first four years of peace, coupled with agricultural and manufacturing depression, made the expansion of foreign demand an urgent necessity. Improved economic prospects after 1820 presented the opportunity to bring about the changes which the experience of the previous few years had shown to be necessary. Commercial reform was thus defensive in origin – in Gash's words 'a policy sired by hope out of necessity' – albeit founded on a conviction that greater freedom of trade was incontrovertably something to be desired.[15]

With the debate which followed the Merchants' Petition, Parliament began the review of commercial policy which was to occupy much of its time for the following few years. The setting up of a Select Committee by the Lords 'to inquire into the means of extending and securing the foreign trade of the country', followed by a similar appointment by the Commons, brought two questions central to shipping interests into immediate focus. Identifying three types of commercial restriction: that supportive of maritime power; that introduced to raise revenue; and that protective of native industries, the Commons Committee decided to look at the first of these – the Navigation Laws. Meanwhile the Select Committee in the Lords devoted itself to the timber trade. The reason for the Lords' choice is evident. The petition, for all its general liberal rhetoric, was concerned with that particular trade.[16] But what is the significance of the Commons choice of the Navigation Laws for their first investigation?; certainly not a desire on the part of government for abolition. It had affirmed its commitment to maritime protection when the Commons was presented with the London Merchants' Petition and the report of the Select Committee itself, of which Wallace as Chairman was author, also made much of their continued merits:

A just respect for the political wisdom from which the enactment of the Navigation Laws originated and a sense of the great national advantages derived from them in their effects on the maritime greatness and power of the Kingdom have rendered them objects of attachment and veneration to every British subject. Nor can your Committee suppose that any suggestions they may offer can lead to a suspicion of their being disposed to recommend an abandonment of the policy from which they emanated; or to advise in favour of extension of commerce, a remission of that protecting vigilance under which the shipping and navigation of the kingdom have so eminently grown and flourished.[17]

No doubt this statement was intended to reassure shipowners, a number of whom had attended a meeting in London on 16 May 1820 to express their fears as to what modifications in the Laws might involve.[18] But in fact despite the optimistic assertion in the Select Committee's report that 'the skill, enterprise and capital of British merchants and manufacturers require only an open and equal field for exertion', there was little in its recommendations to which shipowners could or did take exception.[19] Still less could the report be construed as a major onslaught on the principle of protection. Indeed, much of what was suggested reflected the shipping interest's concerns about the practical working of the laws as expressed by the Shipowners' Society. McCulloch's claim in an 1827 article in the *Edinburgh Review* (by which time relations between government and shipping had become distinctly hostile in the wake of the reciprocity issue) that Wallace's Acts were a response to the shipowners' own demands was not without some justification.[20]

The Select Committee's recognition of the undue complexity of the regulations and the case for codification of 'the vast and confused mass of legislation' was uncontroversial, while the extent to which regulations had been often been relaxed 'whenever a new state of political circumstances appeared to parliament to afford sufficient reasons for such a change' offered a precedent for ending the long outdated restrictions on Dutch and German trade. In their evidence the shipowners Buckle and Lyall made no objection to these proposals and they had only slight reservations, in respect of Mediterranean business, about allowing entry of cargoes from non-producer European ports; in most cases such a change would benefit British shipping. Only the question of permitting non-European goods to be imported from European ports, even in British vessels, aroused their hostility. This concern to reserve the 'long voyage' to the national fleet was sufficient to ensure that Wallace's 1821 Act allowed such imports only for re-export. [21]

The essentially conservative, non-controversial nature of the Wallace reforms, was unwittingly testified to by McCulloch:

the feebleness of the opposition to the bills introduced in spring 1821 by Mr Wallace, for the improvement and amendment of the Navigation Laws, is indeed a curious and gratifying circumstance . . . such, however, and so rapid has been the progress of more enlarged and liberal opinion that even the shipowners approved of the new bills; and they were carried through both houses with but little debate and by triumphant majorities. [22]

McCulloch's optimism was naive. If shipowners seemingly approved of the Wallace reforms, this was a reflection not of their acceptance of the new political economy, but of the continued force of a much older principle – self-interest.

Under the Liverpool administration, then, the Navigation Laws were updated and simplified, but their fundamental character remained unaltered. In contrast, Huskisson's Reciprocity of Duties Act in time had considerable implications for sections of the shipping industry, exposing some trades to greater competition from foreign owners. Nevertheless, to conceive the Act as an intentional attack on protection for shipping is to misunderstand the thinking behind it. Huskisson's motive was his concern to expedite bilateral trade flows, which he believed to be hampered by the widespread international practice of charging discriminatory duties on foreign goods shipped in non-national vessels. But there was nothing unilateral in Huskisson's commercial treaty approach; reciprocity implied not a gift but a bargain. The aim was to secure for British merchants uninhibited access to foreign markets at a time when a number of countries, but most significantly Prussia, threatened further discriminatory imposts. In return, the British government was prepared to forgo the revenue from discriminatory customs duties and to compensate local port and other authorities for loss of income. Huskisson's view was that the offer of reciprocity treaties constituted a pragmatic response to changed conditions. That the dues and duties affected also acted as a protection for British shipping was incidental. They formed no part of the formal navigation code.

Huskisson aimed to replace an antiquated scheme of protection with one seemingly better suited to the needs of a threatened commerce and fretful colonies. A recurrent motif in his speeches on these themes was the necessity to appreciate the significance of 'the altered state of the world' if national interest was to be served. Imposing discriminatory duties on foreign ships and risking retaliation in return was a contest out of which Britain was unlikely to emerge 'with dignity and advantage'.[23] Furthermore, if colonists were not to rebel, attention must be paid to their demands: 'a colony is not a plantation'. Alexander Brady has argued (interpreting the administration's unwillingness to tackle the timber and sugar questions as a matter of choice not political necessity) that Huskisson sought to substitute imperial preference for protection. Certainly when much else was considered alterable, inter-imperial carriage was treated as inviolate; trade between Britain and its colonies remained the domain of the national mercantile fleet.[24]

With this central exception, the navigation system as it affected the colonies was not static, reciprocity saw to that, but by the same token progress depended on the response of other powers. When in 1826 the United States of America refused to respond to colonial concessions, the Board of Trade took retaliatory measures. There was little echo here of the bold free trade assertion in the 1820 London Merchants' Petition that 'our restrictions would not be less prejudicial to our own capital and industry, because other governments persisted in preserving impolitic regulations'.[25]

Against this view of Wallace and Huskisson as very limited liberalisers as far as shipping was concerned must be set an alternative judgement which sees these men as the first warriors in a long battle to abolish protection. This interpretation was later popular among free traders, enabling them to invoke the shade of the Tory Huskisson in support of their cause.[26] Certainly both the government's free trade friends and protectionist critics tended to believe that its ultimate intentions were more far-reaching than public utterances suggested. In a speech at the Annual Dinner of the Shipowners' Society in December 1822, Lord Liverpool assured the diners of his belief that 'we owe our security to the Navy, and we owe our Navy to that system of Navigation Laws under which our country has so long acted with so much advantage to our best interest', and stressed his rejection of 'fanciful and impracticable theories'. David Ricardo interpreted this as an attempt by Ministers to conciliate the shipping lobby – 'I am sure they did not speak their real sentiments' – a suspicion, no doubt, also harboured by some shipowners.[27] However, if the shipping interest could not be ignored, there is no reason to suppose that its influence diverted the government from doing what it wanted, a point confirmed by the reciprocity legislation.

Indeed, it seems inescapable that the Liverpool administration's policy towards shipping was shaped more by a conviction that some protection was justified than by any tension between commercial liberalisation and concern for vested interests. In a speech of May 1826 Huskisson encapsulated the dilemma faced by those of a liberal economic persuasion confronting the Navigation Laws. Commercially, he argued, they were disadvantageous: 'the regulations of our navigation system, however salutary they may be, must, more or less, act as a restraint on that freedom of commercial pursuit, which it is desirable should be open to those who have capital to employ'. Nevertheless they were based upon 'the highest ground of political necessity': the need for national safety and defence, security of colonial possessions, protection of commerce from the risks associated with war and the 'necessity of preserving ascendancy on the ocean'. In pursuing these ends, Huskisson contended that the interests of the shipowner should not be allowed to cramp commerce beyond what state necessity required. But nothing he said can be taken as a denial of the efficacy of protection in serving that national need. [28]

Such opinions were not inconsistent with the teachings of the new political economy. Adam Smith's view is well known, but is worth quoting in full:

When the Act of Navigation was made though England and Holland were not actually at war, the most violent animosity subsisted between the two nations . . . it is not impossible, therefore, that some of the regulations of this famous act may have proceeded from national animosity. They are as wise, however, as if they had all been dictated by the most deliberate wisdom. National animosity at that particular time aimed at the very same object which the most deliberate wisdom would have recommended, – the diminution of the naval power of Holland, the only naval power which could endanger the security of England. The Act of Navigation is not favourable to foreign commerce, or to the growth of that opulence which can arise from it. The interest of a nation in its commercial arrangements to foreign nations is, like that of a merchant with regard to the different people with whom he deals, to buy as cheap and to sell as dear as possible. But the Act of Navigation by diminishing the number of sellers, must necessarily diminish that of buyers; and we are thus likely not only to buy foreign goods dearer, but to sell our own dearer, than if there was a more perfect freedom of trade. As defence, however, is of much more importance than opulence, the Act of Navigation is, perhaps, the wisest of all the commercial regulations of England.[29]

Smith's argument, by implication profoundly pessimistic as to the ability of British shipping to compete, would seem to be that the Navigation Laws, while admittedly economically damaging, represented a special case, an acceptable exception to the general rule. Not all historians of economic thought, it should be said, accept this interpretation of Smith's statement. Samuel Hollander considers that Smith saw acceptability of Navigation Laws as subject to cost, and limited his approval perhaps only to those elements directly affecting British import and coastal trades.[30] Nevertheless, Smith's intellectual descendants were not inclined to dispute his support for the Laws, only its validity in current circumstances. As McCulloch put it in his *Dictionary of Commerce*: 'the real question which now presents itself for our consideration is not what are the best means by which we may rise to national greatness? but – what are the best means of preserving that undisputed pre-eminence in maritime affairs to which we have attained?'[31] Liberal political economy could allow no theoretical distinction between Navigation Laws and other protective measures. All reduced economic welfare by distorting the natural pattern of economic activity, all were therefore undesirable. But where maritime protection was singled out for separate consideration, as by McCulloch himself in an article on the Navigation Laws which appeared in the *Edinburgh Review* in May 1823, he made no attempt to argue the case for total repeal.[32]

This rather relaxed approach to the issue mirrored that of Ricardo. In his writings, Ricardo was unexplicit on Navigation Laws as on much else; Mark Blaug has pointed out 'there was no such thing as a Ricardian theory of economic policy'.[33] In his parliamentary role he naturally welcomed all the administration's liberalising measures but, from Ricardo's comments in the debate on the reciprocity bill, it would appear that he did not disapprove of proceeding conditionally:

It certainly was a question of policy whether England should take off the duties without receiving reciprocal advantage from foreign powers but if foreign powers recognised the same liberal principle, there could be no doubt that the advantage to England would be double the advantage which any other country could derive from the regulation.[34]

Further insight into free trade attitudes to the Navigation Laws is provided by what is known of the deliberations of the Political Economy Club before mid-century. The shipowner and merchant George Lyall, a Chairman of the Shipowners' Society, was a founder member of the club. Shipping appeared on the agenda only three times before 1850 – on each occasion on Lyall's initiative. In March 1823 he led a discussion under the heading 'What effect have the Navigation Laws produced upon the political and commercial interests of Great Britain?' In June 1831, and again in February 1832, he went rather further with the question: 'What effect have the Navigation Laws had upon the shipping and commerce of this country and is their continuance essential to the maintenance of its commercial ascendancy?' We have no record of the debate at the meetings in 1823 and 1831, but fortunately the diarist J. L. Mallet noted what took place on 3 February 1832 – an occasion when the Vice-President of the Board of Trade, Poulett Thomson, joined in the argument:

The Navigation Laws have been so modified by the Act of 1824, that they are very unlike their original of 1650; but the great majority of those who spoke, and [Poullet] Thomson particularly, were clearly of opinion that whatever remains of them ought to be done away with; that they were clearly injurious to the wealth and not necessary to the naval pre-eminence of this country.

McCulloch, Tooke and Norman took the view that Smith had been wrong to attribute the gradual increase in Britain's shipping to the protection offered by the Laws. It was, they thought, due to 'our superior skill and naval advantages'. Further discussion focused on the sources of competition with British ships, with McCulloch identifying the United States of America as the main threat.[35]

If this account suggests that opposition to the Navigation Laws was a commonplace of classical liberal orthodoxy, it equally demonstrates the extent to which the 'nursery' concept formed part of the thinking of free traders on the subject and the degree to which support for repeal was seen as connected with a practical issue – the ability of British shipping to compete. Some years later J. S. Mill's *Principles of Political Economy* revealed a similar concern:

The Navigation Laws were founded, in theory and profession, on the necessity of keeping up a 'nursery of seamen' for the navy. On this last subject I at once admit that the object is worth the sacrifice; and that a country exposed by invasion by sea, if it cannot otherwise have sufficient ships and sailors of its own to secure the means of manning in an emergency an adequate fleet, is quite right in obtaining the means, even at an economic sacrifice in point of cheapness of transport . . . But English ships and sailors can now navigate as cheaply as those of any other country; maintaining at least an equal competition with the other maritime nations even in their own trade. The ends which may once have justified Navigation Laws require them no longer and afford no reason for maintaining this invidious exception to the general mode of free trade.[36]

It should, however, be noted that this approach to the question of protection for shipping was not characteristic of all strands of liberal economic opinion. Richard Cobden and his followers, 'the Manchester School of Economics', believed in the subordination of national power to wider, internationalist, objectives and aimed, with radicals such as Joseph Hume, at reductions in defence expenditure. For these men, the Navigation Laws exemplified a mistaken obsession with military strength. Classical liberals, such as McCulloch and Mill, did not dispute the legitimacy of the objectives of national defence which the Laws were intended to serve, only their continued necessity. But Cobdenite liberals repudiated these ends and were therefore left free to regard the issue as purely economic; a simple matter of opposition to monopoly power which raised shipping costs.[37]

To emphasise the somewhat diffident and conditional fashion in which most free traders approached the shipping question is not of course to argue that they were not in principle opposed to its protection. But given other more straightforward and potentially popular causes, notably Corn Law repeal, the Navigation Acts were necessarily assigned a lower priority. Moreover, the formation of the Anti-Corn Law League in 1838 represented a tactical determination to focus the free trade campaign on this issue. 'I was always for confining the public mind to that question. I call it the keystone of the arch, the rest will fall of itself', recalled Cobden in 1849.[38]

Thus although Poulett Thomson, Political Economy Club member, Vice-President of the Board of Trade between 1830 and 1834 and then President, had gone so far as to characterise the Navigation Acts as 'from the beginning prejudicial instead of advantageous to British commerce, and even shipping' in a speech early in his career, and his successor in 1839, Labouchere, was to be the Minister who eventually presided over repeal in 1849, the Whigs contemplated no reduction of protection, other than that associated with reciprocity or lower timber duties. Indeed they introduced a new, updating, Navigation Law which extended the list of enumerated products.[39] Nevertheless, notwithstanding this general lack of interest in the subject amongst parliamentary free traders, developments in the 1830s affecting the Board of Trade had a longer term impact on the prospects for repeal. In these years the Board acquired a free trade colour as a government department. By 1842, Lucy Brown writes, 'there was no senior official in the Board of Trade who was neutral in the controversial problems of political economy'. It also gained a Statistical Department under Porter, whose work was to contribute much to the style of debate over the Laws in the late 1840s. Finally, bruising experience of the problems of negotiating reciprocity treaties which would prove genuinely advantageous left many of the Board's officials profoundly sceptical as to the benefits of this approach to trade liberalisation.[40]

Despite what has been said, it would be wrong to conclude that protective policy towards shipping was an altogether settled question in the twenty years following Wallace and Huskisson. There was an impulse for re-examination of the issue – but it came not from free traders but from shipowners, whose quarrel was not with the reformulated Navigation Laws but with reciprocity. The immediate response of the Shipowners' Society in 1823 to the prospect of reciprocity treaties had been a petition to the government 'not to exercise the powers given to you', followed by a reasoned report which set out to demonstrate the competitive difficulties those in North European trades were already facing and the need for 'still further assistance and protection', rather than less. The government had no difficulty in confining its reaction to a courteous acknowledgment.[41] But three years later, with shipping sharing in general economic distress, Huskisson was forced to defend his policies in a major parliamentary speech on the state of the shipping interest. There ensued a concerted campaign of petitions from London and the outports, culminating in May 1827 with a motion from General

Gascoigne, Huskisson's fellow member for Liverpool, for an inquiry into the depression in shipping. This initiative proved a debacle, and he was forced to withdraw. 'The hearty zeal of General Gascoigne, and the manly independent conduct of Mr Liddell deserve the highest praise; but they had no supporters', commented the sympathetic author of an article in *Blackwoods*. The following year the untiring Gascoigne tried again, with a similar result and no doubt for the same reason – the support Huskisson's liberal measures tended to attract from the Whigs.[42]

Although the change of government in 1830 might have been expected to offer no additional encouragement to further initiatives on behalf of shipping, this did not prove to be the case. The struggle over the Whig proposal to reduce the protection given to colonial timber enabled the representatives of shipping to regain some credibility as a parliamentary force. If the government's defeat owed less to the merits of the case than to the shadow of Reform, and the desire of the opposition to impose the greatest humiliation possible, it nevertheless signified the potential for forging effective coalitions with colonial interests. Furthermore, as we have seen, one side-effect of the Whig attack was to encourage the re-establishment in London of the Shipowners' Society, this time under more protectionist leadership than that previously offered by George Lyall. With the entry into Parliament of G. F. Young, the industry gained a redoubtable public champion. Young, noted the author of the *Parliamentary Guide* in 1836, 'is a steady and strenuous supporter of the shipping interest in particular and devotes much attention to the business of the House'.[43]

Shipping again came to the fore in 1833, with debates on general public distress initiated by the Attwoods in March and April, and the setting up of two Select Committees (one on Agriculture, the other on Manufactures, Commerce and Shipping), which the Ministry was grudgingly forced to concede as a result. 'Their appointment would have the effect', Althorp, told the House of Commons when proposing his motion, 'of showing that the expectations of the country on the subject of the redress of grievances in the way desired were impossible.' The shipping interest had by now been campaigning for an inquiry into the industry for a number of years, but by lumping this together with manufactures and commerce, the government's proposal fell short of what was wanted. As G. F. Young commented in reply, 'he could assure the Noble Lord that the proposed inquiry, as far as it related to the shipping of the country, would be perfectly unsatisfactory to those connected with that branch of industry.'[44]

Nevertheless, the Select Committee provided the chance to put over the shipping case and the General Shipowners' Society enthusiastically responded to the invitation to provide names of those prepared to give evidence, suggesting one of its members for each branch of trade. Its involvement went further than this to include not only gathering information on shipbuilding and equipment costs but also briefing witnesses. A minute of 2 July records the work of a special committee which 'proceeded to consider and discuss the points at which the evidence of the parties who were to be examined should be most particularly directed'.[45] As a result the members of the Select Committee heard much of the evils of reciprocity treaties from the representatives of the shipping interest who came before them.

The following year G. F. Young, though still a relatively in-experienced MP, took the initiative in pressing the shipowners' case against reciprocity still further. On 5 June he moved for leave to bring in a 'Bill to repeal the Act 4th George IV, c.77, commonly termed the "Reciprocity of Treaties Act", with the view of restoring to Parliament its constitutional control over all treaties with foreign powers, involving the commercial interests of the British community'. In a long, detailed analysis Young explained the nature of the protective system as it affected shipping, describing the discriminatory duties on goods imported in foreign ships as 'the most important protection which British navigation possessed', and argued that that the effect of reciprocity treaties in removing these and discriminatory local dues had been to increase the share of foreign shipping in the trade with Prussia, Denmark, Sweden, Norway and Germany.

This was straightforward enough but a secondary theme of his speech, which conveniently ignored the substantial protective impact of the Navigation Laws themselves, was that a gross act of injustice had been done to the British shipowner because he was less protected than agriculturalists or manufacturers: 'There was no article produced by the skill or industry of British artisans which did not meet with legislative protection, save British shipping alone.' Moreover, the shipowner was subject to an 'exclusive burthen', because forced to purchase ships built with timber on which duty had to be paid, to undertake most repairs in Britain, to man his ships with British sailors, as well as being prevented in the interests of agriculture from freely carrying foreign corn to British ports. Young challenged the House to be consistent. It should 'either repeal the Navigation Acts and the Registry Acts – either leave them to build and navigate their ships as cheaply as they could – or give them a protection equal to the disqualification imposed upon them'. This was dangerous territory into which to stray deliberately, particularly after the timber duty controversy. As Joseph Hume commented in the ensuing debate, such an argument might reasonably be construed as one for free trade. But Young was trying to encompass the full range of shipowning concerns, which included a lively sense of grievance at any limitations on their freedom of operation.[46]

Such an approach underlines the point already made that shipowners were protectionist not out of any political conviction but because it suited them to be. In time Young himself was to move beyond the confines of sectional interest into the wider protectionism of the National Association for the Protection of British Industry. But he was exceptional in this. Most shipowners were content to appreciate the shelter the Navigation Laws offered, but, like Young in this debate, saw no inconsistency in at the same time campaigning against other restrictions. It is also of interest to note that on this occasion, as was sometimes the case subsequently, those who spoke for the shipping industry did not evoke the naval argument. This reflected the fact that while some shipowners regarded protection as the condition for their economic survival, others put the emphasis rather differently – protection was the quid pro quo for the burden of serving as the 'nursery' of seamen.

Responding on behalf of the government, Poulett Thomson spoke of shipping as 'the foundation of our naval defence and the basis of the welfare and prosperity of our national commerce', but questioned whether repeal of the Reciprocity Act would do more than remove the power of retaliation, given that the power to conclude treaties was contained in another statute. The twelve existing treaties would not be affected by any change in the law. Thomson defended the principle of reciprocity on the grounds that re-imposition of duties would simply encourage retaliation. He went on to dispute the charge that shipping was in a ruinous state, pointing out that if all foreign and colonial trades were taken into account the British share of voyages had remained constant at approximately two-thirds between 1819 and 1832. Britain had maintained its position, and surely that was sufficient? 'What right had we to expect to do more than keep our ground?', he continued magnanimously, 'It was absurd to suppose that, after the war was at an end, and the commerce of other countries came to be set free, that we should keep all the commerce of the world.'[47]

Besides Young, eight members spoke in the debate. With the exception of Hume, all were representatives of maritime constituencies. Hutt and Lushington were opposed to Young's motion. Lushington, member for Tower Hamlets, particularly acknowledged the claim of his constituency: 'he should not be an Englishman, he should not be worthy to represent the place he did, if he did not deeply feel for the distress of the shipping industry', but he could see no benefit in ending reciprocity. When the House finally divided, fifty-two members voted in favour, 117 against.[48]

The issue of protection was not to be raised again in Parliament on the initiative of a representative of the shipping industry until 1841, then under rather different circumstances. When Young lost his seat in 1838, shipping was deprived of an active spokesman. George Lyall's re-election as Member for the City of London in 1841, after a five-year absence, once more strengthened the shipping element, but not in ways that the General Shipowners' Society leadership approved. Lyall, by now Chairman of the East India Company, moved a motion for the appointment of a Select Committee:

to enquire into the effect produced upon our trade, navigation and colonies by the important alterations which have been made within the last twenty years in the Navigation Acts and to consider whether the objects contemplated in the framing of these acts might not how be more effectively attained and secured by some further modifications of them in reference to existing interests, and to the present commercial relations of this and other countries and also to take into consideration how far it may be practicable and expedient to adopt what measures to enable the shipping of this country to enter into competition, upon more equal terms, with the shipping of other nations and at the same time to promote the extension of its commerce.

This motion, which obviously owed much to Lyall's position as an MP for the City of London and to his own free trade convictions, not surprisingly appalled the shipowners who served on the Committee of the General Shipowners' Society. Confronted with a worried deputation from the society, Lyall's defence was that his interest was merely to establish facts, but as the shipowners pointed out 'when such a committee was once appointed, it might adopt conclusions which however favourable to commerce in general would be injurious to shipping interests in particular'.[49]

Three years later, with no sign of the depression in shipping coming to an end, the society was prepared to support Lyall in his campaign for a Select Committee, which it saw as a means of showing the 'hardships and difficulties' facing the industry. Ironically, it was now the government which had reservations about the direction such a committee's investigations might take. Responding to Lyall's motion of June 1844, Gladstone, Vice-President of the Board of Trade, told the House that the government was not opposed to the appointment of a Select Committee but warned that 'mischievous effects might ensue if the notion went abroad that after the lapse of so many years there existed any intention of departing from those treaties'. Any proposition to abandon reciprocity treaties was, in his view, 'wholly visionary'.[50]

Nevertheless, the witnesses nominated by the General Shipowners' Society to the 1844 Select Committee on British Shipping saw to it that reciprocity received a fair share of attention as a cause of the depression and, on balance, the evidence submitted proved to be if anything weighted towards the protectionist case. No final judgement on its impact on the members of the Committee is possible because, although re-appointed the following session, it took no further evidence and presented no report. It is hard to see how the Select Committee, chaired by a free trade shipowner, but in the main taking evidence from protectionists, could have reached any consensus. The reasons given for the failure of the Committee to complete its work – the pressure of railway bills and Lyall's ill health – seem likely to have been judicious excuses.[51]

One proposal for a further extension of protection which surfaced in the evidence submitted to the 1844 Select Committee was that of the General Shipowners' Society for a tax on colonial-built shipping referred to in an earlier chapter. Given the liberalising commercial policy of the Peel government, and the opposition from North American shipping interests to this idea, it seems surprising that the shipowners should have supposed that there was any chance that the government would lend its support. Gladstone predictably told a deputation from the General Shipowners' Society which raised the issue with him at the Board of Trade in October 1843 that he saw no possibility that Parliament would accept such a measure.

A later phase of the same ministerial interview, when contradictorily Gladstone was told 'that the greatest benefit the shipping interest could receive would be to be left alone', perhaps more accurately reflected the realistic limit of the shipowners' ambitions at this time as

far as government policy was concerned.[52] Once more a Tory
government was committed to commercial policies which attracted
support from its opponents and in this respect the contrast with the
political situation in the 1830s, as also some similarity to the 1820s, did
not bode well for protection. As Nassau Senior noted in the *Edinburgh
Review*, 'the liberal policy of the Whigs was constantly thwarted by the
Opposition; that of the Tories is actively supported. To the Whigs the
Opposition was a drag; to the Tories it is a stimulus.'[53]

There was no sign of a direct threat to the Navigation Laws from
Peel's government, although the lifting of a discriminatory duty on
coal exported in foreign ships in 1843 suggested little concern for
shipping interests. Instead it was responsible for the introduction of a
routine consolidating navigation measure. However, the general
direction of policy was unmistakeable. 'It need scarcely be stated',
observed the General Shipowners' Society in 1844, 'that the vital
principle of the Navigation System is protection, while the prevailing
doctrines pervading and guiding legislation are those of Free Trade.'[54]
Those 'prevailing doctrines' were not unattractive to sections of the
shipping industry which saw no harm in measures which could only
increase the demand for their services. But, whether the liberalisation
of commerce was welcome or not, there could be no assurance that this
ebbing tide of protection would leave the Navigation Laws safely
afloat.

Notes

1 The Navigations Laws were contained in a number of statutes. The Act of
   1849 repealed 8 & 9 Vict. c. 88 (An Act for the Encouragement of British
   Shipping and Navigation), sections of 8 & 9 Vict. c. 86, c. 89, c. 90, c. 93;
   sections of 7 & 8 Vict. c. 112 and 5 & 6 Vict. c. 14; 5 Geo. IV. c. 1, 4 Geo.
   IV. c. 77, 4 Geo. IV. c. 80 s. 20; 37 Geo. III. c. 117.
2 Lucy Brown, *Board of Trade*, pp. 34–5.
3 See R. Taylor, 'Manning the Royal Navy: the reform of the recruiting
   system, 1852–1862: first part', *Mariner's Mirror*, LXIV, 1958, pp. 302–13;
   'second part', LXV, 1959, pp. 46–58; J. S. Bromley (ed.), *The Manning of
   the Royal Navy: Selected Public Pamphlets 1693–1873*, Navy Records Society,
   London, 1974, pp. xiii–xlvii; C. J. Bartlett, *Great Britain and Sea Power 1815–
   1853*, Oxford, 1963.
4 *Lords S. C. Navigation Laws*, PP 1847–48 XX Pt. II, Q. 8217.
5 *Lords S. C. Navigation Laws*, PP 1847–48 XX Pt. II, Appendix G, p. 907.
6 *Correspondence between the Board of Treasury and the Board of Admiralty on the
   Subject of the Manning of the Royal Navy, together with copies of a Report of a
   Committee of Naval Officers*, PP 1852–53 [1628] LX, p. 11.

7 *Lords S. C. Navigation Laws*, PP 1847–48 XX Pt. II, Appendix G, p. 907.
8 For a number of such schemes, see *Extracts of Report and Appendix of Committee of 1852 on Manning the Navy*, PP 1859 Session 2, (45) XVII Pt. II, Appendices 1–14, pp. 329–51.
9 'Draft of a plan for a better and more systematic organisation of Her Majesty's naval forces', *Lords S. C. Navigation Laws*, PP 1847–8 XX Pt. II, Q. 5836.
10 5 & 6 Wil. IV. c. 19; 4 Geo. IV. c. 25.
11 On the history of the registry, see the statement by J. H. Brown, Registrar of Seamen, *Lords S. C. Navigation Laws*, PP 1847–48 XX Pt. II, Appendix M, pp. 970–5 and V. C. Burton, 'Counting seafarers: the published records of the registry of merchant seamen', *Mariner's Mirror*, LXXI, 1985, pp. 305–14. On apprenticeship, see E. G. Thomas, 'The Old Poor Law and maritime apprenticeship', *Mariner's Mirror*, 63, 1977, pp. 153–61 and Burton, 'Apprenticeship regulation'.
12 PD, Third Series, XXVI, 17 March 1835, c. 1121.
13 See, for example, Barry Gordon, *Political Economy in Parliament 1819–23*, London, 1976; Barry Gordon, *Economic Doctrine and Tory Liberalism 1824–30*, London, 1979; J. E. Cookson, *Lord Liverpool's Administration; the Crucial Years 1815–1822*, Edinburgh, 1975; Norman Gash, *Lord Liverpool: the Life and Political Career of Robert Banks Jenkinson, Second Earl of Liverpool 1770–1828*, London, 1984; Frank Whitson Fetter, *The Economist in Parliament: 1780–1868*, Durham, NC, 1980; R. Hilton, *Corn Cash and Commerce: the Economic Policies of the Tory Governments 1815–1830*, Oxford, 1977.
14 See Thomas Tooke, *Free Trade: Some Account of the Free Trade Movement as it Originated with the Petition of the Merchants of London*, London, 1853; Hilton, *Corn, Cash and Commerce*, pp. 173–6. The text of the London Merchants' Petition is given in J. R. McCulloch, *A Dictionary of Commerce*, London, 1844 edition, pp. 364–5.
15 Gash, *Liverpool*, p. 170.
16 William Smart, *Economic Annals of the Nineteenth Century*, London, 1910–17, provides a useful summary of this review of commercial policy. See also *First Report from the S. C. of the House of Lords on the Means of Extending and Securing Foreign Trade (Timber Trade)*, PP 1820 (488), III, p. 381; *S. C. Foreign Trade*, PP 1820 II.
17 *S. C. Foreign Trade*, PP 1820 II, p. 5.
18 *The Times*, 17 May 1820.
19 *S. C. Foreign Trade*, PP 1820 I, p. 1.
20 J. R. McCulloch 'The complaints of the shipowners', *Edinburgh Review*, XC, 1827, pp. 446–58.
21 *S. C. Foreign Trade*, PP 1820 II, p. 28, p. 34.
22 J. R. McCulloch 'Navigation Laws', *Edinburgh Review*, XXXVIII, 1823, pp. 478–94.
23 BL, Huskisson Papers, Add. MS. 38766, ff. 67–77, Minute dated 17 February 1824.
24 Alexander Brady, *William Huskisson and Liberal Reform: an Essay on the Changes in Economic Policy in the Twenties of the Nineteenth Century*, London, 1928, p. 133.

25 McCulloch, *Dictionary of Commerce*, p. 364.
26 See, for example, the speech by Sir James Graham, PD, CIV, 23 April 1849, c. 464. Not all free traders were so impressed. See the article by Nassau Senior, 'Free trade and retaliation', *Edinburgh Review*, LXXVIII, 1843, pp. 1–47.
27 David Ricardo, *The Works and Correspondence of David Ricardo* (ed. by Piero Sraffa, with the collaboration of M. H. Dobb), IX, Cambridge, 1965, pp. 269–70.
28 PD, New Series, XV, 12 May 1826, c. 1146.
29 Adam Smith, *An Inquiry into the Nature and Causes of the Wealth of Nations*, ed. by R. H. Campbell and A. S. Skinner, 2 vols, Oxford, 1976.
30 Samuel Hollander, *The Economics of Adam Smith*, London, 1973, pp. 264–5.
31 McCulloch, *Dictionary of Commerce*, p. 850.
32 McCulloch, 'Navigation Laws'. D. P. O'Brien, in his *James Ramsay McCulloch: A Study in Classical Economics*, London, 1970, argues that McCulloch was not an extreme advocate of free trade. A useful recent study on the history of this area of economic thought is Leonard Gomes, *Foreign Trade and the National Economy: Mercantilist and Classical Perspectives*, London, 1987. See also Bernard Semmel, *The Rise of Free Trade Imperialism 1750–1850*, Cambridge, 1970.
33 Mark Blaug, *Ricardian Economics: a Historical Study*, Yale, 1958, p. 194.
34 Ricardo, *Works*, V, pp. 305–6.
35 Political Economy Club, *Minutes of Proceedings 1899–1920. Roll of Members and Questions Discussed 1821–1920 with documents bearing on the History of the Club. Vol VI*, London, 1921, p. 19, 35, 37–8.
36 John Stuart Mill, *Principles of Political Economy with some of their Applications for Social Philosophy. Collected Works of J. S. Mill, III*, (general editor, F. E. L. Priestley), Toronto, 1965, pp. 916–17.
37 W. D. Grampp, *The Manchester School of Economics*, Stamford, 1960, pp. 116–17. See also Donald Reed, *Cobden and Bright: a Victorian Political Partnership*, London, 1967; N. C. Edsall, *Richard Cobden – Independent Political Radical*, Cambridge, Mass., 1986.
38 John Bright and J. E. Thorold Rogers (eds), *Speeches on Questions of Public Policy by Richard Cobden M.P.*, I, London, 1870, p. 406.
39 PD, New Series, XVII, 7 May 1827, c. 617; 3 & 4 Will. IV. c. 50–61.
40 Brown, *Board of Trade*, p. 29, pp. 71–93, pp. 116–40.
41 *Correspondence relative to Petitions of the Ship Owners of London*, PP 1826–27 (28) XVIII, pp. 1–17.
42 PD, New Series, XVI, 12 May 1826, c. 1144–202; XVII, 7 May 1827, c. 592–665; 'Mr Huskisson's speech on the shipping interest', *Blackwood's Edinburgh Magazine*, XXII, July, 1827, p. 3: PD, New Series, XIX, 17 June 1828, c. 1416–37; XXIV, 6 May 1830, c. 453–84.
43 Brock, *Reform Act*, pp. 173–4; R. B. Mosse, *The Parliamentary Guide: a Concise History of the Members of Both Houses of Parliament, their Connexions, Pursuits etc.*, London, 1836.
44 PD, Third Series, XVII, 3 May 1833, c. 958–9.
45 GSS, Minutes, III, 24 June 1833, 2 July 1833. The trades and names linked by the Society were E. India – G. Palmer, W. India – J. Steele,

North America and Canada – Robert Carter, Mediterranean – J. Nickels, Baltic – J. Chapman, Fisheries – C. Enderby, Hamburg – E. Cohen, S. America – D. Powles, Spain and Portugal – A. Anderson, Coal trade – Messrs. R and R. Brown, coasting – Sheriff Humphrey.

46 PD, Third Series, XXIV, 5 June 1834, c. 185–211.
47 *Ibid.*, c. 192; c. 233.
48 *Ibid.*, c. 211–29. Members who took part in the debate were Chapman (Whitby), Hume (Middlesex), Ingham (South Shields), Lushington (Tower Hamlets), Hutt (Hull), Alderman Thompson (Sunderland) , Lord Sandon (Liverpool), Ruthven (Dublin).
49 GSS, Minutes, IV, 16 November 1841, 14 December 1841.
50 PD, Third Series, LXXV, 4 June 1844, c. 275.
51 *S. C. British Shipping*, PP 1844 VIII; GSS, *Report of Annual Meeting*, 16 June 1845.
52 GSS, Minutes, IV, 21 November 1843, p. 206; *S. C. on British Shipping*, PP 1844 (VIII), Q. 213; *Letter*, PP 1846 XLV, p. 347, p. 351.
53 Senior, 'Free trade and retaliation', p. 7.
54 GSS, *Report of Annual Meeting*, 18 June 1841, 31 July 1844.

Chapter Five

From corn to ships

Parliament paid little attention to Navigation Laws in the intense and wearying debates on free trade which dominated business for the first five months of 1846 and culminated in the repeal of the Corn Laws in May. The proposal to lower timber duties attracted the attention of seaport representatives, but as always on this issue their responses reflected the familiar conflict within the industry itself between Baltic and North American interests. Opinion was divided even among north-eastern MPs. Liddell, member for North Durham, and Hinde, the Newcastle representative, found their case against any further reduction undermined by a petition in favour from the shipowners of Sunderland presented by William Hutt.[1] But ending protection for shipping was no part of Peel's scheme for commercial reform which he presented to the Commons on 27 January 1846 any more than it had featured in his earlier measures. For Peel the Navigation Laws remained a separate issue – a view shared by shipowners.

Lord George Bentinck was later to claim that he had recognised that 'when the Corn Laws were repealed, it followed as a matter of course that the Navigation Laws must follow' but such perspicacity was not general, even among others on his side.[2] When, for example, the shipowning protectionist stalwart Alderman William Thompson mocked at the government for inconsistency in the debate on the Corn Laws on 19 February, he seemed to take it for granted that the Navigation Laws were inviolate:

If we were to have free trade in corn, he wanted to know if the farmers had not a right to bring their produce to market by that ship which would convey it at the cheapest rate? He wanted to know if they had not a right to demand the abolition of the monopoly possessed by the shipowner in the coasting and colonial trade? ('Hear, Hear') Hon. Gentlemen opposite might say 'hear!' but he apprehended that if a proposition to that effect were made it would be met by Hon. Gentlemen on that side of the House telling them 'Oh, the national safety and national honour alike deter us and demand that we should not have our coasting trade or colonial trade destroyed.'[3]

As for the shipping interest itself, in the main its spokesmen saw little reason to oppose free trade in corn, which could only bring the industry more business, and there was no constituency dimension involved which might have affected their decision. Parliament in 1846 contained seven members with some identifiable direct personal association with the industry and a further three members who specialised in shipping issues. This first group comprised George Barnard, Aaron Chapman, George Duncan, George Lyall, Thomas Mitchell, William Thompson, James Wawn; the second, Joseph Henley, William Hutt and Henry Liddell. Of these only Chapman, Liddell, Henley and Thompson voted against repeal; a lack of protectionist solidarity which subsequently called forth a bitter taunt from Bentinck: 'When I saw the representatives of the shipping interest hurrying on to deprive the the agriculturalist of his protection, I thought their protection would be the first to follow.'[4]

In fact, such behaviour cost the shipping interest little in terms of support when this was needed. The desire of the agriculturalists for revenge on the free traders outweighed any reservations about making the navigation cause their own. But the industry's representatives were profoundly mistaken in assuming that all that was at stake in that vote was simply free trade in corn. The repeal of the Corn Laws created a context in which repeal of the Navigation Laws became for the first time a real possibility. Most obviously in the wake of repeal came Peel's defeat on the Irish Bill, his resignation and a new administration. Lord John Russell's Whig cabinet was by no means united in its attitude to the Navigation Laws or certain of what, if any, steps needed to be taken, but it could not ignore the demands of some of its more radical liberal supporters that it should confront the issue. The free traders in their turn, having won a great victory, now had an opportunity to extend their triumph by putting pressure on a government which they saw as more nearly their own.

As significant was the impact of Corn Law abolition on colonial interests. Along with the abolition of preference on bacon, beef and hides, and lowering of the duties on sugar and timber, it meant for British possessions a major further loss of protection. The Canadians protested vigorously against these liberalising measures, citing the

85

St Lawrence improvements as one development which would be particularly affected by the loss of a guaranteed market for their wheat and flour. But once the measures came into effect, they turned their attention to finding means of meeting foreign competition.[5] In this increasingly free trade setting, the remaining restrictions confining shipments to British ships appeared anachronistic and burdensome. Moreover, repeal was followed by the British Possessions Act, passed in July by a thin summer Parliament, with, according to Bentinck, 'half the house gone to the moors and another fourth to the continent'. The implications of this measure, which granted full freedom over their tariffs to the colonies, were considerable for shipping. The Peelite Goulburn was one of those who expressed misgivings. With power over tariffs, he suggested, colonies would want freedom for navigation. Bentinck was more forthright: 'The consequence of passing this Bill would ultimately be to abolish the Navigation Laws.'[6]

In New Brunswick the strength of timber trade interests maintained support for protectionism.[7] But in some parts of Canada, as also for the West Indies in respect of sugar, opposition to free trade as it applied to commodities was transformed by repeal into support for free trade as it applied to shipping. In the summer of 1846 the Free Trade Association of Montreal, composed mostly of grain exporters now looking for unrestricted shipment of American grain to Britain, petitioned the Colonial Office for repeal of the Navigation Laws, so as to end 'the twofold inconvenience of removal of protection and prohibition of free trade'. An equivalent call came from the Toronto Board of Trade and, a year later, from the similar body in Hamilton. July 1847 saw the provincial government adding its voice, with an appeal for sanction of 'the free use of the navigation of the River St. Lawrence by all nations'.[8]

In the West Indies planters and merchants in Jamaica, Antigua and Trinidad asked for similar relief. Modification of the Navigation Laws 'would enable British colonists to avail themselves of the cheapest 'bottoms' to enable them to carry their produce to the home market as well as bringing their outward supplies, an advantage at present denied them, but at the command of their opponents, the slave holders'.[9] Paradoxically, then, abolition of the Corn Laws and the attack on the sugar preference helped to foster a colonial movement for a further free trade measure – the abolition of the Navigation Laws.

It was not only in Britain and its possessions that these measures were discussed. The movement to free trade attracted considerable attention abroad, particularly in those countries anxious to secure closer commercial ties. Accustomed to negotiations confirmed by Orders in Council and reflecting the priorities of the executive, Prussian and United States Ministers in particular were impressed by the evidence of the power of the British Parliament in overthrowing vested interests which repeal of the Corn Laws seemed to offer. Prior to the repeal of the Corn Laws, in April 1846, the Prussian Minister Bunsen, acting for the *Zollverein,* had given notice that it was not prepared to renew the 1841 Treaty, due to expire on 31 December 1847, in its existing form. What Prussia sought was the freedom for *Zollverein* vessels to carry cargoes into British and colonial ports, irrespective of where these goods were produced. The justification for this request was that Prussia itself placed no restrictions on indirect traders. As Bunsen recognised, such a concession exceeded that which could be granted under normal reciprocity arrangements and would require a relaxation of those navigation regulations affecting the long voyage and third party carriers. The British Ministers concerned, setting the claim within the broader context of Prussia's generally ungenerous tariff policy, saw little merit in the case and refused to enter into negotiations. In May of the following year Bunsen re-opened the subject, threatening to impose differential duties on colonial goods imported in British vessels via other countries if Britain did not relax its Navigation Laws.[10] The perception that there now existed in Britain a genuine wish, and majority, for freer trade helped to stiffen Prussian resolve to pursue these negotiations more aggressively and encouraged it to doubt the political capacity of the Foreign Office to resist their demands. Similar considerations also led the United States to look for progress towards its long-established objective of gaining access to Britain's colonial trade.

Such links between corn and navigation are those apparent from a historical perspective. In late 1846 the connection was much more direct. Concern at the continued shortage of grain supplies led to the suspension of the Corn Laws in January 1847 and with them, initially until the following September, the Navigation Acts applying to grain. That this latter modification was a limited measure, forced on Russell by political necessity rather than by any conviction of practical efficacy, is clear from his letter of 28 December to Henry Labouchere:

I do not think the suspension of the Navigation Laws likely to be useful. The French have a small mercantile marine, we have a very large one. American ships can, as the law stands, bring produce from America and Russian ships from Odessa. We should gain nothing by a discouragement of British ships at the present moment.[11]

In addition, neither Russell nor Clarendon, President of the Board of Trade, had any enthusiasm for tackling the Navigation Laws in the longer term. On 21 December 1846 Clarendon had confidently assured a delegation from the General Shipowners' Society that the government had no intention of altering them in any way, adding that he hoped the question would not be raised in Parliament. Others in the cabinet were also anxious for the government to act with general caution. On 26 December the Chancellor, Charles Wood, no doubt worried about possible Palmerstonian excesses, told the Foreign Secretary that in his view, 'the character we have to acquire and maintain as a government is that of being prudent, steady people'.[12]

But among the government's supporters on the back-benches there were men who feared precisely that. With the beginning of the new session it rapidly became evident not only that ending protection for shipping was now a prime target for the parliamentary radical free traders but that this cause had been adopted as his own by an energetic young MP eager to make his mark at Westminster. John Lewis Ricardo, always 'full of bravado' as his fellow member for Stoke-on-Trent later somewhat unkindly recalled, had entered Parliament in 1841 at the age of thirty-three. Son of the financier Jacob Ricardo, he was one of an increasing number of members with interests in railways, as well as the founder and Chairman of the Electrical and International Telegraph Company. As nephew of the economist, a member of the Political Economy Club and brother-in-law of G. R. Porter, Ricardo had impeccable free trade credentials but appears to have shown no interest in the Navigation Acts before he raised the issue of repeal on 19 January 1847.

Entrusted with seconding the Address in response to the Queen's Speech, Ricardo, having in the judgement of the *Illustrated London News* 'almost a hereditary title to be heard', expressed what he described as 'merely my own opinion' on the Navigation Laws. In his view, it would be better to trust to British talent and enterprise than to rely on

the miserable remnant of a law made for other times and under other circumstances – a law, be it remembered which failed when it was adopted, which in later times had been the main cause of our separation from the our former colonies of America, and which even now is a fruitful source of discontent in your dependencies.[13]

Four days later Joseph Hume, the radical MP for Montrose, created some embarrassment for the government when he seized the opportunity offered by the debate on the suspension of the Navigation Laws as they affected corn (a measure agreed by all sides) to call for an end to every duty affecting shipping and to urge the government to 'take a comprehensive view of the whole subject, and repeal those laws, both as regarded the colonies and the mother country'.[14] The free trade stalwarts John Bright and William Ewart then spoke in similar vein. Finally, on 9 February, Ricardo pushed the matter still further with a proposal for a Select Committee to investigate 'the operation and policy of the Navigation Laws'. Disingenuously disclaiming any prior commitment to repeal, and acknowledging the commercial marine to be the 'nucleus and nursery' of the navy (though then subjecting the laws to detailed criticism), Ricardo argued that such an investigation would merely continue the work done by the 1844 Select Committee on shipping, which had made no report. This view was endorsed by the Vice-President of the Board of Trade, Thomas Milner-Gibson, who suggested that the many changes which had recently taken place in commercial policy themselves justified impartial investigation.[15]

Opposing Ricardo, Liddell (who with Hudson, MP for Sunderland, had presented petitions against repeal at the beginning of the sitting) denied that any further investigation of shipping was needed – 'a gleam of prosperity having manifested itself', there had been no need to reappoint the Select Committee – and asserted that Ricardo's predetermined object was repeal. 'Was England', he asked the House of Commons, 'to be made merely the workshop of the world? Did we look for the recruiting of our army and the equipment of our navy from the stunted population of our manufacturing districts?' Directing his attention to the Prime Minister, Liddell warned of the political dangers of an investigation: 'Was it wise to enter into this large and complicated inquiry, involving such enormous interests, exciting agitation and feelings of dismay and want of confidence in every seaport of the kingdom?'[16]

Privately Russell may well have shared such reservations. He certainly had no strong feelings against the Laws. Indeed, in the debate on the British Possessions Bill the previous year he had reminded the House, though with no great passion, that any changes in the Navigation Laws might risk endangering British naval supremacy. Certainly, as he admitted to the House, he had had no intention himself of proposing a Select Committee on the subject.[17] But once suggested, there was no possibility that the government would withhold its support. Not only had Milner-Gibson spoken up for an inquiry on behalf of the Board of Trade, the proposal was also approved by Peel:

There can be no reason given why there should not be an inquiry into the operation and effect of the Navigation Laws; nor why there should not be an opportunity given of ascertaining whether the maintenance of those laws, as they at present exist, is for the interest of British commerce, or for the interest of British shipping.[18]

Ricardo having succeeded in forcing a Select Committee on the government, it remained for the membership to be decided. Several of those who had spoken in favour of its appointment had expressed the view that it should be genuinely impartial in its membership. But when, on 12 February, Ricardo moved the names of those chosen to serve, free traders dominated to such a blatant extent that the sixteen-name list failed to gain approval. Four days later, Ricardo brought forward a further list, this time consisting of fifteen names, four of which were new. This was accepted, though some opponents of the Select Committee saw little improvement in protectionist representation. One member commented that since it could be seen beforehand that the Committee would divide ten to four, 'the report might as well be drawn up at once without further trouble'. Russell, who described the Committee's composition as 'fair and honest', likewise identified only four members as upholders of the Navigation Laws but claimed that of the remainder only four were committed to repeal; the rest were undecided.[19]

The government was represented by the Manchester MP Thomas Milner-Gibson, Vice-President of the Board of Trade and formerly an active member of the Anti-Corn Law League. Milner-Gibson, was under some unenviable moral pressure 'to do something', as Cobden put it, in the liberal cause in a situation in which he was 'allied with a party that has not been been very successful in statesmanship; and succeeds a government which has proved itself eminently strong in practical measures'.[20] This was perhaps one reason why he had lent his support so enthusiastically to the proposal for a Select Committee, on which he served as Chairman. Ricardo deputised for him on the few occasions when he was absent. Other free trade luminaries appointed were John Bright and Joseph Hume, although Bright played little part in the Committee's work, attending only eight of its thirty-three sessions – the poorest attendance record. Of the three shipowning members of the Select Committee, Thomas Mitchell, MP for Bridport was a Liberal, as also in some respects was George Lyall. However, the latter's position on the Navigation Laws was equivocal, while that of the Protectionist Alderman William Thompson was not. Henry

Liddell similarly ranked on the Protectionist side, as did the Conservative financier Thomas Baring. Its most distinguished member, Sir Robert Peel, was possibly more uncommitted on the question than his opponents supposed, but clearly did not consider the Laws to be sacrosanct. The Peelites Sir George Clerk and George Villiers were similarly probably predisposed to some amendment, as was also the Liberal Alexander McCarthy. The position of Admiral Sir James Dundas, MP for Greenwich, and Sir Howard Douglas, MP for Liverpool, was unclear.

For Ricardo and other radical free traders in the Commons, the appointment of the Select Committee marked the first stage in their campaign to persuade the government to tackle shipping protection. No doubt they already appreciated that much of the pressure that they could exert would have to come from within the political system, at parliamentary and governmental level, and in this context a Select Committee, properly handled, could prove effective. Outside the parliamentary sphere it was already apparent that valuable support for their case might be found in petitions from the colonies, where such signs of discontent carried a longer term threat to imperial integrity. With this in mind, Ricardo took due care to refer to the colonial dimension when moving the Select Committee.

What the free traders could not offer at this stage was evidence of any popular demand for repeal of the Navigation Laws such as it had proved possible to show in the case of the Corn Laws.[21] Within the British Isles, though not always perhaps in British possessions overseas, the navigation code operated at such a distance from the consumer as to be virtually invisible; whatever the effect on freight rates, the final impact on the retail price was negligible. (Ironically, those with greatest awareness of its restrictive elements were the shipowners themselves, forced to comply with manning regulations and to purchase British-built vessels.) The minority with mercantile interests who might be affected by its operation were not as yet persuaded by what were minor, accustomed inconveniences to devote much time or energy to campaigning for repeal. Predictably only in Manchester, the free trade capital, was there any interest in the subject prior to 1847. In 1850, when the battle for repeal was over, the Manchester Chamber of Commerce was to claim some part in this victory as the first public body to call for repeal. Its *Report on the Injurious Effects of the Restrictions on Trade*, published in 1841, had referred to the Navigation Acts, and in September 1846 the Chamber addressed a memorial to the Treasury, demanding their 'immediate reform or abolition as against the world'.[22]

In contrast, the campaign in support of protection for shipping had a considerable extra-parliamentary dimension. In part this resulted from the established role of the General Shipowners' Society as a representative body. It also owed much to the depth of feeling on the subject in some east-coast seaports, which had manifested itself over the years in petitions and memorials directed against reciprocity. With the very heart of the maritime protective system now under threat, it might be expected that this would evoke a still stronger reaction, and so indeed it was to prove. But the problem which faced those who sought to defend the industry from legislative threat was, as always, how to hammer the outrage of shipowners and shipbuilders into an effective political weapon.

For the General Shipowners' Society the appointment of the Select Committee was the first unequivocal sign that repeal, or at best modification, of the Navigation Laws was on the political agenda. But it could hardly have been an unexpected development. The society's Annual Report of August 1846 had pondered 'whether the special circumstances connected with navigation will induce the continuance of maritime commerce as an exception to the general rule' but by October it was sufficiently worried by the evidence of interest in the subject at Manchester to convene a special meeting and to seek to make representations to government.[23] Any reassurance felt as a result of the interview in December with Lord Clarendon was rapidly dissipated once Parliament re-convened and the free trade radicals demonstrated their determination to pursue the issue.

In the past, when faced with the prospect of a Select Committee, the General Shipowners' Society had required no special organisation in order to provide a response, but on this occasion the society departed from past practice. On 2 March 1847 it set up a special body, 'The Central Committee for Upholding the Navigation Laws', to direct proceedings in what it termed 'the present emergency'.[24] Two reasons may be suggested for this decision; one practical, the other political. First, there was the question of money. Any campaign would prove costly and, because annual subscriptions to the society had been falling off for a number of years (in 1845 amounting to only £242), funds were low.[25] A separate organisation devoted to a single issue would be more likely to attract the necessary support than would attempts to enlarge membership or appeals to existing members. If this was indeed a motive, then it proved only moderately successful. It has not been possible to discover exactly how much was raised over the three years of the Central Committee's existence, but, whatever the sum was finally, it proved insufficient to cover all costs. Nevertheless, the available records show it in receipt of a total of £908 by April 1849, contributed by sixty supporters, including port associations at Tynemouth, South Shields and Sunderland and marine insurance clubs at Yarmouth.[26]

Another factor encouraging the General Shipowners' Society to set up a special body to deal with the question may well have been the perception that on this issue its members would not prove to be of one mind. It is evident from the minutes of meetings of the society's Committee in August and October 1846 that there was some disagreement as to how much prominence at the annual meeting should be given to the threat to the Navigation Laws and also some interest in simply urging on government that it undertake a 'full investigation' before acting. Those who saw shipowners as at every turn 'impeded, taxed and prevented' were not so inclined to feel that all change in the navigation code would prove disadvantageous, or to disapprove of the appointment of a Select Committee.[27]

For the most committed protectionist activists in the General Shipowners' Society, like Young and Buckle, the effect of the appointment of the Central Committee for Upholding the Navigation Laws was to give them a rather freer rein to promote their views. Matters relating to the Navigation Laws issue were no longer dealt with by the Committee of the General Shipowners' Society, where they might have caused division, but were left to those who had no free trade sympathies. Nevertheless the Central Committee appears to have had no genuinely independent existence. Appeals in 1849 for additional funding for its campaign against repeal came from Duncan Dunbar, the society's Chairman that year, and the Central Committee was never referred to by any of the society's spokesmen when giving evidence before either of the Select Committees on the Navigation Laws.[28]

Despite the somewhat tendentious nature of the General Shipowners' Society's claim to be able to speak for the British shipping industry, the small number of individuals concerned had undoubtedly acquired over the years a considerable degree of skill and experience in organising opposition to government proposals. In October 1846 three immediate tasks had been identified: first, 'to enlighten the public mind on the real merits of this improperly understood question'; second, to make representations to government; and third, to alert the outports and gain their support.[29] Over the longer term public opinion, government and the outports were to remain the focus of their attention as a pressure group. But in the spring of 1847 the immediate concern was to assist the small number of protectionist sympathisers on the Commons Select Committee.

Hearings of the Commons Select Committee 'on the Operation and Policy of the Navigation Laws' extended over five months, from the beginning of March to mid-July, finishing almost at the end of the parliamentary session before any final report could be made. The evidence taken by the Committee was, however, periodically set before the House in a series of five reports, a device which ensured that the question remained in public, and government, view.[30] Thirty-four witnesses were interviewed: an unrepresentative group according to the 1849 Annual Report of the General Shipowners' Society: 'With the exception of three official functionaries, all zealous advocates of free trade, and one naval officer standing in his opinion alone in his profession, they consisted wholly of foreigners or persons little known in the commercial world.'[31] This was a somewhat selective recollection, given that witnesses included Duncan Dunbar, then Chairman of the society and G. F. Young himself, whose examination lasted five days. Nevertheless, the shipowners' charge that the Select Committee was 'in composition and proceeding partial' was understandable. Merchants predominated among witnesses, and of those interviewed who gave their opinion of the Navigation Laws, thirteen expressed themselves in favour of repeal and seven against.

For all this, it would be wrong to regard the work of the Commons Select Committee as in any way perfunctory. This was not a inquiry like those of 1833 and 1844, where the questions and answers followed a predefined, repetitive, course, owing everything to artifice, little to spontaneity. The free traders were anxious to pursue certain issues, which provoked defensive alternative themes from the protectionists, but the complexity of the subject imposed its own shape, or rather shapelessness, on the Committee's deliberations. As a result, the mass of detail accumulated in the answers to 8,060 questions asked in thirty-three sessions is arguably of more use to historians than it would have been to the Committee itself had it been in the position to produce a summary for a final report. Even those most attentive and informed Committee members were unable to assimilate the amount of information presented. At one session, for example, G. F. Young reeled off a list of shipbuilding costs in British and European ports in response to a question from Mitchell. This showed the price per ton of ships in some European countries to be half that of those in Britain, and Ricardo immediately interjected to ask where the figures came from. Young had great pleasure in replying: 'I have principally had recourse to the evidence given before this Committee by parties who are hostile to the views which I entertain', and went on to cite his sources in particular answers given by earlier witnesses.[32]

The foundation of the free trade case as presented to the Committee was the evidence of the three Board of Trade officials, Macgregor, Porter and Lefevre. The association of the Board with liberal economic opinions was by this time well established. Peel and his Ministers had viewed these officials with suspicion and, having no very high opinion either of their political probity or of their practical ability, had tended to bypass them whenever possible. With the change of government, the political match between Board officials and Ministers was once again close. In an age when the political neutrality of public servants was neither assumed nor expected, Macgregor and Lefevre both had close links with the Whigs. Indeed, in the winter of 1847 Macgregor was taking steps to obtain a candidature in Glasgow, where he was to be successful in the General Election later that year.

Porter and Macgregor had some experience of business; the former as a sugar broker, the latter as a schoolmaster turned shipbuilder in Prince Edward Isle and subsequently as a merchant. Neither had been successful in these careers; they were, in the hostile words of the Liverpool shipowner Henry Chapman, 'gentlemen who as merchants and tradesmen could not conduct their own business rightly'. Both had published books on trade: Porter, the mainly statistical work *The Progress of the Nation*; and Macgregor, *The Commercial and Financial Legislation of Europe and America*. Lefevre, a barrister from a more elevated professional background, was generally more incisive than Macgregor, though no less liberal in his economic views. Gladstone, who had had to deal with the two Assistant Secretaries in connection with the 1842 tariff reforms, was later to contrast them: 'one, Macgregor, a loose-minded free trader, the other, Lefevre, a clear and scientific one'.[33]

Only Lefevre's powers of exposition, not his economic views, came through in his evidence which uncontroversially set out for the Committee the main features of the Navigation Laws as the starting point for their investigations.[34] Macgregor's evidence dealt principally with reciprocity and the commercial relations with the United States of America, where Macgregor's 'terms of intimacy with many leading statesman of that country' led him to believe that relaxations by Britain would be met by an equal response from the United States. In response to questions from Ricardo, he referred to complaints against the Navigation Laws from the colonies, the United States of America, Russia, Prussia and Denmark. In Macgregor's view, provided taxes and restrictions on the British shipowner and shipbuilder were removed, the British shipowner could compete; and where shipbuilding costs were lower, as in Norway and Sweden, British capital would be employed. Asked by Sir Howard Douglas to explain his 'astounding proposition' that the increase in British tonnage was achieved in spite, not because, of the Navigation Laws, Macgregor affirmed, with a rhetorical flourish, his free trade faith:

I consider that the increase of British shipping has not depended upon the Navigation Laws, but that it has depended upon the demand for British ships; and I come to the conclusion that the prosperity of our trade and navigation in this country, the improvement of our ships and the increase of our ships in this country, has been as independent of the Navigation Laws as if they had not existed at all; and that our trade has not depended upon the Navigation Laws any more than the fertility of the banks of the Nile has depended upon the pyramids.[35]

G. R. Porter did not come before the Committee until June, when he was probably called in order to counteract criticisms of his shipping statistics made by protectionist witnesses. His evidence, as might be expected of the Head of the Statistical Department, was more overtly based on quantitative material, making particular use of entry and clearance figures to demonstrate the growth in both British and foreign entries over the preceding two decades. By differentiating the protected colonial trades from all other foreign business, and comparing 1824 with 1846, Porter was able to contrast growth in entries between these dates of 94.4 per cent in protected trades with 182.98 per cent in unprotected. Porter, like Macgregor, then took the liberal economist's leap of faith – concluding that without the 'mischief' of the Navigation Laws, trade would have increased still more, hence they should be expunged.

For all his figures, Porter's evidence to the Select Committee indicates that his commitment to free trade owed much to theoretical concepts. Asked by Liddell about Baltic trade profits, Porter replied that for the British shipowner, 'his profit has been larger in proportion to the average rate of profit in this country than the profit of the foreign shipowner in proportion to the average rate of profit in their countries, otherwise the foreign shipping would have increased in a far greater degree than it has increased', but agreed that this was hard to prove to the satisfaction of the shipowner:

I remember some time ago looking at the accounts of a British shipowner, and he showed me every ship which he had, in every voyage that it made produced him a serious loss and yet he went on carrying on his trade and increasing his shipping; that presented a difficulty which I could not solve; there was something in the accounts which did not exactly meet my comprehension.

Like Macgregor, Porter favoured total repeal. He had no truck with reciprocity, telling the Select Committee: 'I should never ask the question, if I were legislating for the good of this country, whether they [foreign countries] would or would not reciprocate with us'.[36]

The attitude of the three senior Board of Trade officials to the Navigation Laws exemplified the classic liberal approach to trade restrictions, but the instigators of the Select Committee recognised that such considerations were of limited value to their case in comparison with arguments for repeal coming from within the commercial sector itself. The Committee's brief was to look at the way the legislation operated and to this end the free traders' witnesses were selected for their experience of particular trades or aspects of business, and of course for their willingness to speak in favour of repeal, or at least not to pronounce against. The protectionists on the Committee had to endure two months of meetings before any of their witnesses appeared.

What did the free traders aim to establish by their questions? First, that the Navigation Laws were a hindrance to commerce. For the merchant Samuel Browning, with interests in the Australian and Indian trade, the fact that foreign-owned vessels could not be used for carriage to Britain from the colonies had significant side-effects:

if we were permitted to import by the ship of any flag that we chose the bulky items of manufacture, we should gain an advantage in the price; and consequently our merchants, by having permission to send their goods to foreign markets, by there being double voyages made, would be able to make a reduction in their price; and in the foreign market a very trifling percentage frequently makes a difference between a sale and no sale.

A similar complaint was made by another witness, Edward Berger. In his experience opportunities for importing African and East Indian produce from the United States of America were lost because of the obligation to use a British ship. Hamburg merchant W. R. Goschen was among a number of witnesses objecting to the law preventing import through Europe when he argued that the price of Cuban sugar was higher because it had to come directly from the West Indies in British vessels. In respect of the East India trade, Francis Carnac Brown alleged that there was commonly a lack of tonnage to carry goods to Britain, though he attributed this to the barriers to employment of Lascar seamen. The copper ore trade had by a quirk come under the Navigation Laws in 1842, when a duty was substituted for smelting in bond, so ruling out import in foreign vessels. Three witnesses produced by Ricardo complained of the effect that this had had on their shipments.[37]

The main thrust of such evidence was the practical proof it provided of the ways in which the Navigation Laws impeded the free flow of goods to Britain, and raised freights so that, in the words of Committee member Joseph Hume, 'if the shipowners gain, they gain at the expense of the community at large'.[38] Necessarily this was an argument primarily focused on the colonial and oceanic trades; with the exception of the restriction on the import of such goods through Europe, which in any case also affected British shipping, it had little relevance for nearer trades. What interested the Committee as far as the Continent was concerned, free traders and protectionists alike, was what the experience of the shipping industry under reciprocity suggested would be the result if *all* protection were to be removed.

Proving that shipowners and shipbuilders, not just merchants and consumers, would benefit from repeal of the Navigation Laws was the second aim of the free traders. That this was part of the free trade case was evident from the beginning. In moving the proposal for a Select Committee, Ricardo had argued at the some length that the picture of the shipping interest as injured by reciprocity, and requiring protection, which had been painted by evidence to the 1844 Select Committee was false. Questions on this theme were put to witnesses in the earliest sessions, but as a flow of petitions against repeal began to make an impact and protectionists on the Committee forced the issue, it became increasingly central to the free trade argument.

In attempting to show that repeal would not damage shipping and shipbuilding, the repealers had given themselves a difficult task, not least because they were unable to produce as witnesses in favour even a single shipowner or shipbuilder. Several of the merchants who appeared before the Committee were either then, or had been in the past, owners of ships but by their own admission only as an adjunct of their main business. Such men were willing to pronounce on shipping questions, in some cases quite forcefully, but their opinions necessarily lacked the authority of the shipping interest's own representatives. Some air of objective assessment was provided by calling witnesses who were not British citizens, one of whom, the Swede William Tottie, attended only under vehement protest. But the fact that a number of the free traders' witnesses were foreigners undermined rather than strengthened their case, providing the opponents of the Select Committee with a valuable suggestive weapon in a debate which centred so much on what constituted the national interest.

A more fundamental problem, and one which was to dog both sides in the whole debate over repeal, was that predictions as to the effect of the removal of protection relied on how the current situation was interpreted and what was considered to be relevant. Eventually the protectionists were able to broaden the discussion to encompass the wider defence implications, but in early 1847 the initiative lay with the radical free traders, who saw the issue as essentially economic. Already, however, the political instincts of the Liberal members of the Committee ensured attention to practical detail here. Porter might speak grandly of flows of factors of production across national boundaries, but such elegant considerations would not persuade the doubtful. What was needed was evidence that the shipping industry had nothing to fear from repeal.

The central question was competition. If foreign shipowners and shipbuilders were given free access to markets hitherto reserved to the British, what would be the result? One part of the answer followed directly from the case against the restrictive effects of protection. In trades where there was a shortage of ships, foreign vessels would move in to meet the demand and freight rates would fall. But then what would happen? Would foreign vessels drive out British in sea carriage? And would shipbuilding decline if foreign-built ships were admitted to British registry?

For the free traders on the Committee the answer was predetermined; British ships and shipbuilders could compete. But if they imagined at the outset that providing proof of this would be straightforward, they must have soon been sadly disillusioned by the performance of their own witnesses. The answer to the following question by Alderman Thompson illustrates two of the problems – lack of information and the speculative nature of much allegedly expert opinion:

Do you possess any information as to the comparative expenses of sailing an English vessel of 400 tons burden, and a Norwegian vessel of the like burden? – We have some statements upon that subject: I do not recollect at this moment what they are; they do sail ships in particular trades cheaper than we do; but in all our calculations we have arrived at this conclusion, that if other nations constructed ships for navigation and trade in a hot climate, and copper fastened and copper sheathed them, and strengthened them in the same degree as we require British ships to be secured, our ships would cost very much the same in their construction as foreign ships.[39]

In this instance the respondent was the Board of Trade official Macgregor, but a similarly conditional approach to British performance was shown by others. Browning called for a reduction of duty prior to repeal 'upon all the materials used in the construction of ships such as timber, copper ore, and old foreign copper sheathing for re-melting, foreign ores and stamps upon marine instruments of all kinds, insurance policy, and light dues', and looked to the breaking of combinations through introduction of foreign shipwrights in British yards in order to reduce costs. Another witness, Berger, acknowledged the superiority of American-built ships but thought that ending protection would encourage 'a better class of English vessels' so would not prove injurious. For Colquoun, competition following repeal would work its own magic on costs, reducing seamen's as well as shipwrights' wages.[40]

The free traders were unable either through the evidence of these merchants or that of sympathetic witnesses associated with marine insurance (who testified to higher rates on goods carried in British vessels) to demonstrate in any convincing fashion a favourable outcome from repeal for shipping.[41] Implicit in much that was said was an assumption that costs in the British industry were higher than for its competitors, but there was little to engender any optimism as to their reduction after repeal, in ways which would not damage some branch of shipping. Furthermore, this approach was hardly consistent with the claim that protection was inflicting considerable damage on commerce. As G. F. Young astutely recognised, there was a logical flaw in the free trade case:

It is difficult to reason with the two sides of the question; on the one hand it is asserted that the benefit which will arise to the consumer is reason enough for taking off from us the protection that we now enjoy, and on the other hand persons attempt to delude us into the belief that the deprivation of that protection would really not place us in a position in which we should suffer from the competition. One of the propositions may be true, but both, in my judgement cannot.[42]

In short, if repeal would have so little effect on British shipping, the impact of the Laws could hardly be as great as was claimed.

In seeking to establish that the British shipping industry did not need protection, the free traders were counteracting in advance one anticipated facet of the protectionist case. A similar motive lay behind the summoning of a distinguished naval officer, Sir James Stirling, to testify on the manning issue. Stirling disputed the claim that the mercantile marine was a nursery of seamen, estimating that only a tenth of 'blue jackets' had seen service in the merchant navy, and argued for a 'fixed peace establishment' for the navy of sufficient size 'to render the two services independent of each other'. This was an argument which sat uneasily with liberal concern to minimise defence expenditure, and Stirling's explanation that a reduction in the number of officers would allow a larger force to be maintained at no extra cost, cannot have been entirely convincing in this respect.[43]

Nevertheless, the free traders were wise to attempt to engender scepticism as to the relationship between defence and merchant shipping, rather than relying simply on their general claim that repeal would bring about an enlargement of the British mercantile marine by expanding the scope for commerce. Belief in an association between national defence and the Navigation Laws was part of a conventional wisdom which extended from shipping protectionists through to the Prime Minister himself. Those who favoured repeal could not afford to allow such an assumption to continue to influence government policy. But providing reassurance on this score was to prove difficult.

The protectionists on the Select Committee called eight witnesses: prominent members of the London-based General Shipowners' Society, Dunbar and Young; two representatives of Liverpool shipowners, Imrie and Lockett, who were proposed by the Liverpool MP Sir Howard Douglas; the steamship company proprietor James Macqueen; shipowner and shipbroker William Phillips; Robert Anderson of the South Shields Shipowners' Society; and William Richmond, representing Tynemouth. Although these shipping interest representatives faced a largely hostile Committee, as a group they had certain advantages over the free traders' witnesses. First, they were presenting a coherent, collective, and above all familiar, case in favour of protection, which in its essentials had last been rehearsed as recently as 1844. Ricardo's argument that a Select Committee on the Navigation Laws would be the successor to that of 1844 was not entirely specious. By devoting much attention to the necessity of restoring protection that Committee had touched on many matters now being examined. Next, a number of the witnesses were old hands at parliamentary committees. Anderson and Phillips had appeared in 1844, Dunbar and Young had given evidence both in 1844 and 1833, as also had William Richmond, who had also come before the Select Committee on Foreign Trade in the early 1820s. Finally, several of these men were able to claim that they did not speak as private individuals but as the chosen representatives of associations, local and national.

However, the greatest advantage possessed by the shipping interest in promoting its case was that it had an exceptionally able spokesman in the person of G. F. Young. Young was undoubtedly something of a bore. W. S. Lindsay described him as 'a most garrulous gentleman, when once his tongue was set in motion, it went on incessantly, without stopping', and it is true that he seems to have been incapable of anwering any question in a few words.[44] But he addressed himself to the task of defending shipping against the free trade attack with considerable industry and talent. Young's role in organising the overall campaign against repeal was to be central, but at this stage his contribution was to ensure that the argument on the protectionist side could not be easily dismissed as simply the instinctive special pleading of a privileged group.

The least convincing, though for the Committee perhaps the most entertaining, witness coming from the shipping side was the elderly Tynemouth shipowner William Richmond. According to Richmond, repeal 'would be followed by the sweeping of British merchant ships from the face of the ocean' because foreign competition would overwhelm the British industry. 'How', he asked, 'is a horse with a heavy burthen to run against a horse without weight?' Richmond, a great dramatiser, asserted that as a result of reciprocity treaties freights had been unremunerative for twenty-five years – 'The shipowners hobble on until they get into the Gazette' – so laying himself open to the obvious question as to whether repeal could make matters any worse. The other protectionist witnesses were less florid in their language but no less certain as to the inability of the industry to compete. Anderson, like Richmond from the north-east, endorsed his view of the lessons of reciprocity. The shipowner and shipbroker William Phillips, sceptical as to whether other countries would or could offer comparable concessions, saw the opening of indirect trade as the means by which the United States of America, 'would meet us in

Calcutta, China, Australia or Cuba'. As for shipbuilding, British shipowners including himself, would buy foreign ships and man them with foreigners. In all, Phillips estimated, such was the scale of employment associated with the shipping industry that 2 million people would be injured by repeal. William Imrie, Liverpool merchant, shipowner and shipbroker, similarly feared United States shipping; while Lockett, of the Liverpool Shipowners' Association, thought that allowing British registration to foreign-built ships would mean that shipbuilding would be 'annihilated'.[45]

Like that produced by the free traders, much of this evidence was impressionistic. And, even when supported by more precise quantitative information, not always convincing. For example, Duncan Dunbar put in a list of ships entering Rio de Janeiro in December 1846 which showed a wide range of nationalities to be represented, among which British vessels were a small number. Dunbar told the Committee that this list, compiled by himself only the previous evening 'changed my opinion with reference to the power of competing with foreigners, because before that I was not so much afraid of them'.[46] Young, however, was better prepared. With Thompson and Liddell prompting him with pre-arranged questions, he presented the Committee with a mass of detail on building and operating costs calculated to support the central protectionist contention – that considerable damage would be inflicted by repeal. The implication of what had happened in consequence of reciprocity, Young argued, was inescapable – foreign ships had come to dominate those trades:

I fail to perceive why, if those nations were placed in the same relative position with British tonnage in the whole navigation of the world, they should not eventually reach the same point of proportion which they are present possess, as rapidly as they could supply themselves with tonnage to displace the tonnage with which they would be placed in competition.

But Young's most original contribution was his assertion that merchants as well as shipowners stood to lose. If it became possible to import goods from distant parts via Europe, the lower costs of warehousing in Amsterdam, Rotterdam and Hamburg would ensure that 'importations would take a different channel' and the Continent, not Britain, would become the emporium of the world.[47]

Rather than simply challenging these witnesses on their estimation of the power of foreign competition, the free traders on the Committee concentrated their attention on a related point, the effect of repeal on freight rates. Interestingly, the shipowners did not deny that protection had the effect of raising freights, though they did not assess by how much, but stressed the infinitesimal share of freight in the final price to the consumer. In the case of tea, for example, it was claimed that a reduction of a quarter in the freight rate would mean a reduction of only a farthing per pound. Some argued that freights would at first fall after repeal, depreciating the value of shipping as an investment by as much as a third, but once British ships were driven out freights would rise again.[48]

Significantly, these protectionist witnesses did not make much of the importance of the Navigation Laws for ensuring a supply of seamen for the navy. Only four cited a connection between these and naval manning. Moreover, whereas Phillips and Macqueen were prepared to say that repeal would damage the country's defences, Young, who spoke most fully on the subject, but in response to a leading question from Ricardo, was unwilling to accord the nursery of seamen a central place in his argument for the Laws. In Young's view the maintenance of British shipping was 'a point of considerable national importance, irrespective of its immeasurable importance as regards the national defence'. And as far as defence was concerned, for Young, the shipbuilder, it was the impact of repeal on this branch of the business, not the supply of seamen, which was the prime issue. If shipbuilding were to be destroyed, he argued, there would be an additional cost to the nation 'in providing a supply of naval artisans, and the means of building and repairing ships for Her Majesty's Navy'.[49]

Young's determination to see shipping in its own right recognised as a great interest in the state was shared by another witness, the founder of the Royal Mail Steam Navigation Company, James Macqueen. Both men put in estimates as to the capital employed in shipping and the level of return. Though the figures differed, and Macqueen's treatment was more explicitly comparative, the reason for their submission was precisely the same – to show that shipping had as great a claim to consideration as did other important trades. Even a year previously the appropriate standard would no doubt still have been agriculture. It was now cotton; a sign of the new political context established by the repeal of the Corn Laws.[50]

The deliberations of the Committee were brought to a close with the end of the session in July 1847. It had served its intended free trade purpose in keeping the Navigation Laws under scrutiny. Prejudices on both sides were duly confirmed but it is doubtful whether any genuine enquirer after truth could draw any clear conclusion from the evidence presented. As one reader, Admiral T. J. Cochrane, complained:

I have taken great pains, in reading over the evidence given before the House of Commons last year prior to my return to this country, to see if I could elicit from that evidence anything to lead my opinions, but really I found it so contradictory, one man declaring that so-and-so is so much cheaper, and the very next person who is examined that it is so much dearer, – in short, it is so contradictory and conflicting that I acknowledge that I have not improved my information very much by reading that evidence.[51]

No report came forward from the Select Committee. Even had time allowed, it would have proved impossible to produce an agreed statement on an issue where divisions ran so deep. Ricardo contented himself with the publication of his own conclusions in *The Anatomy of the Navigation Laws*, a polemical work which appeared in the summer of 1847. Ricardo's book was to serve as the bible for free traders arguing the case for repeal, and inspired several ripostes from the protectionist side, such as that by an anonymous author, *Mr Ricardo's Anatomy of the Navigation Laws Dissected*, which appeared in 1848.[52]

Further progress towards repeal would be made only after the General Election of late summer 1847. But one of the last acts of the waning Parliament had been to agree that the period for suspension of the Navigation Laws as they affected corn should be extended. In the debate on 2 July, Bentinck argued that there was no longer any justification for admitting third party vessels; the supply of shipping was adequate. Continuing the suspension was, in his view, simply 'a flimsy pretext to undermine the principle upon which we continue those laws for the protection of British shipping'.[53] Mindful no doubt of the benefits freer trade in corn had brought to the British shipowner, Liddell and Chapman did not join with the Protectionist leader in opposing the measure. Yet the lifting of restrictions on the carriage of corn had provided the opportunity to judge what might happen if this freedom were to be extended to all trades. Not only did foreign shipping continue to dominate the corn trade but half of the foreign vessels which carried grain to Britain between January and June 1847 were third party traders, loaded with the produce of other countries.[54] Suspension had not damaged the interests of British shipowners in any obvious way, they were in general satisfied with their share of the greater trade in corn, but it had demonstrated the ability of foreign fleets to seize new opportunities. There was here to be had a glimpse of the future, but those who spoke directly for shipping once again demonstrated the limits of their vision.

Notes

1 PD, Third Series, LXXXIII, 23 February 1846, c. 46; 20 March 1846, c. 1287.
2 PD, Third Series, XCIII, 2 July 1847, c. 1140.
3 PD, Third Series, LXXXIII, 19 February 1846, c. 1202–3.
4 PD, Third Series, XCII, 2 July 1847, c. 1140.
5 On the colonial response, see Ben Forster, *A Conjunction of Interests: Business, Politics and the Tariffs 1825–1879*, Toronto, 1986; W. P. Morrell, *British Colonial Policy in the Age of Peel and Russell*, Oxford, 1930, pp. 210–17; Robert Livingstone Schuyler, *The Fall of the Old Colonial System: a Study in British Free Trade 1770–1870*, Oxford, 1945, pp. 177–93.
6 PD, Third Series, LXXXVIII, 13 August 1846, c. 739, c. 679–80, c. 740–1.
7 Forster, *Conjunction of Interests*, p. 14.
8 'Copies of extracts of any Correspondence between the Secretary of State, and the Governors of the several Colonies respecting the Operation of the British Navigation Laws, since 1845', Appendix K, *Lords S. C. Navigation Laws*, PP 1847–48 XX Pt. II, pp. 912–946.
9 *Ibid.*, pp. 947–953; p. 952.
10 PRO, BT 1/466/1536/47 'Zollverein'; J. H. Clapham, 'The last years of the Navigation Acts', *English Historical Review*, XXV, 1910, reprinted in E. M. Carus-Wilson, *Essays in Economic History*, III, London, 1962, pp. 166–8.
11 G. P. Gooch (ed.), *The Later Correspondence of Lord John Russell 1840–1878*, I, London, 1925, p. 167.
12 GSS, Minutes, IV, 12 January 1847; SUL, Broadland Papers GC/ WO/ 20, Wood to Palmerston, 26 December 1846.
13 Boase, *Modern English Biography*; F. Levenson Gower, *Bygone Years: Recollections*, London, 1905, p. 240.
14 *Illustrated London News*, 23 January 1847; PD, Third Series, LXXIX, 19 January 1847, c. 75.
15 *Ibid.*, 21 January 1847, c. 233; PD, Third Series, LXXXIX, 9 February 1847, c. 1005–12, c. 1030.
16 *Ibid.*, c. 1025–30.
17 PD, Third Series, LXXXVIII, 13 August 1846, c. 740–1; LXXXIX 9 February 1847, c. 1058.
18 *Ibid.*, c. 1049.
19 PD, Third Series, LXXXIX, 12 February 1847, c. 1317; LXXXX, 16 February 1847, c. 27.
20 Manchester Record Office (MRO), Wilson Papers, M29. Box 449. Letter from Cobden to Wilson, 29 December 1846. Cobden's suggestion was that Milner-Gibson should equalise all colonial and foreign duties including coffee. He made no mention of Navigation Laws.
21 On the methods of the Anti-Corn Law League see Norman McCord, *The Anti-Corn Law League, 1838–1846*, London, 1958 and Patricia Hollis, *Pressure from Without in early Victoria England*, London, 1974.
22 MRO, Records of the Manchester Chamber of Commerce and Manufactures, M8/2/5, Twenty-ninth Annual Report, 11 February 1850;

Manchester Chamber of Commerce, *Report of the Directors* ... on *the Injurious Effects of Restrictions on Trade*, Manchester, 1841; Manchester Central Library (MCL), Records of the Manchester Chamber of Commerce, M8/2/4, 30 September 1846; A. Redford, *Manchester Merchants and Foreign Trade*, 2 vols, Manchester, 1934–56.

23 GSS, Minutes, IV, 12 August 1846; 20 October 1846.

24 GSS, Minutes, V, 2 March 1847.

25 GSS, Minutes, IV, 14 April 1846.

26 GSS, *Miscellaneous Papers*, 'Central Committee'.

27 GSS, Minutes, IV, 13 October 1846, 4 August 1846.

28 Unfortunately the records of the General Committee which survive in the General Shipowners' Society archive do not include any minutes.

29 GSS, Minutes, IV, 13 October 1846.

30 All the reports are printed in PP 1847 X. Since the questions are numbered consecutively and the five reports are indexed as a whole, they have not been cited separately.

31 GSS, *1849 Annual Report*.

32 Commons *S. C. Navigation Laws*, PP 1847 X, Q. 5243–5.

33 Speech at Liverpool reported *Shipping Gazette*, 19 February 1849; John Brooke and Mary Sorensen, (eds), *The Prime Minister's Papers: W. E. Gladstone, I: Autobiographica*, London, 1971, p. 44.

34 *Commons S. C. Navigation Laws*, PP 1847 X, Q. 1–220.

35 *Ibid.*, Q. 457–8, Q. 619, Q. 554, Q. 637.

36 *Ibid.*, Q. 7595, Q. 7677, Q. 7685, Q. 7797.

37 *Ibid.*, Q. 835, Q. 1511, Q. 1716–34, Q. 3770–82, Q. 2824–3048, Q. 4472–5558, Q.2622–705.

38 *Ibid.*, Q. 1818.

39 *Ibid.*, Q. 559.

40 *Ibid.*, Q. 839–40, Q. 1592, Q. 4171, Q. 4184.

41 *Ibid.*, Q. 6328–35, Q. 6573.

42 *Ibid.*, Q. 5913.

43 *Ibid.*, Q. 4596–8, Q. 4615–6.

44 NMM, Lindsay Papers, *Journal*, II, p. 102.

45 *Commons S. C. Navigation Laws*, PP 1847 (X), Q. 7994, Q. 7381, Q. 7001–5, Q. 6734, Q. 6829, Q. 6805, Q. 6640, Q. 7489–93, Q. 7226–8.

46 *Ibid.*, Q. 4389.

47 *Ibid.*, Q. 5524, Q. 5300.

48 *Ibid.*, Q. 6769, Q. 5482, Q. 5219, Q. 4557–60, Q. 7486–9.

49 *Ibid.*, Q. 5643–4

50 *Ibid.*, Q. 6101–20, 6222–9.

51 *Lords S. C. Navigation Laws*, 1847–48 XX Pt. II, Q. 8205.

52 J. Lewis Ricardo, *The Anatomy of the Navigation Laws*, London, 1847. (The copy in the Goldsmiths' Library, Senate House, University of London belonged to Sir Robert Peel); A. Barrister, *Mr. Ricardo's Anatomy of the Navigation Laws Dissected*, London, 1848. Among examples of other protectionist works are J. Allen, *The Navigation Laws of Great Britain, Historically and Practically Considered*, London, 1848; Houston Browne, *The Navigation Laws – their History and Operation*, London 1847; J. Dibs, *The*

Navigation Laws. Three Letters to Lord John Russell M. P. showing the Justice, Necessity and Economy of Protection to British Shipping, London, 1849; J. Revans, *England's Navigation Laws, No Protection to Shipping*, London, 1849.

53 PD, Third Series, XCIII, 2 July 1847, c. 1136, c. 1150.

54 Entries of all foreign vessels carrying grain totalled 538 (63,555 tons). Of these foreign vessels 304 (28,292 tons) were indirect traders. See *Return and Further Return of the Number of Foreign Ships admitted into the United Kingdom under suspension of the Navigation Laws to June 1847, PP 1847* (557)(670) LX, p. 333, p. 335.

Chapter Six

'A better question to raise': tactics and principles

The General Election of 1847 was a lacklustre affair. Only 235 out of 656 seats were contested and party allegiances were confused by a variety of issues. Religion and education featured more than economics, in so far as local campaigns were affected at all by national concerns. Neither protection in general nor the Navigation Laws in particular were central questions.[1] Even had the Whigs' intentions in respect of shipping protection been clearer, this would not have ensured greater attention to the issue nationwide. The benefits of modification were too intangible for the issue to exert widespread appeal, while those who stood to lose were the minority of voters associated with shipping. Nevertheless, despite the still undeclared position of the government, with a Select Committee at work, few in the seaports can have been unaware of the threat to the maritime protection. Indeed, already a number of petitions and memorials had been dispatched to Westminster on the subject. The question is how much, if at all, did the navigation question affect elections in these constituencies.

In London and Liverpool, where the electorate was divided, candidates treated the subject with some caution. In Liverpool the Peelites scored their greatest success with the victory of Cardwell, who replaced Lord Sandon. Cardwell's platform was 'Commercial Freedom and Religious Toleration' but he had seen fit to muffle his free trade principles in respect of the Navigation Laws. There was considerable ambiguity in his election address pledge to 'support no change in the Navigation Laws calculated to interfere with the growing prosperity of the shipping and commercial interests'. A similar political dexterity characterised the reply he gave at one meeting: 'How can I be supposed to be hostile to the Navigation Laws, supported as I am on one side by the Chairman of the Dock Committee and on the other by the Chairman of the Shipowners' Society?' In London, the Peelite John Masterman, looking to protectionist support, declared himself to be 'very jealous' of the Navigation Laws.[2]

In Glasgow, where political opinion was seemingly overwhelmingly liberal, electors had a choice of four candidates 'all liberals in their politics, free traders in commerce, and Scotchmen to the backbone'. However, the only candidate who did not specifically pledge himself to support modification of the Laws was Hastie, who, along with the Board of Trade's Macgregor, was returned for the city.[3] At Bristol, where political power was comfortably divided between the two parties, the sitting Tory member, Philip Miles, who successfully defeated a Peelite challenger, was able to be straightforward; his nomination speech cited the Navigation Laws question as of 'greater importance to this town than any other'. There was, Miles said, 'a duty to maintain any law which tends to supply hardy and experienced seamen to man our navy'.[4]

In the north-eastern constituencies the Navigation Laws question came more to the fore in some local campaigns, although even here it did nothing to reverse the region's established political trend, which tended to run against the Tories throughout the decade.[5] Indeed in Newcastle the only candidate who had pronounced against repeal, the sitting member Tory Richard Hodgson, was ousted by a Liberal. In Tynemouth the Grey nominee was returned unopposed, but his election address suggests that the Navigations Law issue was potentially sensitive. 'I am not an advocate for their total repeal and I should watch with great jealousy any proposed alteration in the present code', was Ralph Grey's message to his constituents.[6] In South Shields the Liberal member, Wawn, likewise indicated support for the Navigation Laws, perhaps with more genuine conviction to judge by his later behaviour, and successfully fought off a Protectionist opponent. In North Durham there was no contest. Here Henry Liddell, who might have been expected to continue to play an active part as a shipping spokesman in the new Parliament, pledged himself to resist any alteration in the Laws, but then stood down. His replacement, Lord Londonderry's son Seaham, likewise pronounced in favour of shipping protection, but as an MP was to show no comparable concern for general maritime questions, despite the Londonderry interest in Seaham Harbour.[7]

If in the north-east the navigation issue perhaps achieved rather more prominence than elsewhere, it was still far from proving a major source of political conflict, not least because most Whig and Liberal candidates refused to take a principled stand on an aspect of free trade which could only cause them electoral trouble, and on which some may have been genuinely undecided. Sunderland was the exception. As the *Newcastle Guardian* noted in February 1848:

In the neighbouring borough of Sunderland the question of the Navigation Laws, which elsewhere has excited extremely little interest, has latterly absorbed much attention, and has been discussed with a vehemence scarcely less intense than that evinced during the progress of the Corn Law agitation.[8]

The election campaign saw the first phase of this vehemence in Sunderland. One of the two sitting members, the Tory railway magnate Hudson, was challenged by a London Liberal, Wilkinson, who chose to focus his campaign on Hudson's support for the Navigation Laws. Wilkinson had the backing of the prominent local quaker shipowner Joshua Wilson, a witness to the 1844 Select Committee on Shipping. But Wilson's view, expressed at a campaign meeting on 23 July, that the Navigation Laws were of 'comparatively trifling moment', merely comparable to 'the loss of a finger or two', was not shared by the majority of electors and Hudson was re-elected. His fellow member, the Liberal London merchant David Barclay, was also returned again, having affirmed in his election address that he considered the Navigation Laws to be ' wholly distinct from the doctrine of free trade, which justifies a departure from this principle'. When Barclay stood down some months later, Wilkinson failed to fill the vacancy, which was taken by Sir Hedworth Williamson, who 'conciliated the shipowners by expressing himself opposed to any alteration of the Navigation Laws'. In the opinion of the Sunderland Lloyd's surveyor, Simey, this election 'hinged almost altogether upon the question of the Navigation Laws', with Williamson's pledge ensuring that he gained 'a very large number of votes which he otherwise would not have had'.[9]

In Hull, Sir James Clay and Matthew Baines, both new candidates, were returned unopposed. Clay was protectionist on shipping, as also, more surprisingly in the light of the fact that Russell in 1849 appointed him President of the Poor Law Board, was Baines. Whether Baines's support for the Laws reflected deep-seated conviction or a sensible respect for local opinion is impossible to say. Certainly Hull, with port charges on foreign vessels arguably the most punitive in the whole country, had a long record of opposition to reciprocity treaties and a short way with candidates who failed to support shipowning interests.[10]

In terms of party support, the effect of a perceived threat to the Navigation Laws may have been to sustain Protectionist candidates in some maritime constituencies. But considered in terms of personalities, the shipping interest in the new Parliament was a depleted force. Liddell was no longer an MP and George Lyall, whose liberal commercial views had given him close access to government over two decades, had also retired at this election. Lyall disliked speaking in public but had been an active committee member and lobbyist.[11] Among the new shipping members there were for the first time representatives of the steamship companies. But while Willcox and Anderson campaigned against the Light Dues – a particular burden on steamer operations because of the number of repeated voyages – they had little interest in wider shipping issues, beyond having a broad prejudice in favour of free trade; Arthur Anderson had been a member of the Anti-Corn Law League. In the election at Poole of George Robinson, former Chairman of LLoyd's, the maritime protectionists gained a member who was prepared to speak on the floor of the House, but of the old band of shipowning activists only the redoubtable Alderman Thompson remained. The shipping case to a large extent came to depend on the efforts of the increasingly discredited George Hudson, exerted largely in self-interested defence of Sunderland constituents, and the expertise of Joseph Henley.

Overall the election of 1847 resolved little, except to confirm any doubt as to the continuance of political disarray. There remained what Stanley described as a 'general confusion of parties, persons and principles', with free trade Conservatives maintaining a sizeable presence of around 113 members.[12] The least confused aspect of the new Parliament was the poor state of the Protectionists. Although numbering about 230, with the impact of free trade seemingly more benign than harsh, there was little except 'No Popery' to provoke cohesion, and this was a cry which was anathema to Bentinck, their nominal leader in the Commons. The government looked with satisfaction at the disarray among its opponents but, despite increased numbers, it also lacked unity, with educational and religious policy, along with the demands of the fifty or sixty radicals, constituting major divisive elements.[13]

In the Parliament of 1847, then, a divided government was confronted by a divided opposition. This had a number of consequences which were germane to the issue of the Navigation Laws. First, the fate of any legislative measure was frequently uncertain. This encouraged caution and head-counting on the part of the administration and much lobbying on the part of opponents. Even though free trade questions were more recognisably party matters, the same applied. Another consequence was the power the situation gave to those prepared to take the initiative, whether in the Board of Trade or on the back-benches. Moreover, as the parliament wore on, with government relying on temporary alliances for support, and MPs increasingly voting according to individual inclination rather than group loyalty, the stability and survival of the administration itself became an issue. Within the narrow political context of Parliament, the inability of the Whigs to command support was of limited importance, judged frustrating or diverting according to political affiliation. But the events of 1848 on the Continent and Chartism at home forced on members a wider perspective. With public order so apparently fragile, what would be the effect of disruption at the centre of power, were the government to be defeated?

In the late summer of 1847 such developments still lay in the future. Once their parliamentary predominance had been confirmed, the main practical issue for the Whigs was what their programme for the forthcoming session should be. With little scope for lowering duties and no chance of being able to reduce taxes, the government's opportunities for liberalising economic measures were severely limited, yet these were expected of them by their supporters. Here, as the Chancellor, Sir Charles Wood, recognised, the Navigation Laws issue might prove very useful. It would, he wrote to the Prime Minister on 20 August, 'be a very good subject to engage the two sides of opinion in the House of Commons' and it had 'the great advantage of costing nothing, in point of revenue, which is no slight matter in the present state of our finances'. Wood continued:

All this renders the Navigation Laws a better question to raise for if we disappoint our people in point of taxation it may be as well to turn their attention to the remaining piece of antiquated legislation which ought to be swept away. Indeed, some of the absurdities resulting from the existing law will hardly bear to be stated.[14]

What Wood seems to have envisaged fell well short of total repeal. All he suggested was a widening of reciprocal arrangements to allow foreign vessels to bring goods to Britain from anywhere in the world, in return for similar concessions. Replying to Wood, Russell accepted the suggested means for achieving this – an Act of Parliament permitting treaties to be made – but reported Dalhousie's view that, although minor changes were permissible, it would be unwise to give foreigners access to colonial carriage. Yet if this were not conceded, Russell wrote, 'I do not see how we could say that an American ship could bring sugar from Cuba here and not sugar from Jamaica. Pray consider this point well.' In answer, Wood suggested that there was no possibility of reciprocity in respect of the colonies, which were unique, so both coastal and colonial business would continue to be reserved to the national fleet, but beyond commenting that 'the colonies may complain perhaps', failed to take up the essence of Russell's point: that the colonies might not only feel, but actually be, disadvantaged.[15]

At the time that Wood was urging modification of the Navigation Laws on grounds of political expediency, others in the cabinet, as Russell was aware, were already engaged in informal discussions on the Navigation Laws with George Bancroft, the United States pleni-potentiary. Bancroft had been appointed by President Polk the previous autumn, with a primarily commercial brief in which reduction of tobacco duties and relaxation of regulations affecting United States trade with the West Indies and Canada were the chief elements. Bancroft, 'most American of American representatives', who had a strong personal philosophical commitment to trade liberalisation, had established a sympathetic relationship with like-minded government Ministers, in particular with Labouchere, who had become President of the Board of Trade in May 1847.[16]

Bancroft's talks with Labouchere and with Palmerston at the Foreign Office initially centred on opening up the indirect trade, so that United States vessels would be enabled to bring goods to Britain from all foreign parts, but by September 1847 his instructions from his government were that he should seek greater concessions. In the view of his superior, the American Secretary of State, to deal only with the indirect trade would be extremely complex, whereas if Britain 'should consent to abandon her entire colonial system, and place her colonies on the same footing with her territories in Europe, the treaty would be completely simple in its provisions'. Bancroft was told 'to continue endeavors in conversation to prepare the minds of the members of the British cabinet for abolishing every restriction in the trade, direct and indirect, between the possessions of the two countries, and placing it on the footing of the most perfect reciprocity'.[17]

Bancroft was not the only individual anxious 'to prepare the minds' of Ministers; a similar concern was apparently felt by some members of the cabinet in relation to their colleagues. On 3 November 1847

Bancroft sent to the Board of Trade a letter which asked whether 'Her Majesty's government is inclined to remove existing restrictions on international commerce'. It continued:

Should Her Majesty's government entertain similar views, the undersigned is prepared, on the part of the American government to propose that British ships may trade from any port in the world to any port in the United States and be received, protected, and in respect of charges and duties, treated like American ships may in like manner trade from any part of the world to any part under the dominion of Her Brittanic Majesty.

The removal of commercial restrictions, while it would be of mutual advantage to the material interests of both countries, could not but give openings to still further relations of amity between them, and by its influence on the intercourse of nations create new guarantees for the peace of the world.

After Palmerston and Labouchere had conferred privately on the American proposal, Labouchere contacted Bancroft and suggested the insertion of an additional paragraph. Bancroft complied, sending an alternative version, dated as was the original and asking Labouchere to 'pray take care that the substitution is properly made in the Foreign Office and send me back the one which is not preferred'.

This incident reveals more than Bancroft's naïvety (for of course the Foreign Office records note the substitution). It suggests that the Board of Trade was anxious for proposals from the United States of America which would, by use of the key word 'reciprocity', seem attractive to those looking for a limited reform of the Navigation Laws, in particular, perhaps, the Prime Minister Russell. The new paragraph, which immediately preceded those quoted above, had the desired effect of altering the whole tone of the United States proposition:

Universal reciprocity, in the widest sense, is held by the American government as the only thoroughly appropriate basis for intercourse between the great nations. The prohibition of the indirect trade has but restrained enterprise, it has done good to neither country. To abrogate it would at once set free dormant commercial wealth without injuring anyone.[18]

When Parliament re-assembled, the Queen's Speech contained a reference to the government's determination to act on the Navigation Laws.[19] At this stage many members of the cabinet possibly still supposed that any changes in the protective system as it affected shipping would be achieved through the conclusion of reciprocity treaties with individual countries. On 19 January, however, Labouchere informed Russell that the opinion of the Law Officers was that direct legislation would be necessary, because of the problems posed by

115

existing most-favoured-nation provisions, and that he was framing his bill accordingly. Labouchere asked the Prime Minister, if he approved, to raise the matter at the next cabinet meeting because 'when the subject was last discussed it was determined to proceed in a different manner'.[20]

It seems probable that Labouchere, with Palmerston's compliance, was seeking to ensure that any action taken on the Navigation Laws represented a genuine advance for free trade. Certainly the steps he took subsequently to push his bill forward suggest a real commitment to the principle of trade liberalisation.[21] This approach ran directly counter to the instinctive preference of others in the government for a more cautious approach. Rumours of differences in the cabinet over this and sugar duties reached the press; the *Shipping Gazette* questioned 'whether the Premier is now inclined to go the whole hog with such men as Mr Milner Gibson'.[22] With no ministerial agreement on how to act, and across the Channel the establishment of the Second Republic keeping defence against the French still uncomfortably high upon the government's agenda, the navigation question was accorded a low priority.

At the free trade banquet in honour of the return to Parliament of the Anti-Corn Law members, George Wilson had anticipated opposition and had promised a bold response:

they will fight us upon the Navigation Laws. Well we will fight them upon the Navigation Laws; and as with the Corn Laws, so with the Navigation Laws, our friends will meet them, and with a long pull and a strong pull, we will defeat them.[23]

Now the Ministry's commitment to some change seemed to be in doubt, while the Protectionists' capacity to mount an effective challenge to the government on the issue was being enhanced with every month that passed.

Finally, frustrated at the inactivity of the government of which he was a part, Labouchere sought the assistance of the back-benches. On 3 April Bright raised the question of United States cotton cargoes at Le Havre. Could they, he innocently inquired, be brought to Britain under present regulations? Labouchere's predictable response in the negative gave Gladstone the opportunity to express his regret that the government was not intending to bring forward its bill for amending the laws until late May. He pressed Russell to confirm that he intended to proceed with the measure that session. The Prime Minister pleaded pressure of parliamentary business as the reason for the delay and the

House moved on to other matters, but the message had been conveyed to the Whig leadership: the radical Liberals and free trade Conservatives were not prepared to let the matter rest.[24]

As far as maritime protectionists were concerned, the fall of Bentinck as Tory leader in January threatened to have serious practical implications for their cause. Despite his reservations about shipowners as political allies, Bentinck had not only shown a willingness to espouse their interests publicly which was not general on his side, but had also developed with enthusiasm his own expertise on the subject. Rash and impulsive though Bentinck could be in debate, he revelled in the mastery of detailed information and had found in the shipping question a fine field for the exercise of this talent. Such skill was, of course, not lost to the shipping interest when Bentinck ceased to be leader – he was to play a full part in the Commons debates on the Laws in May and June – but his departure from the opposition front bench, like the disunity which it signified, called into question the ability and will of the Protectionists in Parliament to mount an effective campaign against any change in the Navigation Laws.

However, Bentinck's resignation as leader proved only a minor setback for the cause of protection for shipping. In the late summer of 1847 Stanley had not been sanguine about the immediate prospects for his cause, telling Croker that 'the game of Free Trade must be played out and its effects . . . must be tested by actual experience before the experiment can be retracted or it would be wise in us to press for its retraction.'[25] By the new year 1848, in the immediate wake of the commercial crisis and with industrial demand still falling, such pessimism began to look inappropriate. If the time was still not yet ripe for a retraction of free trade, the case against any further such experiments was much strengthened. Moreover, if differences with the Peelites over the Navigation Laws issue was one factor preventing Conservative reunion, equally their defence offered Stanley the prospect of re-establishing his own group's unity on its firmer, original protectionist basis.[26]

Faced with a clear commitment in the Queen's Speech to some alteration in the Laws, but no doubt aware of the misgivings of some senior Whigs, Stanley was determined that there should be strong Protectionist opposition and that full advantage should be taken of any government delay in bringing forward legislation. With the aid of material provided by Bentinck in early February, which came accompanied by an assurance that although the papers required 'two or three days for thought and consideration after this they would afford the elements of a great case', Stanley briefed himself on the issue, paying particular attention to colonial carriage.[27] In the Commons, it now fell to the seventy-year-old Herries to act as Protectionist economic spokesman, but Herries was enthusiastic about Stanley's stance – 'I heartily rejoice that you are determined to fight out the battle of the Navigation Laws' – and was to prove for the most part a not ineffective performer.[28] More important, at the end of February the Earl of Hardwicke successfully moved for a Select Committee of the Lords to investigate the Navigation Laws. If the free traders had their Select Committee, so now did the Protectionists.[29]

The new-found determination among the Protectionists at Westminster to fight with vigour on the Navigation Laws owed everything to considerations of party, nothing to the interests of shipping as such. Had G. F. Young been an MP at this time no doubt he would have aimed to play a prominent role, but among the few members of the 1847 Parliament having any connection with shipping, supporters of Stanley were in a minority. Leading Protectionists were happy to use as debating points the evidence of support for the Laws offered by petitions or public meetings, but they sought no connection between the campaign in the country and the campaign in Parliament. Lord Stanhope's efforts in 1849 to build a general protectionist movement enjoying mass support were to be regarded as misguided and dangerous in Tory circles. Popular protest was not something to be encouraged.

What then of the protectionist response outside Parliament? The year 1847 had seen petitioning and meetings in a some ports, but there was no great activity, perhaps because the government's intentions were still only a matter of rumour until the beginning of 1848. Indeed, the appointment of the Central Committee to work for the preservation of the Navigation Laws by the General Shipowners' Society had apparently made so little impact in shipping circles that, noting the formation of an anti-repeal association in Liverpool, the *Shipping Gazette* called for such a body to be established:

The time has now arrived when it behoves the friends of British Shipping to be up and doing in the City. . . . The material is ample: all that is wanted is organisation. There are members still living belonging to the Pitt club; there are members of the Shipowners' Association; there are hundreds of subscribers to Lloyds, and the other coffee houses – the Jerusalem and Jamaica for instance – who would enrol their names as members . . . One great effort, a spirited public meeting in the City, would put the people in the right course and prevent Ministers mistaking the apathy of despair for acquiescence in revolutionary national and colonial confiscation . . . Let not future historians have to recall the fact, that, when called upon the citizens of London permitted the best interests of the nation to be sacrificed without an effort.[30]

But if the shipping elite was slow to respond to the challenge, the same charge could not be levied against those lower down the social scale. At the beginning of February Londoners witnessed an unusual spectacle, a seamen's demonstration on the Thames, culminating in the presentation of a memorial for the Queen to the Home Secretary by a deputation consisting of representatives of seamen from London, the Tyne, South Shields, Sunderland and Weymouth. The plan for a procession 'when the fleet now here arrives in London' originated in the north-east. Its instigator was James Mather, a South Shields radical shipowner who had been active in the Anti-Corn Law League, but was nevertheless in favour of the Navigation Laws. Mather, who in the General Election had called for the return of 'such English-hearted men as will protect the nation's honour and safety by securing the commercial marine from destruction', was concerned that the seamen appeared apathetic about repeal and saw such a demonstration as a means of countering this impression.[31] The original plan was for a march through the City, but when the Lord Mayor refused permission on the grounds that 'so great a body, passing through the streets, would put a stop to business, and might lead to tumult', it was decided instead to process by water, taking advantage of an offer from G. F. Young to provide some boats and flags.

At 12 o'clock there were about 100 boats lying off the entrance to the London Docks, the crews and masters being dressed in their blue jackets, and, having blue ribbon in their hats with 'Navigation Laws' in yellow, some of the Masters had their names in gold.

Bad weather and the problems in maintaining the line of vessels caused delay and 'the loss of much of the inherent gaiety of such a scene', but by the time the procession reached London Bridge it consisted of some 500–600 boats, a further 200 having been left at Woolwich as a result of wind and weather. *The Times* reporter, who noted with irony that many of the foreign vessels down river unaware of the object of the procession had shared in the festive mood by flying their bunting, was struck by the size of the demonstration. He observed that, 'when the steamer in tow of the first division reached Southwark Bridge the last of the monster tail of boats had just cleared London Bridge'. The seamen

then disembarked at Westminster Stairs and marched to Trafalgar
Square, impressing the *Shipping Gazette* with their good behaviour:

Perhaps a more imposing sight had never been witnessed in the Metropolis –
this vast body of men being dressed in their best clothes; and, as far as our
reporter had the opportunity of witnessing them, every man was orderly and
well conducted.

The seamen's leaders then left them to go the Home Office,
accompanied by Wawn, the Liberal MP for South Shields, where they
handed over their memorial to Grey. This reminded the Queen,
slightly obliquely, of the appeal of the United States mercantile
marine:

Your Memorialists will be driven to seek employment in another state,
speaking the same language and possessing similar laws, where seamen's
interests and seamen's rights are carefully attended to and where thousands of
British seamen have already found protection – so weakening Your Majesty's
empire, and giving protection to an already great maritime competitor.[32]

As is often the case with demonstrations, the exact number
participating is difficult to establish. In this instance the *Shipping
Gazette*'s estimate of 5,000–6,000 has to be set against that of the less
sympathetic *Illustrated London News*, which suggested that those
involved amounted to a maximum of 3,000. Nevertheless, the seamen
did succeed in gaining valuable press attention for their cause, not least
from that paper's engravers. More significantly, they had directly
confronted a government based in London with the seafarers of the
north-east, a group peaceful enough on this occasion, but with a
reputation for combination.[33] Subsequent events suggest that the
seamen's procession succeeded in exerting no small influence over
government policy.

Faced with the threat of unlimited admission of foreigners into the
British mercantile marine, these seamen found it easy to make common
case. Their understanding of the issues may have lacked sophistication;
John Bright was told by some of the demonstrators that 'that some of
the people down river had told them they were to eat black bread if the
Navigation Laws were abolished'. But Bright's conclusion that this
indicated 'the sort of delusion attempted to be practised upon them'
betrayed ignorance of the extent to which the 'black bread' provided
on Scandinavian vessels symbolised for British seamen low wages and
poor standards of victualling.[34] If shipowners, not renowned for
magnanimity, were to be allowed freely to employ foreigners in the

coasting trade it was not unreasonable to expect that this would encourage them to depress wage costs.

Organising other maritime groups proved more difficult. A meeting later the same month of 'persons engaged in the outfit and equipment of ships' chaired by the London shipbuilder Money Wigram merely succeeded in revealing the divided state of the industry. Duncan Dunbar injudiciously observed that 'as a shipowner he would like to buy in the cheapest market, but as a patriot he would be ashamed to do so', while the prominent shipbuilder, shipowner and philanthropist Richard Green excused his absence in a letter which frankly declared, 'I wish you every success but I very much fear the Navigation Laws are doomed.' While it seems unlikely that shipbuilders were in favour of repeal – even a free trade contributor to the *Economist* conceded that they had 'the deepest interest in the continuation of the Navigation Law' – such attempts at concerted action seem to have been rare.[35] Shipbuilders, many of whom were also investors in shipping, relied on the General Shipowners' Society to fight on their behalf and no national campaign specifically reflecting shipbuilding interests emerged in response to the threat to expose the industry to competition from foreign yards.

But the main weapon adopted both by those opposing repeal of the Navigation Laws and by free trade groups was the parliamentary petition. Before 1842 petitions to the House of Commons were dealt with on the floor of the Chamber and could have an impact simply by the delay this could cause to parliamentary business. After this date petitions were referred to the Committee on Public Petitions and the only way in which petitions could directly influence proceedings was 'through their size and novelty or by being the subject of a special report from the Public Petitions Committee', in which case the petition, or an extract, was printed.[36] Petitions addressed to the House of Lords were unaffected by this system, but, as the less influential body, in general the Lords proved less attractive to petitioners. As the result, then, of this change, the petition had been considerably weakened as a means of influencing parliamentary opinion and it has been suggested that the explanation for its continued popularity with various movements was that, as with Chartism, the petition became an end in itself. It is also possible that some of those who organised petitions in the later 1840s were not sufficiently aware of parliamentary processes to appreciate the significance of the change in procedure. A more convincing explanation, and one that certainly seems to fit the present context, is that the extensive use of the petition as a political device in particular by the Anti-Corn Law League had made it an an obligatory ingredient in any agitation. Appeals from the public might exert very little positive influence, but if they were absent, then the conclusion to be drawn by the legislators was that what was proposed was generally acceptable.

When used in national campaigns rather than to press local demands the petition was a radical device; the extensive use made of it by shipping protectionists constitutes an intriguing, and forgotten, exception. In the parliamentary session 1847–48, 139 petitions indicating support for the retention of the Navigation Laws were submitted to the House of Commons. The number of signatures appended to these petitions totalled 49,231, some representing individuals, others various associations. Over the same period, the House of Lords received thirty-three petitions, with 13,330 names. In the 1849 session the balance altered. The Commons received a further fifteen petitions (2,029 signatures) and the Lords 133 (133,805 signatures) 'against any alteration', plus a further 134 (31,956) 'against the Bill'.[37]

What we have here, of course, is not a spontaneous upsurge of outrage but a thoroughly organised campaign, with the Central Committee for Upholding the Principles of the Navigation Laws acting as the prime instigator. The timing of petitions, and whether they were directed at the Commons or the Lords, reflected the parliamentary progress of the issue. In 1848, assuming (mistakenly as it turned out) that the government would legislate that session, the shipping interests directed their main onslaught to the Commons, although in some quarters it was felt that little could be expected here and that the Lords would be a better target, 'it being in vain to reason with the rabid free trade House of Commons led by a reckless ministry'.[38] At the same time, there was concern at the partial nature of the work being undertaken by the Commons Select Committee on the Navigation Laws, and a subsidiary campaign developed for the appointment of a Lords' Select Committee, with forty-nine petitions coming forward to the House of Lords on this.[39] Although, as it transpired, the government was unable to proceed with a bill that session, the Commons vote on the navigation question in the early summer of 1848 encouraged the petitioning campaign to concentrate its attention on the Lords the following year.

Further evidence of organisation is provided by the petitions themselves, most of which were identical or very similar, as the reports of the Commons Committee on Public Petitions noted. There were exceptions, such as the petition submitted in May 1848, signed by three Sunderland shipbuilders, which set out details of comparative costs in justification of their assertion that 'successful competition is utterly impossible'.[40] But a majority of petitioners were content to make use of forms emanating from the Central Committee. The Greenock ship-builder John Scott, for example, in February 1849 ordered twenty copies of such a draft, which he dispatched to protectionist sympathisers in the area, assuring the campaign organisers that he would do all he could 'for the good cause of getting up petitions in this place and neighbourhood, although there is much opposition by many who sacrifice their interest for the cry of free trade'.[41] Scott was responding to an Address from the Central Committee which recommended that

In all Sea-port towns in which it may be practicable and prudent, public meetings should be held for the adoption of the Petition; that shipping tradesmen be everywhere roused to exertion; that Local Committees be formed where they do not already exist, to correspond with this Central Committee and assist its operations; that subscriptions be raised and transmitted; that no effort be spared to influence County as well as Borough members to support the Petitions; – in short, that every exertion should be used to give to the opposition all the weight and effect to which the earnest remonstrances of a powerful national interest are constitutionally entitled.[42]

This printed statement reflected the public strategy of the Central Committee in relation to petitions. More private instructions sent to supporters in connection with the earlier petition for a Lords Select Committee give a better insight into the considerations at work:

It is of course advisable that the petitions should be as numerously signed as possible, but it is of even greater importance that the petitions themselves should be multiplied, than that dependence should be placed alone on the number of signatures. Thus shipowners, seamen and the various classes of tradesmen and artificers connected with the building and outfit of ships, commercial associations, (parishes as interested in the question of national security) all may separately petition in their several capacities where their number is sufficient.[43]

Sunderland, at least, proved responsive to this suggestion. On 25 February 1848 the Commons Committee on Petitions reported receipt of separate petitions on this subject from 'the Shipwrights of Sunderland, the Sailmakers and Ropemakers of Sunderland, the Chain and Anchormakers of Sunderland, the Grocers and other tradesmen of Sunderland, the Master Mariners, Seamen and Pilots of Sunderland, the Block and Mastmakers and Boat Builders of Sunderland, the Shipbuilders of Sunderland and the Shipowners of Sunderland'.[44]

If the petition was necessarily a somewhat artificial political device, it should not therefore be concluded that the evidence of concern over the Navigation Laws which they offer is false. Those petitions which came forward in the last phase of the campaign in the first half of 1849 from 'the Owners and Occupiers of Land' in such places as Dorchester, Crewkerne, Petersfield and Shrewsbury were promoted by supporters of agricultural protection, and must be seen in that light.[45] But the bulk of petitions was from the seaports, with the north-east contributing the greatest evidence of opposition. Opinion was not wholly on the side of protection; it also proved possible to organise pro-repeal petitions in London, Liverpool, Sunderland, Yarmouth, Dundee and Belfast. But the numbers which could be rallied in favour of repeal were a tiny proportion of those against. Had the fate of the Navigation Laws depended on the evidence of interested opinion provided by petitions, they would have survived.

Notes

1 Robert Stewart, *The Politics of Protection: Lord Derby and the Protectionist Party 1841–1852*, Cambridge, 1971, p. 108.
2 *Liverpool Times*, 10 May 1849; *Shipping Gazette*, 14 March 1849; William Devereux Jones and Arvel B. Erickson, *The Peelites*, Ohio, 1972, p. 15.
3 *North British Railway and Shipping Journal*, 5 June 1847, 26 June 1847.
4 *Bristol Poll Book*, 1847.
5 Nossiter, *Influence*, p. 34.
6 *Newcastle Guardian*, 24 July 1847.
7 *Sunderland and Durham County Herald*, 11 June 1847, 9 July 1847.
8 *Newcastle Guardian*, 12 February 1848.
9 *Sunderland and Durham County Herald*, 18 June 1847, 23 July 1847, 13 August 1847, 23 March 1849; *Lords S. C. Navigation Laws*, 1847–48 XX Pt II, Q. 4112.
10 *Hull Advertiser*, 16 July 1847; 16 February 1849.
11 *Dictionary of National Biography*.
12 LCL, Derby Papers, (14) 177/2, Derby to Croker, 7 September 1847. (This letter, reprinted in L. J. Jennings (ed.), *The Croker Papers*, 3 vols, London, 1884, p. 107 is mistakenly given a June date.)
13 On the politics of this period, see J. B. Conacher, *The Peelites and the Party System 1846–52*, Newton Abbot, 1972; Jones and Erickson, *The Peelites*; William Devereux Jones, *Lord Derby and Victorian Conservatism*, Oxford, 1956; S. Maccoby, *English Radicalism 1832–1852*, London, 1934; Donald Southgate, *The Passing of the Whigs 1832–1886*, London, 1962; Stewart, *Politics of Protection*.
14 PRO, Russell Papers, 30/22 6E f. 154.

15 *Ibid.*, 30/22 6E f. 199; Gooch, *Russell*, pp. 182–3.
16 Bancroft to Labouchere, 23 August 1847, Russell Papers, PRO 30/22 6E f197; *Dictionary of American Biography*, pp. 564–70; Lilian Hendlin, *George Bancroft: the Intellectual as Democrat*, New York, 1984; Buchanan to Bancroft, 6 October 1846, in John B. Moore (ed.), *The Works of James Buchanan*, VII, Philadelphia, 1909, p. 92.
17 Buchanan to Bancroft, 29 September 1847, Moore, *Buchanan*, p. 422.
18 PRO, FO 5/478, f121, f125, f139; 5/482 f 69, f86, f90.
19 PD, Third Series, XCV, 23 November 1847, c. 14.
20 PRO, Russell Papers, 30/22 7A f. 69.
21 Palmerston also raised the issue with Russell. See Southampton University Library (SUL) Broadlands Papers, GC/RU/ 914-1148.
22 *Shipping Gazette*, 20 January 1848.
23 *Shipping Gazette*, 28 January 1848.
24 PD, Third Series, XCVII, 2 April 1848, c. 1202-13.
25 *Croker Papers*, Stanley to Croker, 12 September 1847, p. 000.
26 LCL, Derby Papers, 290 Der(14) 177/2.
27 Derby Papers, 290 Der(14) 132/13.
28 Derby Papers, 290 Der(14) 152/1.
29 PD, Third Series, XCVI, 25 February 1848, c. 1313.
30 *Shipping Gazette*, 18 January 1848.
31 Boase, *English Biography*; James Mather, *An Address to the Electors of the Seaports of the United Kingdom on the Navigation Laws: and their duties at this critical juncture*, South Shields, 1847, p. 21.
32 *Shipping Gazette*, 9 February 1848, 15 January 1848, 2 February 1848; *The Times*, 10 February 1848.
33 *Illustrated London News*, 12 February 1848. See Stephen Jones, 'Community and organisation: early seamen's trade unionism on the north east coast, 1764–1844', *Maritime History*, III, 1973, pp. 35–66; D. J. Rowe, 'A trade union of the north east coast seamen in 1825', *Economic History Review*, 2nd ser., XXV, 1972, pp. 87-98.
34 PD, Third Series, CI, 10 August 1848, c. 59.
35 *Shipping Gazette*, 24 February 1848; *Economist*, 12 February 1848.
36 See House of Lords Record Office, B. J. Enright, 'Public Petitions in the House of Commons' (unpublished typescript, 1960).
37 House of Lords Record Office, *Reports of the Select Committee of the House of Commons on Public Petitions*, 1847–48, 1849; *Lords S. C. Navigation Laws*, 1847–48 XX Pt. II, Appendix Hh, p. 1051.
38 *Shipping Gazette*, 16 February 1848.
39 *Lords S. C. Navigation Laws*, PP 1847–48 XX Pt. II, Appendix Hh, p. 1051.
40 House of Lords Record Office, *49th Report of the Committee on Public Petitions*, Appendix 1020.
41 Glasgow University Archives, (GUA) GD 319/11/1/18.
42 LCL, Derby Papers, 920 Der(14) 38.
43 GSS, Miscellaneous Manuscripts, Address, dated 26 January 1848.
44 *Lords S. C. Navigation Laws*, PP 1847–48 XX Pt. II, Appendix Hh, 1051.
45 *Lords Journals*, 1849 LXXXI.

Chapter Seven

'More safely and more wisely' : debates on repeal

On 15 May 1848, after months of delay during which the deliberations of the Lords Select Committee had given some advantage to the Protectionist side, the government's intentions on the future of the Navigation Laws at last became clearer. Even then Labouchere put before the Commons for approval not a bill but a resolution:

That it is expedient to remove the restrictions which prevent the free carriage of goods by sea to and from the United Kingdom, and the British possessions abroad, subject nevertheless, to such control by Her Majesty in Council as may be necessary and to amend the Laws for the Registration of Ships and Seamen.[1]

While what was suggested went less far than had been anticipated, or hoped for, in some quarters, it nevertheless represented a major departure. Hitherto, whatever the demands of the radical free traders, Whig talk had been of modification or amendment, not repeal. As Herries pointed out, until that day 'no legislator, however strong his opinions of free trade, or however disposed towards reform, had ever yet proposed the abrogation of the Navigation Laws.'[2]

In fact, Labouchere's proposals still fell some way short of total repeal, and reflected far more shades of opinion than was sensible for this major measure. It was not intended to open the coasting trade, the restrictions on British registry were to be maintained, and the only relaxations of manning restrictions were in respect of Lascar seamen and apprenticeship. Here the government had paid some attention to shipowners' complaints, but rather more to the fears of seafarers and those concerned about national defence; the seamen had not processed up the Thames in vain. The reciprocal principle, favoured by some members of the cabinet, survived in the power retained to refuse concessions if similar benefits were not forthcoming. Leaving their coasting arrangements to local legislatures was intended to avoid a dispute over colonial interests.

Neither the content of what was proposed nor the way it was brought forward were calculated to inspire much confidence even among the government's supporters. The imprecision inherent in discussion of proposals which were still not formally incorporated in a bill and which relied on ministerial explanation lent an air of improvisation to government exposition of points of detail. In addition, the elements of compromise satisfied neither enemies nor friends of repeal (Gladstone, for example, questioned the wisdom of retaining the provisions on manning), while the method of proceeding by resolution rather than a bill, perhaps because drafting was still in progress, gave the Protectionists the opportunity to table an alternative motion:

That it is essential to the national interests of this country to maintain the fundamental principles of the existing Navigation Laws; subject to such modification as may be best calculated to obviate any proved inconvenience to the commerce of the United Kingdom and its dependencies, without danger to our national strength.[3]

The leading Protectionists had determined their strategy at a meeting on 17 May to which Hudson and Miles were invited as the only seaport members in this camp.[4] Forcing a division on the issue as defined in terms of their own choosing, rather than simply reacting to Labouchere's proposal, had both political and tactical advantages. It enabled the Protectionists to focus attention directly on the central principle of shipping protection as an issue of national importance, while admitting the possibility of some alteration. The division on the opposition motion could not be expected to result in government defeat but ensured a fuller discussion than would otherwise have been probable. By this means the Protectionists were enabled to build on the extra-parliamentary campaign of the previous months, to take full advantage of the ammunition provided by evidence to the Lords Select Committee and to prolong the discomfiture of those members of the government who were still unhappy about what was proposed. Above all, this tactic made it much less likely that the bill itself would be brought forward that session – as, in fact, proved to be the case.

Proposing his resolution the following day, Labouchere set out the immediate background to the Laws proper, running through the history of alteration, and emphasised not only the importance of the

Huskisson measures but also what he described as the 'breach' made by the relaxations relating to the Danube ten years earlier. He justified further reforms in terms of demands from overseas, citing the addresses submitted the previous year from Montreal and Trinidad; the note from Prussia of 10 May 1847; and the evident interest of the United States government in reciprocity as conveyed by Bancroft's note of the previous November. Labouchere went on to explain the inclusion of the laws on registration and merchant seamen in his reform proposals on the grounds that 'the system hangs so together', but stressed that he wanted only to do away with compulsory apprenticeship and the limitations on Lascar employment. As far as other matters of interest to shipowners were concerned, he reminded the House that he was dealing with the question of Trinity Dues and the Merchant Seamen's Fund separately, and expressed a hope that the question of pilotage and education of merchant seamen might be the subject of future legislation.[5]

Reports of the government's announcement brought a flurry of public meetings in the seaports over the weeks which followed, and encouraged a renewed spate of petitions. *The Liverpool Times*, reporting on one such meeting, noted that a free trade motion had been defeated, and concluded that 'there is no decided feeling amongst any numerous portion of the people of Liverpool in favour of the abrogation of these laws'. The general opinion was, it said, in favour of some amendment but not 'the unnecessary and dangerous experiment' of total abrogation.[6] In Glasgow 'a most repectable assemblage' signified its opposition to repeal, despite the fact that the meeting included men whom, in the judgement of the *North British Railway and Shipping Journal*, 'have been the foremost to advocate radical politics and to tear from the agriculturalist everything in the slightest degree approaching to protection'.[7] At Sunderland, however, where Duncan Dunbar attended a protectionist meeting of shipowners and shipbuilders on behalf of the Central Committee, a rather different assembly of shipwrights and seamen demonstrated that working-class support in the town for the anti-repeal campaign could not continue to be relied upon. James Dunn, an organiser of the seamen's procession earlier in the year, proposed a protectionist resolution, which was accepted. But then a speaker from the floor introduced a class dimension, arguing that this was 'a shipowners' question'. 'When he saw them kicking against the repeal of the Navigation Laws', he told the meeting, 'he thought it would be to the advantage of sailors.' A resolution in favour of repeal then followed, which attracted an overwhelming majority, and the meeting broke up in disarray. Such a reversal was perhaps not surprising. Labour relations in Sunderland tended to be tense, and any alliance between shipbuilders and shipowners on the one side, and their employees,on the other, was necessarily problematical. Some days prior to the meeting petitions to the Commons in favour of repeal had already attracted the signatures of 650 seamen and 250 shipwrights. This may well have owed more to a desire to demonstrate defiance of local capitalist interests than support for the government. But, in any case, once Labouchere's decision to maintain manning restrictions and not to open the coasting trade became known, one element of working-class concern on which protectionists had been able to play had been removed.[8]

Elsewhere, there was concern about parliamentary representation on the issue. At a crowded meeting in Tynemouth Town Hall, the Chairman told the meeting that 'it seemed to him of great importance that they should know how the Member for Tynemouth would deport himself on this occasion', though since the man in question was the Whig Ralph Grey there could hardly have been much doubt. In Scarborough the shipowners were more deferential. It was decided to send an Address to Sir John Johnstone and the Earl of Mulgrave 'as representatives of our maritime borough'.[9] Nothing in the way of meetings was organised in London, however – a symptom of a general lack of activity which drew the following critical comment from the *Shipping Gazette's* correspondent 'A Looker On':

if the shipowners of London intend to offer no greater or more vigorous opposition to the repeal of the Navigation Laws, which so vitally affects their interests than the mere expression of their views in your journal, it must be obvious that any hope they might entertain of defeating the government measure will be deceived.[10]

Despite the fact that the Central Committee was based in London and led by London shipowners, it seems clear that in the capital the protectionists could not rely on the degree of support for their cause which was to be found elsewhere. May and June saw petitions come in from artisans in the Thames shipbuilding industry, the joiners, shipsawyers, caulkers and riggers, and Herries was able to present a petition with 1,932 signatories, from 'Merchants, Bankers, Shipowners and Trades'. But, given the size of London's shipping industry, this showing was hardly impressive; Liverpool had raised 6,687 signatures on a single petition and Bristol 4,613. The City petition emphasised the dangers to social harmony from embarking on such a measure at such a time (only a month earlier much of central London had been turned into a virtual fortress in anticipation of a Chartist uprising), noting that 'the success of commercial affairs is essentially dependent on quiet and stability'. But it was decidedly muted, indeed almost neutral, in tone. A separate petition signed by sixteen members of the General Shipowners' Society Committee, including Dunbar and Young, was concerned mainly with another measure, the Merchant Seamen's Fund Bill, which it identified as an additional burden on shipowners 'at the very moment at which they are required to embark in the severe struggle of a competition most unequal and injurious'. If the Navigation Laws were repealed, then shipowners should be relieved from 'numberless harrassing and vexatious regulations' to which they were subject. Such an approach, which seemed to accept the inevitability of repeal, sat strangely alongside the efforts of the Central Committee for Upholding the Navigation Laws to stop it happening, but reflected the need to preserve some degree of unity in the society.[11]

But if the capital proved comparatively apathetic about the protectionist cause, their opponents faced a much greater difficulty in arousing interest, not only in London but also elsewhere. Free traders had been able to provide some extra-parliamentary support for Labouchere in the form of a 292-signature petition from 'Merchants, Bankers, Manufacturers, Shipowners, Traders and Other Inhabitants of the City of London', designed, as it stated, to avoid any mis-construction arising from 'the silence hitherto observed'. This argued that after repeal shipowners would be 'fortified by a spirit of greater self reliance' and went on to challenge the commonplaces of protectionist rhetoric:

phrases such as 'Independence of Foreigners', 'Our Wooden Walls', 'Ships, Colonies and Commerce', 'Nursery for Seamen', made use of one some occasions by the advocates of class legislation, are, in the opinion of your Petioners and others, unjustly and inappositely applied, and will not reconcile our seamen to the laws of impressment, or our colonies to the oppression of our Vice-Admiralty laws.[12]

In addition to those from shipwrights and seafarers, Sunderland produced a free trade petition from eighty-seven shipowners. Petitions calling for repeal also came from 'Merchants and Bankers' at Liverpool, from Great Yarmouth, from the Belfast Chamber of Commerce and from the Staffordshire Potteries (a reflection of Ricardo's interest there). Manchester provided two petitions: one, predictably, from the Chamber of Commerce; the other, didactically, from 'taxpayers'.[13] In all, excluding those that came in from the colonies, just nine petitions favouring repeal were submitted to the Commons in May and June 1848. These were the product of local effort alone. There was no centrally organised petitioning campaign by free traders, which is one reason for the extent of the contrast with the performance of the protectionists here; over the same period there were fifty-one petitions in opposition. But any popular movement in favour of repeal would have required much more sedulous fostering than was needed on the protectionist side. As the Tory Croker commented to Bentinck: 'Who wants it, who is to get anything out of it?'[14]

In the Commons the Protectionists' counter-proposition was introduced by Herries on 29 May. Protesting at the sudden speed with which it was now acting, after six months of doing nothing, Herries argued that the government had failed entirely to make out a case for so fundamental a change. Noting that all the demands for repeal to which the Minister was allegedly responding at that stage came from outside the country – 'they had received not a few petitions, but on which side were they?' – and questioning the unanimity of the West Indian interest (though remaining silent on the Canadians), Herries stressed the relationship between the Navigation Laws and defence, pointing out that Labouchere had failed to address the question of how the navy was to be manned. Moreover, 'extensive class interests' were involved, whose existence 'lay at the foundation of our national defences'. If the Navigation Laws were, as was claimed, indeed hampering trade, Herries conceded that some modification would be acceptable, but he could see no justification for total abrogation.[15]

The debate on the future of the Navigation Laws arising out of these two resolutions continued intermittently until 9 June, when the Herries' amendment was defeated by a vote of 294 to 177. *The Times* professed itself disappointed with this first airing of the question in the Commons, commenting that it was 'not conducted on either side in the most masterly style'. 'One is apt to suspect', its editor continued, 'that all the speakers have been fairly worn out by the toil of turning over the leaves of their Blue books. There are facts and counter-facts or at least what seem to be such; there are statements, replies and rejoinders and some declamation. But the subject somehow is frittered to pieces.' Certainly, high-flown rhetoric was a rarity and, as with the two Select Committees, one of which was still meeting, detail continually threatened to overwhelm argument as speaker after speaker pursued the ultimately unrewarding themes of shipping costs, freight rates and the quality of British seamen, this last nicely satirised by *The Times*; 'One member produced a sober British captain at Riga, another a drunken one at Crondstadt, another one half drunk at Buenos Ayres.'[16]

Behind the debating points, however, lurked some more substantial issues. One was the necessity for action. The government case for repeal relied on its assessment of the intentions of foreign governments. In Disraeli's words, it was placed between the United States of America and Prussia, 'on the one side the bland smiles and the winning accents of Mr. Bancroft; on the other Mr. Bunsen, with the dagger and the bowl'.[17] Not unnaturally, the Protectionists made much of the self-interested nature of communications from these parties. But promises and threats from foreign powers were not the whole story; the colonies were involved also. There was a certain awkwardness felt by both sides here. Free traders were unwilling to admit that the sufferings of the West Indians and Canadians were a result of their policies, but made the most of petitions emanating from those sources in their arguments. The Protectionists, on their side, welcomed evidence of the harm inflicted by liberalisation ('if ever', averred Bentinck, 'there was a part of the Queen's dominions which had been deprived of its legitimate protection, which had been attacked by the action of free trade in the foulest way, it was the British West Indies'). But they could only respond to evidence of colonial requests for repeal by questioning the petitions' provenance or suggesting that the colonists did not understand their own true interests.[18]

How much weight should be attached to these international and imperial considerations as a cause of repeal? For Clapham they were central. 'Every statesman of mark', he wrote in 1910, 'recognised that importance.'[19] He noted that Peel cited the following reasons for giving his support to the government: the attitude of the colonies, the attitude of foreign powers, the complexity of the reciprocity treaty system and the degree to which the Navigation Laws had already been eroded. But while undoubtedly such factors may have contributed to support for the measure among some sections of the Commons, as far as the Russell government is concerned, it is wise to recognise, first, that not all had equal force; and, second, that they reinforced the argument for repeal rather than created it. Party politics, rather than foreign or colonial relations, played the key role here.

That said, it is clear that the pressure from the colonies certainly made the greatest impact on Russell himself, while Labouchere was impressed by offers from the United States of America. However, the effect of the threat from Prussia to impose differential duties on British vessels in indirect trades can be overestimated. This was but the latest phase in a long commercial negotiation and the Foreign Office detected a fair element of bluff in the Prussian position. As Palmerston noted in his reply to Bunsen of 14 June 1847, the previous year only four British vessels had entered Prussian ports from third countries.[20] Looking also to Britain's other partners in reciprocity, no doubt the Foreign Office was happy to identify in repeal the end to the demands for equal treatment which had followed on the Austrian Treaty of 1838. But there was nothing urgent about this, nor much sign that, had the repeal of the Navigation Laws not been in the offing, Palmerston would not have felt free to continue to resist Prussian demands. Although the government could invoke colonies and foreign powers in support of its cause, it was in greater difficulty nearer home. The arguments for repeal would have been stronger if there had been evidence of a popular movement in favour. Its sensitivity on the question is indicated by Labouchere's presentation of a London merchants' petition in support of the government immediately before this debate. Milner-Gibson might argue that 'the present question stands on better ground because it was not backed by clamour', a remarkable statement from someone so closely identified in the past with the campaign against the Corn Laws, but the imbalance between the few petitions in favour and the many against was undoubtedly an embarrassment.[21]

In fact, the inescapable popular clamour of 1848 was that of the Chartists and some back-benchers were not slow to make a connection between the impact of repeal on seaport employment and political unrest. 'What effect', asked Robinson, member for Poole and a shipowner, 'would Chartist demagogues have if they did not find a distressed population?'. With plenty of evidence already on hand of working-class opposition to repeal, and memories of the seamen's demonstration in February still fresh, suggestions linking the two questions cannot have seemed entirely fanciful. A similar charge as to inappropriate timing was made by some speakers in relation to the international situation. With so much confusion on the Continent, it was argued, this was hardly the best moment to make changes which had implications for national defence.[22]

Though the Protectionists put up a formidable performance in terms of mastery of detail, there was little in the case they presented to surprise the government or to require more than a reiteration of familiar arguments. Of far greater interest and importance was the response of those outside the government but not opposed to it. The radicals, who had in April formed themselves into a separate parliamentary group, were now an increasingly unreliable element in Whig calculations but presented little threat on this issue. Predictably, Hume attacked what was proposed on the grounds that it left untouched many restrictions on the freedom of shipowners: 'let the shipowners alone to conduct their own affairs and they will beat the world'. But there was no risk that their call for 'a clear field and fair play' for the shipping industry would lead them to oppose the measure. Better some approach towards repeal than none at all.[23]

More uncertain was the response of the Peelites. There was no doubt that the majority of Peel's followers in Parliament were prepared to support major amendment of the Laws. In January one of their number, Goulburn, had identified the issue as one which made Conservative reunion an impossibility. Indeed, as his earlier inter-vention had shown, Gladstone was particularly committed to this, writing later of 'my endeavours to force the government to bring forward the Navigation Laws which they were manifestly inclined to avoid: for which Labouchere thanked me individually saying I had much helped him'.[24] But although Gladstone had been pleased to assist Labouchere in putting pressure on the Whigs, he had considerable reservations about the quasi-unconditional approach they had adopted. It was his opinion that foreign powers should be asked for concessions in advance.

At this time Gladstone's support for free trade was still rooted in practical and administrative considerations rather than theoretical concepts. His father, steeped in the hard-headed values of the Liverpool mercantile class and with whom Gladstone was in disagree-ment over the Navigation Laws question, harshly accused him here of siding with those who espoused 'impracticable doctrines . . . sentiments beautiful in the abstract but totally incapable of application to the conduct and habits of mankind'.[25] But this charge, which may have stiffened Gladstone's resolve to press for reciprocity, was wide of the mark. There was nothing Cobdenite or trusting in his approach to the ending of protection for shipping, neither in respect of other powers nor indeed in respect of the motives of those nearer home. Communicating his thoughts on the subject in a letter to Peel on 2 May, Gladstone made it clear that he regarded the Law Officers' advice on which the government was acting as suspect. Ministers were, he said, possibly influenced by 'those below them'. That is, by the Board of Trade's permanent officials, Porter, Macgregor and Lefevre.[26]

Gladstone, then, found himself at odds with the government over the navigation issue; not over ends but means. What became clear in the debate was that on this he was also in disagreement with Sir Robert Peel. Gladstone told the Commons, in what Bancroft described as 'an able and graceful speech', that he believed the best way to proceed would be by treaties of reciprocity:

You will proceed more safely and more wisely by undoing the present system piecemeal than by abolishing the whole of it at one sweep and then, by the same act of parliament, to retain a power which enables you to build upon it again and which in all probability, you will very shortly do.

He regretted that it was not intended to open the coasting trade, because this would be a useful concession to exchange with the Americans, and argued for an end to restrictions on the freedom of shipowners freely to purchase and man their vessels.[27]

Peel's contribution revealed both the extent to which he was prepared to back the government – his effective speech left Russell, by his own account, with little left to say – and how careless he could be of the feelings of supporters. If the booing and jeering which greeted the early part of his contribution demonstrated the depth of personal animosity still felt towards him by the country gentlemen, and the impossibility of any end to the Conservative rift, it also showed strains within the Peelite camp. Peel dismissed Gladstone's reciprocity proposals, playing the elder, more experienced statesman – 'when you come to act practically upon those treaties you find they involve you in very great difficulty' – and went on argue against any conditional element at all. What was proposed, he suggested, reversed the normal relationship between the executive and the legislature, 'the House of Commons will be the source of favour – the House of Commons will relax and the Crown will restrain'.[28]

The government's decision, announced on 17 July 1848, not to proceed any further that session with a bill on the Navigation Laws surprised no-one. There was insufficient time left to deal with such a major measure and the Ministry simply contented itself with the publication of a bill a few weeks later, framed along the lines already proposed by Labouchere. Some critics of repeal continued to detect a lack of enthusiasm in the administration for its own policy. Delay, suggested the *Shipping Gazette*, was 'not entirely disagreeable to the government'; the measure had been forced on Russell and 'it was easy to see that his Lordship never entered upon repeal of the Navigation Laws *con amore*'.[29] Certainly, the free trade radicals felt demoralised by the general lack of progress on liberal measures. Cobden's judgement was that Russell,' has allowed himself to be baffled, bullied and obstructed by Lord George Bentinck and the Protectionists, who have been so far encouraged by their success in sugar and the Navigation Laws that I expect they will be quite ready to begin their reaction on corn next'.[30]

If the Protectionists had some reason to be satisfied with their performance on the floor of the House of Commons, the same was true out of the Chamber. Hardwick's Select Committee on the Navigation Laws not only more than matched the previous years' Commons Select Committee in terms of industry – their Lordships saw fifty-four witnesses between March and July – but it also lived up to its sponsors' expectations as a Protectionist counterweight. According to the Whig Granville, the proceedings were very much dominated by Stanley's followers:

I found Lord Hardwicke always at his post actively examining, from a brief which I believe was prepared by G. F. Young, witnesses who were for the most part Protectionists – Lord Colchester was useful to him, having great industry and knowledge of the subject. Lord Auckland was the only cabinet minister able to attend, and excepting during occasional absences, conducted the government case. I was the only other peer connected with the Govt. who attended and Lord Radnor was the only independent peer on our side who took an active part.[31]

This ensured both a preponderance of witnesses expressing opposition to repeal and a rougher ride for free traders like G. R. Porter than they had experienced the previous year. But, with a number of witnesses making their second appearance and after such recent lengthy examination of the issue by the Commons Select Committee, the overall effect was in general repetition not novelty: the amassing of more details favourable to the Protectionist case rather than the provision of new insights.[32]

There was one major exception to this – the treatment of the naval manning question. The only expert witness on this question who had come before the Commons Select Committee had been Sir James Stirling, an officer with controversial views of the current value of the merchant service as a nursery of seamen and equally controversial proposals for manning reforms. The Protectionists were determined that Stirling's attack on the conventional wisdom should not pass unchallenged, and in addition to subjecting Stirling to some further questioning, they called four navy witnesses, Rear Admiral Cochrane, Admiral Sir Thomas Martin, Captain J. T. Nicholas and Captain Berkeley MP. Berkeley was the Chairman of the Admiralty Committee on the Supply of Seamen from the Merchant Navy, which had reported the previous April. On the basis of the evidence of the muster books for the previous eight years, that Committee had concluded that 40 per cent of seamen of all grades entering the Royal Navy had come from the merchant service. This was in direct contradiction of Sir James Stirling's estimates, which put the figure much lower. But the two statistics were compiled on a different basis; Stirling's excluded ordinary seamen.[33]

However, whether or not the navy currently drew to any great extent upon the merchant service was not the central point at issue between Stirling and Berkeley. The question was whether the navy might be manned differently in the future, in particular in wartime. Berkeley told the Select Committee of his reaction to Stirling's plan for a permanent force: 'I thought that it was not only expensive, but that it was impossible to be independent of the Merchant Service; it was wholly out of the question.'[34] Admiral Martin took the same view: 'the mercantile marine is everything to the Navy and the Navy could not exist without it', but the example he used to justify this was hardly recent. Martin reminded the Committee that, when war broke out in 1793, 'we had not as many as 20,000 men and those scattered over the globe, when war broke out; it was therefore the Merchant service that enabled us rapidly to man some sixty sail of the Line, and double the number of frigates and smaller vessels.'[35]

Since acceptance of free trade measures did not necessarily imply rejection of such arguments, the Protectionists on the Committee were anxious for evidence that repeal would damage the historic connection between the two services. Given that by the time these witnesses were examined the government had already indicated that its intention was to continue to limit the employment of foreigners, and that shipowners approved of the ending of compulsory apprenticeship, the argument once again reverted to the question of what size the merchant navy would become in the wake of opening all overseas trades to foreign shipping, and how shipbuilding capacity would be affected. And here the navy's representatives could offer no greater authority than their private opinion.

By July 1848 the business of taking evidence was judged completed, but there remained the question of the report, a matter of some urgency in the light of the pending dissolution. Hardwicke, as Chairman, prepared a draft which he showed to Stanley, whose reaction was not favourable. 'I wish', he wrote to Hardwicke on 2 August, 'you had a little more time to consider, and talk out with our friends the form of this report; for although I agree in the conclusion at which you arrive, I think that the summary of the actual effect of the Laws, the mode of their working, the objections raised and our views upon them might have been somewhat more methodically arranged, if we had some opportunity for private consultation.' Despairing, as he told Ellenborough, of producing 'a creditable report raissoné' at this stage of the session, Stanley set out for Hardwicke's use a set of aggressively protectionist resolutions which might be agreed by the Committee and reported to the House, leaving the opportunity to summon it again next session in order to devise a detailed response.[36]

Stanley left it to Hardwicke to judge whether the pattern of attendance at the final meeting would offer any chance of success for his resolutions, and it appears that they were not discussed. Rather, Hardwicke contented himself with an undertaking given by Auckland, on behalf of the government, that the Committee would be re-convened to consider its report as soon as Parliament reassembled. But the Protectionists were not content to allow the matter to rest there. Over the recess Select Committee members were circulated by Hardwicke with his draft, which Granville found 'long and badly written', then by Stanley with an alternative version, which Granville thought 'equally prolix' and, finally, with a useful digest of evidence by Colchester which Granville judged, 'clearly done, but with its semblance of fairness is not so'.[37]

The Protectionists were not the only ones to find the question of the Navigation Acts intruding into the recess. At the Board of Trade officials and Ministers were anxious to make use of the extra time which postponement of their measure, followed by the ending of the parliamentary session, had given them. For the Whigs the scrutiny of their proposals by the Commons had proved a disconcerting experience. Viewed as a dress rehearsal for the performance which would take place next session, the reception in the Commons suggested that some further work was necessary. It was true that at the end of all the debate, the government had succeeded in defeating the Herries amendment but this was only to be expected. What was equally the case was that its vote was not very impressive, that the Protectionists had proved more talented in pressing their case than might have been anticipated and that the mere identification of repeal as a free trade question had been demonstrated to be not in itself any guarantee of support. Some erstwhile supporters of commercial liberalisation, regarding the Navigation Laws as a special case, had shown themselves willing to break ranks on this issue and to vote against the administration. Of the seventy-one free trade Conservatives who voted, eighteen supported the Protectionists.[38] Furthermore, despite Peel's own position, some more junior free trade Conservatives associated with Gladstone had given notice that they were far from satisfied with the way the amendment was being approached and were looking for changes – in the direction of reciprocity.

Anxious to be assured of Peelite backing, and aware of the force of the charge of rashness in offering unconditional repeal, the Board of Trade wanted a clearer indication of the reaction of foreign countries. In a memorandum to the Foreign Office dated 26 October 1848, the Board set out the position as it saw it. Noting that the Commons had now virtually affirmed the principle of revising the Navigation Laws, the Board suggested that 'Parliament will enter upon the arduous and complicated task it has undertaken with much more advantage if previously advised of the views of other powers.' What was needed at this stage, it argued, was not the formal negotiation of treaties. Such a course would present difficulties if several countries rejected Britain's overtures, compelling the government either to proceed only by reciprocity or placing it 'at great disadvantage in pursuing the line of independent action'. Rather, the Board looked for 'an interchange of communication of a sufficient formal character to induce parliament to judge with confidence of the course which other nations would be prepared to follow in certain events'. This memorandum is one more indication that the repeal of the Navigation Laws should not be seen as a response to pressure from foreign powers.[39] The public pronouncements of Ministers might reasonably lead to the historical judgement that ending protection for shipping was thought necessary for the progress of free trade because 'the Acts stood in the way of its adoption by others'. But in 1848 neither the politicians concerned nor their officials had any clear idea of how the commercial policy of other powers might be affected by repeal. Furthermore, when in the spring of 1849 they received some indication of the likely response, the replies from foreign governments suggested that the Navigation Laws were by no means the most substantial barrier to more liberal trade relations.[40]

Palmerston, never a man to accept any direction on Foreign Office business with equanimity, was affronted by this blatant proposal to use time-consuming diplomatic initiatives for parliamentary political ends. He told the Board that the time was not propitious for what was suggested. In reply, the Board felt constrained to explain 'somewhat more distinctly the precise nature and meaning of that suggestion which Lord Palmerston appears to them to have partly misapprehended'. The approach adopted by the government last session, the Board of Trade official Le Marchant informed this senior member of the cabinet, was a middle course between unconditional repeal, which might conceivably injure British shipping, and reciprocity treaties which would lead to 'great intricacy of legislation'. Discretionary powers were required because of what appeared a material distinction between custom duty reciprocity and navigation reciprocity, with the lack of one frustrating the other. Hence there was a need to establish the views of other countries, but the Board was, of course, aware that any approach must be subject to 'wider political considerations'.[41]

Palmerston, unimpressed by the claim that there was a genuine need for negotiations, responded by suggesting that the Board should itself draft the communication to go out to Her Majesty's Ministers abroad and indicate which countries were to receive it. With the Foreign Office proving so unwilling to co-operate, the Board of Trade decided to retreat. Since France and Germany could not be approached because of the present turbulence in those countries, Le Marchant conceded on 14 December, it would be unwise to approach other powers. Instead, Ministers abroad should simply be asked to 'furnish the government – before the present meeting of Parliament – with any particulars which they may have to communicate as to the present or probable policy of the governments to which they have respectively been accredited'.[42]

While Whig Ministers and their officials sparred, their Conservative allies bickered. The differences in the Peelite camp on the Navigation Laws which had been evident the previous June were minor compared with those that had emerged subsequently over the question of relief for the West Indies, where Gladstone, Cardwell, Goulburn and Lincoln had voted with the opposition. But Gladstone had been chagrined by Peel's attitude to his navigation proposals, writing later of Peel's performance in the debate that 'while he nominally reserved his judgement on the question of reciprocity (we all having spoken in favour of it) he virtually declared against it, but not only this but showed he had not understood me, treating it as if I had meant treaty reciprocity whereas I meant no more than legislative reciprocity, a very different thing.'[43] (By legislative reciprocity Gladstone meant proceeding by means of an Act of Parliament which would make the free entry of vessels under foreign flags contingent on like concessions.)

Gladstone was determined not to let the matter rest. On 12 December 1848 he talked to Peel, who agreed that Gladstone should see Labouchere to advise him against ruling out reciprocal arrangements in advance by any official declaration that Britain was bound because of its treaties to proceed unconditionally. This was for Gladstone a welcome acknowledgement of the validity of his position, but amounted to no more than this, as events were to prove.[44] For Labouchere, Peelite advice no doubt confirmed the continuing political importance of securing some promise of mutual concessions, however vague. Tackling the Navigation Laws was proving a far more difficult task than any of the Whigs could have anticipated a year earlier.

Notes

1 PD, Third Series, XCVIII, 15 May 1848, c. 1021.
2 PD, Third Series, XCVIX, 19 May 1848, c. 13.
3 *Ibid.*, 29 May 1848, c. 9–26.
4 LCL, Derby Papers, 290 Derb(14) 178/1.
5 PD, Third Series, XCVIX, 15 May 1848, c. 991–1014.
6 *Liverpool Times*, 1 June 1848.
7 *North British Railway and Shipping Journal*, 17 June 1848.
8 See James Dunn, *A View of the Navigation Laws*, Sunderland, 1847; *Sunderland and Durham County Herald*, 26 May 1848.
9 *Shipping Gazette*, 26 May 1848.
10 *Ibid.*, 23 May 1848.
11 House of Lords Record Office, *51st Report of the Committee on Public Petitions*, Appendix 1065; *57th Report*, Appendix 1209.
12 *Ibid.*, 49th Report, Appendix 1024.
13 Manchester Chamber of Commerce, M8/2/4, 25 May 1848.
14 Hughenden Papers, Microfilm, B/XX/Be/114, 13 June 1848.
15 PD, Third Series, XCVIX, 29 May 1848, c. 9–26.
16 *The Times*, 3 June 1848.
17 PD, Third Series, XCVIX, 9 June 1848, c. 644.
18 PD, Third Series, XCVIII, 15 May 1848, c. 1031.
19 Clapham, 'Navigation Acts', pp. 169–70.
20 PRO, BT 1/466/1536/47, Palmerston to Bunsen, 14 June 1847.
21 PD, Third Series, XCVIX, 1 June 1848, c. 225.

22 As reported in *The Times*, 16 May 1848; PD, Third Series, XCVIII, 15 May 1848, c. 1000.
23 *Ibid.*, c. 1029–30.
24 BL, Gladstone Papers, Add. MS. 44777 f. 278.
25 H. C. G. Matthew, 'Introduction', in M. R. D. Foot and H. C. G. Matthew (eds), *The Gladstone Diaries III, 1840–47*, Oxford, 1974, Introduction, xxxviii–iv; S. G. Checkland, *The Gladstones: a Family Biography 1764–1851*, Cambridge, 1971; *Shipping Gazette*, 15 June 1848, reprinted letter from John Gladstone to W. E. Gladstone, 17 March 1848, originally published in *Montrose Gazette*. On Gladstone's economic views see Richard Shannon, *Gladstone I 1809–1865*, London, 1982, pp. 207–8. On Gladstone's attitude to reciprocity generally see F. E. Hyde, *Mr Gladstone at the Board of Trade, London*, 1934, pp. 106–11.
26 Institute of Historical Research (IHR), *The Papers of Sir James Graham* (Microfilm) Reel 17, Bundle 105.
27 PRO, FO 5/506 Bancroft to Buchanan, 16 June 1848; PD, Third Series, XCVIX, 2 June 1848, c. 251 .
28 *Ibid.*, c. 661–2.
29 PD, Third Series, CI, 10 August 1848, c. 57–60; *Shipping Gazette*, 17 July 1848.
30 MRO, Wilson Papers, M20/583, John Bright to George Wilson, 3 June 1848; Richard Cobden to George Combe, 23 July 1848, quoted in John Morley, *The Life of Cobden*, II, London, 1881, p. 23.
31 PRO, Granville Papers, 30/29/23/1, Granville to Grey, draft, 6 February 1849.
32 *Lords S. C. Navigation Laws*, PP 1847–48 XX Pt.II.
33 *Ibid.*, Q. 3823–6010; Q. 8414–19.
34 *Ibid.*, Q. 8417, Q. 8472.
35 *Ibid.*, Q. 8365.
36 LCL, Derby Papers, 290 Der(14) 178/1, Derby to Hardwicke, 2 August 1848; 290 Der(14), 32.
37 PRO, Granville Papers, 30/29/23/1, Granville to Grey, Draft, 6 February 1849.
38 Conacher, *Peelites and the Party System*, Appendix A, pp. 220–5.
39 PRO, BT 3/38 f. 47.
40 P. J. Cain and A. G. Hopkins, 'The political economy of British expansion overseas, 1750–1914', *Economic History Review*, 2nd ser., XXXIII, 1980, p. 478.
41 PRO, BT 3/38 f. 72, 7 December 1848.
42 PRO, BT 1/470/4106/48 [B], 9 December 1848; BT 1/470/4106/48 [c], 14 December 1848.
43 BL, Gladstone Papers, Add. MS. 44777 ff. 278–80, 12 December 1848.
44 *Ibid.*, Add. MS. 44777 f. 276, 12 December 1848.

Chapter Eight

'To free trade is now added free navigation'

Slow though progress had been to date on the Navigation Laws, when Parliament re-convened in January 1849 there was no doubt that the matter would at last come forward for full consideration by both Houses. Whether the precise terms would be the same as those published the previous August was still uncertain, even at government level, but there was every expectation that the abolition of the Navigation Acts would be the great political battle of the year.

Had repeal been pushed forward rapidly when it was first mooted, there would have been opposition from the Protectionists but little fight. But over 1848 much had happened to guarantee that this would be a measure which the Protectionists would and could resist, in Stanley's words, *totis vitibus*.[1] Although the problem of finding a leader in the Commons remained, the Protectionists had gained confidence from the ineptitude and lack of direction which had been the hallmark of the Whigs in the previous session, and took satisfaction in the restlessness of some of Peel's followers. Moreover, free trade was no longer in the ascendant – a downturn in economic activity had seen to that. On the contrary, the Protectionists detected a reaction inside as well as outside Westminster. Bentinck's prediction that 'till the landed interest, and the colonial and shipping interests, all together feel intolerable distress we shall do no good' had come nearer to fulfilment than could have been anticipated even a year before.[2] Increasing Protectionist optimism underlay Stanley's determination to make the Navigation Laws a major trial of strength with the government, building on what had already been achieved the previous session. One problem facing him in January 1849 was that Hardwicke, who had led the campaign against repeal in the Lords, had been posted abroad and was no longer available. Fortunately, Colchester, an active member of the Select Committee, who had a good grasp of the issues, was an obvious replacement and readily agreed to take this on, telling Stanley that he felt the Navigation Laws 'cannot be abandoned without shaking the foundations of that naval superiority on which national greatness so mainly depends'. Colchester was willing to see some modification but this was not Stanley's view. 'In our position', he wrote to him on 13 January, 'we should not volunteer any alteration whatsoever.' Stanley admitted that there were some minor details which might be changed, but 'for the sake of legislating on these you open a door which you may find it afterwards find it impossible to close'.[3]

This stand on the point of principle, to which Colchester acceded, had the merit of simplicity and provided a clear political focus. For those more directly affected, however, such an all-or-nothing strategy carried a heavy penalty in the event of failure. In consequence, certain nominally protectionist shipowners found themselves out of step with their Tory defenders in Parliament. These had begun to perceive advantages in volunteering concessions; they were anxious to salvage some element of protection in the event of a total bonfire. One such proposal had been first mooted by the prominent Liverpool merchant and shipowner Henry Chapman, the previous March. Taking the view that the Navigation Laws were doomed unless some compromise was offered, by January 1849 Chapman had drawn up an alternative bill which was circulating in Liverpool shipping circles. This proposed the modification of the Laws to permit import of the produce of Asia, Africa and America via Europe in vessels of any nationality, so conceding the 'long voyage' to foreign shipping. Since some of the most anomalous, and easily ridiculed, aspects of the navigation code as it operated in practice arose from the long voyage provisions, such a change would have served to meet some justified criticisms, without seriously disadvantaging the British shipowner, who would gain the same freedom.[4]

Another shipowner prepared to countenance some modification of the Laws was W. S. Lindsay, at that time a relatively unknown figure in the shipping world but later to achieve prominence as a Liberal MP and as the author of a major work on maritime history. On 10 January 1849 the first of a series of letters addressed to Russell appeared in the *Morning Herald* and in the *Shipping Gazette*. Writing as a 'plain man of business' who inclined to free trade ideas, Lindsay's early letters testified eloquently to the valuable service the Navigation Laws had performed over the centuries. As such they were seized upon eagerly by the leaders of the Central Committee for Upholding the Navigation Laws who undertook to republish his work. G. F. Young had himself written a similar series which appeared in the the *Standard* the previous year and was an assiduous contributor to correspondence columns, but the appearance of a new protectionist advocate from within the industry was a welcome development. However, when Lindsay's subsequent letters began to argue the case for reciprocity, the Central Committee's patronage abruptly ceased. What Lindsay suggested was precise individual treaty reciprocity, 'making the extent of trade which the one contracting power had to offer the *basis* of what the other is to get'. This was not dissimilar to what Wood had originally suggested to Russell but had little in common with what Gladstone proposed, and was decidedly illiberal, as well as fairly impractical. Lindsay's articles may however have been the inspiration for the attempt by the Kilmarnock MP, Bouverie, at the committee stage of the repeal bill to make abrogation dependent on 'strict reciprocity'. [5]

The reaction of the Central Committee to Lindsay's apostasy was an indication of its determination to resist any modification of the Laws, such as that proposed by Henry Chapman in respect of the 'long voyage'. Like the Protectionists in Parliament, the Central Committee was set on defending the principle of protection for shipping. There were good reasons for this. As was explained at the Annual Meeting of the General Shipowners' Society on 2 March: 'If distracted by varied and opposing schemes, they allow themselves to be drawn into controversy and discussion, the object of the general enemy will be effectively obtained, and successful resistance will be impossible.'[6], But this strategy may also have been influenced by another development: the efforts of some agriculturalists to form an extra-parliamentary protectionist movement which would encompass all sections of the economy, including shipping. The previous June the Duke of Richmond, President of the National Association for the Protection of Agriculture and Industry, had issued a manifesto in support of the shipowners:

Although we have not as a society been brought into connection with the shipowners, and although on some occasions those who represent the shipping interest have refrained from supporting the general principle of protection, still, as we are not united for the aggrandisement of a class, we resist the present measure no less than every other attack, which has been directed against the welfare of our domestic industry.

G. F. Young was among those who responded to this initiative, which had resulted in a flow of petitions against repeal from agricultural areas.[7]

The more immediate issue facing Stanley in January 1849 on the Navigation Laws was not how his group should react to the government's proposals but whether to press for reappointment of the Select Committee when Parliament re-assembled. Auckland's death at the end of December had weakened the government side, but Hardwicke's departure arguably had a similar effect on the Protectionists. Stanley did not feel sufficiently certain of the views of all the Committee's members to be sure that re-appointment would be sensible. 'My fear', he told Colchester, 'is that – though in the teeth of evidence – a very free trade report may be carried.'[8] Ironically, the Whigs themselves were far from sure that they would be the victors if the Committee were allowed to report. Granville's assessment, confided to Grey on 6 February, was pessimistic:

If we meet now the numbers of Liberals and Protectionists, whether all voted or whether only those who sometimes attended voted, would be about equal. The question would be decided by Lords St Germains, Ellenborough, Harrowby, Londonderry, Waddington. I am inclined to think that the government would be outvoted.[9]

He advised that a report should be resisted. In the event, the government told the Protectionists that it would have no objection to re-appointment, provided there was no delay to the progress of the bill. But Stanley, deciding that the outcome was too unpredictable to warrant the risk, chose not to pursue the matter. Thus the Lords Select Committee, like its predecessor in the Commons, left as its monument a mass of evidence but no conclusions.

While Stanley and Colchester planned their defence of the Navigation Laws, Labouchere and his officials at the Board of Trade were contemplating the fruits of their approaches to other powers as to what changes in their maritime policy Britain might expect to see as a result of repeal. The replies, published in February and March, were by no means entirely helpful. Prussia promised to put British vessels on 'a perfectly liberal and equal footing', but the other German states and Austria were unwilling to commit themselves and the United States of America was content with a bland general assurance. France volunteered no concessions and Belgium made its commitment to protectionism clear: 'No Belgian vessels could compete on equal terms with British vessels in the intercourse between the two countries.' As

Herries later commented: 'They asked foreign powers what they would do and the vast majority answered "Nothing now"'. His judgement that the whole exercise of consultation had been a 'signal failure' was necessarily biased, but undoubtedly the results of this consultation exercise were not those looked for by the government. They had produced no indication that repealing the Navigation Laws would redound to Britain's benefit, serving instead to suggest rather the contrary.[10]

On 14 February 1849 Labouchere introduced his 'Bill to Amend the Laws for the Encouragement of British Navigation' to the House. It followed the lines of his previous year's proposals, ending all limitations on foreign shipping in overseas trades, continuing to reserve to the Crown the power to re-impose restrictions, should other nations not respond in kind, and maintaining the limitations on manning. There was, however, one innovation. It was now intended to allow all vessels, whether British or foreign owned, carrying cargoes from overseas to Britain to touch at intermediate British ports before finally getting customs clearance. This was a significant departure which amounted to a partial opening of the coasting trade to foreign vessels. Already Labouchere had made clear in his contribution to the debates of the previous session that he believed the United States of America would match any British concessions point for point; now he indicated that this unexpected additional concession would guarantee such a response and so open the American coasting trade to British vessels. Pressed by Alderman Thompson for a further assurance that this would indeed be the outcome, the Minister referred with enthusiasm to his recent interview with the American envoy; Bancroft had said 'he would be willing the next day to sign any convention which should include the coasting trade'.[11] In the event, the coasting provision enjoyed only a very short life as part of government policy. Five weeks later, on 23 March, Labouchere announced that he was withdrawing it from the bill. The explanation offered by Labouchere to the Commons for this sudden change of plan was that the Board of Customs had expressed reservations. So indeed it had, but four weeks earlier, before the second reading. The real reasons for Labouchere's retraction were rather more complex.[12]

As has already been seen, Britain's commercial negotiations with the United States of America were conducted through the medium of the American plenipotentiary George Bancroft. Bancroft's personal commitment to free trade was strong, but there is no reason to suppose that his encouragement of the British government over the Navigation Laws went beyond the brief given him by the Polk administration. However, in November 1848 the political climate changed with the victory of General Zachary Taylor, which meant a more protectionist direction for United States policy. At the time of the introduction of the Navigation Bill, Bancroft was still in post in London, but now as the representative of a government with views very different from his own. By his own account, Bancroft was taken by surprise when Labouchere announced his new intentions for the coasting trade and assured the House that the United States of America would reciprocate. Nevertheless, faced with this unexpected development, he tried to make good Labouchere's claim: 'I resolved instantly to sustain the minister in whose hands the fate of the Bill rested; this I could do only by holding myself ready to sign a convention.' But on 15 March Bancroft was to be seriously embarrassed and mortified to receive a dispatch from his political masters instructing him immediately to suspend all negotiations; the United States government was not yet ready to make any undertaking to admit British vessels to its home waters. [13]

But Bancroft's humiliation was nothing compared to that felt by the British Ministers. Palmerston was outraged. Until mollified by a sight of Bancroft's correspondence with the United States government over the previous year, he took the view that the envoy had deliberately misled the British Ministers. Labouchere, concerned more directly with progress of the legislation and with much personally at stake, told the American that the United States response had seriously undermined government policy; it presented 'a very serious impediment to the passage of the Bill'. Labouchere was subsequently to deny that the United States attitude had any effect on the final terms of the legislation, including the decision to alter the date of implementation from 1 September until the New Year to allow for further negotiation. Nevertheless, Bancroft's belief that it did have an influence seems credible.[14]

The muddle over the American coastwise trade did little credit to either side. Bancroft was foolish not to appreciate that his government's support for free trade could no longer be taken for granted after the change of administration. Equally, Labouchere erred in failing to establish in advance exactly what the reaction to his proposal partially to open the British coasting trade would be. But the reason for so rashly seeking an exchange of concessions at this late stage, having always in the past excluded all aspects of the British coasting trade from discussions, was rooted in immediate domestic political circumstances: the need to build a majority for the bill. As Greville noted on 16 March: 'the Government are (as heretofore) hampered with measures which they have brought forward with very doubtful means of being able to carry them.'[15] Without the support of the free trade Conservatives, the government could not survive, and it was impossible to ignore the fact that a number of these had reservations about the wisdom of opening the seas to foreign shipping without getting something in return. Gladstone had made clear his commitment to an alternative formulation – conditional reciprocity – and nine months later, despite scant support from Peel, still showed no sign of modifying this position.

Although Peel had told Gladstone, Goulburn, Clerk and Cardwell on 6 March that he would not vote against the government and so risk its defeat, this group of his younger followers continued to be set on their cause.[16] Despite Labouchere's promise that a convention with the United States of America was in the offing, when the debate opened on 12 March Gladstone gave notice of his intention to move at the committee stage of the bill an amendment for conditional reciprocity. Gladstone rooted his argument in practical considerations. It was unwise, he argued, to open the colonial trade so readily:

The long and the short of the argument was this – if we proceeded by unconditional legislation, we should not get the coasting trade of America; but if we proceeded by conditional legislation and refused to give America our colonial trade unless she gave us her coasting trade, we should get what we wanted.

Furthermore, it was easier to 'stand upon a system that exists . . . and to make a relaxation in that system a question of time and circumstance', than it was to 'sweep away that system', allowing new interests to develop, and then to retaliate when concessions were not forthcoming.[17]

Gladstone was confident that he had the support of a number of leading Peelites. His private notes on their attitudes to the bill list Peel, Graham, Young, Lord St Germains and the Duke of Wellington as for the government, Lords Lyndhurst and Ellenborough as outright opponents and nine names under the heading 'For Conditional Act, failing that for Government', including those of Aberdeen, Herbert and Lincoln. However, even within this last group there were varying shades of opinion, with Cardwell and Clerk prepared to act unconditionally in certain cases.[18] These differences were not lost on outside observers. On 12 March, when the house divided 266 votes in favour and 210 against on the second reading, Malmesbury noted that 'the Peelites voted different ways, some for and some against the bill'.[19]

Had interest in reciprocity been confined to these few Peelites, Gladstone's initiative could have been dismissed by the government as simply one more example of growing disunity in this faction; certainly the numbers involved could not have been judged as any threat to the bill. But, while Gladstone had produced his own plan for how reciprocal concessions might best be obtained, there was nothing peculiarly Peelite in the notion of reciprocity itself. As has been shown, the first instinct of the Russell administration, when faced with the question of the Navigation Laws, had been to proceed conditionally. By the time the measure was first put before Parliament in May 1848 the government had abandoned any hope of immediate progress on reciprocal arrangements. Nevertheless, in practice the government had continued to treat the response of other countries as an important consideration, not least by reserving the power to retaliate against them. Whatever the parliamentary political calculations behind the approaches to other countries instigated by the Board of Trade in late 1848, the attempt to gauge their reaction to repeal of the Navigation Laws inevitably had the effect of continuing to keep reciprocity very much on the agenda.[20]

Undoubtedly this option continued to be attractive to some Whigs. Dining at Aberdeen's on 14 March, Gladstone found Edward Ellice Senior ready to agree that reciprocity was the only sensible approach, but unwilling to go any further: 'For if one does not vote with one's party when they are in the wrong one might as well not vote with them at all.'[21] Such men could be relied upon to support the bill, whatever their private misgivings. The same could not be said for some other elements. Gladstone was not the only member prepared to push for reciprocity. Bouverie, the liberal Kilmarnock representative, wanted an exact match of concessions before any country was admitted to the British colonial or coasting trade.[22] Furthermore, any Protectionist MPs impressed by the shipowner Chapman's argument that some concessions were necessary might possibly be persuaded to support an amendment directed to this end.

When giving notice of his motion to the House prior to the committee stage, Gladstone had spoken of his wish to assess the reaction of the shipping interest. Some months later, in a letter to his father, he explained that when 'the ship owners and their friends . . . would not adopt a plan upon the basis I propose' he could proceed no further. Certainly the shipowners showed no signs of modifying their views. A fifty-strong deputation to Russell on 9 March offered no concessions, despite the fact that their number included the more moderate Henry Chapman.[23] But there is no indication that Gladstone actively sought support in this quarter. His aim all along had been to persuade Labouchere himself to accept some alteration. On 21 March Peel again warned Gladstone of the danger to the administration should the Navigation Bill be defeated, and they agreed that the latter should see Labouchere to establish his reaction to the proposed amendment. When the two men met the following day, Labouchere, by now well aware that little could be expected from the United States of America, told Gladstone that the government had decided not to accept his amendment 'but if beaten to reconsider the matter and see what they could do'. This brought the matter to an end. Gladstone was not prepared to be responsible for a government defeat.[24]

On 23 March the bill took its final shape. Up to this point the discussion had contained no surprises. Each side had rehearsed the now familiar arguments on a subject which *The Times* leader writer compared to the catacombs of Paris: 'a small portal conducts you to an infinite labyrinth in which you may wander for days'.[25] Herries naturally made much of the feeble nature of the correspondence with foreign countries, noting also the disappearance of the Prussian threat from the government's case, as well as commenting on the protectionist nature of recent Canadian representions, in contrast to those received the previous year.[26] But in general the Protectionist performance was competent rather than inspiring, and G. F. Young, no doubt frustrated at his position as an onlooker, regretted that the death of Bentinck had deprived the opposition of a spokesman with the ability to dissect free trade arguments.[27] Now that the committee stage had been reached, the argument promised to be more interesting, with a number of amendments expected, including that of Gladstone, and some risk of government defeat. *The Times*, apprised in advance of Labouchere's retreat on the coasting trade but unaware that Gladstone had been persuaded not to pursue reciprocity any further, warned that 'petty collisions' and an extended debate would erode support to 'leave the balance only just in its favour' and predicted that if that happened, 'the Lords will step in and throw the 'national defences' into the scale of the Navigation Laws. The new bill will kick the beam'. 'Are the country gentlemen and the Peers', *The Times* asked, 'prepared for a General Election?'[28]

In the event, Labouchere's announcement that the government had decided after all to leave the coasting trade untouched (which meant that the government was itself responsible for deleting fourteen of the thirty-two clauses of the bill), together with Gladstone's failure to press for conditional reciprocity meant that the debate took an unexpected turn. Labouchere's explanation, that his change of heart on allowing foreign vessels some entry to coasting trade was due to advice from the Customs as to the difficulty of preventing smuggling, can have convinced few. Herries was swift to make the connection between government retreat and the American note: 'The contents of that dispatch, and the sudden change made by the government were too manifestly connected with each other to leave much room for doubt on the motives.' This provoked a revealing, and unnecessarily defensive, response from Labouchere as to the 'honourable and straightforward' behaviour of Bancroft.[29] Following hard on the announcement of the government's retreat came Gladstone's statement. He explained that, although disappointed that the government had not responded to his proposals, support for the bill seemed to him preferable to its defeat.[30]

Disraeli was later to make the charge that the administration's altered stance was the price it had paid for Gladstone's support. Other Protectionists took the same view, to judge from the Younger Stanley's diary, but there was nothing in this.[31] Once it was clear that the United States of America would not commit itself to opening its coasting trade to British shipping, there was no advantage to the government in making this further concession, which in any case had not found favour with all its supporters. The member for Greenwich, Dundas, had privately given notice that he would resign his seat at the Admiralty Board should the coasting trade be even partially opened.[32] The *Shipping Gazette*, comparing the vote in support of the government in June 1848 on the Herries amendment with its much smaller majority in the vote on the second reading, was near to the mark:

> if the reply from the United States Government had not since been received and if the majority of 117 had not fallen to 56, we should have heard nothing of this newly discovered and insurmountable difficulty on the part of the Custom-House.[33]

With the two most contentious topics out of the way, and some sense of anti-climax, the House moved to dispose of the remainder of the bill. Bouverie's reciprocity amendment, which looked for a perfect balance on both sides, and would have been unworkable under any most-favoured-nation clause in existing treaties, was overwhelmingly defeated, gaining the support of only fifteen members. Gladstone expressed opposition to Clause Eleven, which reserved the home coasting trade, but accepted Labouchere's argument that it was not wise to increase the sense of damage done to the shipping interests affected and did not divide the House. Peel and Gladstone were united in their objection to the proposal to permit the colonies to regulate their own coasting trade, but the government gained a majority of fifty-four on the division on this.

The Protectionists stood by their resolve to offer no amendments to the bill but to concentrate on the central principle of the Navigation Laws. The only proposal of a protectionist nature to come forward was unsolicited, and Captain Harris, who sought to restore apprenticeship, was persuaded by Herries not to divide the House. Two free traders tried to address shipowning concern about the restrictions on manning which remained. Labouchere pointed out that the technical effect of the amendment which the Glasgow member, Hastie, had devised would extend to the whole concept of British registry, exciting 'alarm and panic' among shipowners. The amendment was defeated. Arthur Anderson, of the Peninsular & Oriental Company, also had a shot at the manning question, but did not persist with his proposal to prevent the navy taking men from merchant ships once Labouchere had suggested that this might weaken support for the bill as a whole.[34]

With the completion of the committee stage, where the only mutilation of the original bill had been performed by the government, it had successfully negotiated the first hurdle. There was now little doubt that the bill would pass in the Commons at the third reading, though the exact margin was still unclear. But there remained the much greater problem of the Lords. By the end of March the parliamentary contest over the Navigation Laws had become no longer simply a question of whether or not the bill would go through. On the outcome there now hinged the survival of the government. Any diffidence in the Protectionist camp about taking office had fully evaporated, and Stanley indicated not only that he was determined to beat the government in the Lords but also that he was prepared to form an administration. There were discussions on the shape of a future government – 'the cabinet is in embryo', wrote Disraeli to his sister.[35] Stanley's only fear, according to his son, was 'lest the reaction against free trade should be so strong as to make it impossible for him to satisfy his supporters out-of-doors'.[36]

On his part, Russell had decided that if defeated by a considerable majority in the Lords the government should resign, and was deliberating whether to declare this in advance. Palmerston disagreed. Writing to Russell on 14 April, he acknowledged that defeat in the Commons would call for resignation, but found it hard to accept that a defeat in the Lords, where the government claimed no majority, should have this result. To threaten resignation in advance would, he suggested, simply 'irritate'.[37] In reply, Russell, who appeared to think a Peelite administration the probable outcome, took the view that 'after having brought forward the Navigation Bill in so solemn a manner for two sessions', there was no alternative. Nevertheless, in the event of only a small majority against the bill in the Lords, Russell informed Palmerston, it was Labouchere's belief that the government would succeed with a second try. In the Prime Minister's view the only part of the bill 'absolutely necessary to carry this year' was that concerning the St Lawrence; evidence of the significance of this aspect of the issue in government eyes and the relative lack of urgency of the measure as a whole.[38]

Against this background of growing political excitement, the Navigation bill received its third reading in the Commons on 23 April.[39] Herries opened the debate, concentrating his attention on the absence of any signs that other countries would reciprocate, on the public reaction against free trade and on the risk to the shipping industry, and thence to national defence. He justified the unwillingness of his side to amend the bill on the grounds that no change could make it acceptable and objected to its 'mendacious title' – it was a bill not for the encouragement but for the *discouragement* of British shipping. There was not much here that was novel and the Younger Stanley's account of Herries's style of delivery – 'he spoke an hour, very slowly, sometimes hesitating, his voice feeble' – belies his conclusion that the Protectionist spokesman 'made every argument tell upon the House'.[40]

Undoubtedly the most valuable contribution as far as the government was concerned came from the Peelite Sir James Graham, for the first time publicly expressing his support for the bill. Graham's only reservation related to the provision for retaliation, which, like Peel, he saw as 'reciprocity in another shape'. He was opposed to such conditionality which, he said, 'makes the folly of others the limit of our wisdom'. Reminding his listeners that as a former First Lord of the Admiralty he had a 'most lively interest in naval affairs', and regarded the navy as the 'arch of our power', he told the Commons that:

The real question is this: will the repeal of the Navigation Laws injure that commercial marine which is the mainstay of the Royal Navy? If I could bring myself to entertain this belief, I should not vote for this bill.

It was his conviction that its effect would be beneficial; it would lead to a lowering of freights, which would increase imports and exports, so stimulating trade and consumption, and hence 'will inevitably lead to an increase in the number of our seamen and our ships'. Graham went on to emphasise the political importance of the measure, earning for himself loud cheers from the radicals. It was 'the capital necessary to crown the work we have already accomplished'. 'Protection or no protection' was the point at stake.[41]

This was by all accounts an unusually effective speech. W. S. Lindsay, sitting in the reporters' gallery found himself impressed in spite of himself. 'Graham's words fell like so many distinct blows from a sledge hammer, clear, concise and pointed. His arguments were in some respects fallacious, still every word seemed to tell.'[42] It was also, as *The Times* mischievously noted, a remarkable retraction, coming as it did from the man who 'only four years since framed, introduced and passed the Navigation Acts in their amended form.'[43]

Nevertheless, despite the efforts of Graham to persuade the doubtful that national defence would be unaffected by what was proposed, and the attempts of Labouchere to take account of their fears by leaving manning restrictions largely untouched, many MPs remained unconvinced. The government majority when the House divided barely improved on the second reading result: 275 votes in favour of repeal and 214 against, a majority of sixty-one.[44] Those voting with the opposition included, by prior agreement with Russell, one holder of a government office, Baines, the President of the Poor Law Board.[45] But this result in the main reflected the continued divisions between free trade Conservatives on the issue. Conacher's analysis of the Commons votes of this group reveals forty-five voting for the Navigation Bill on the third reading, but thirty-four against. Comparison of these votes with those on the Herries amendment of the previous June also confirms the extent to which the fate of the Navigation Laws had remained a genuinely open question. Three of those who had supported repeal in 1848 subsequently voted against, while twenty-one of this group failed to vote at all the following year. Twenty-seven free trade Conservatives who had not voted in 1848 turned up to vote on 23 April 1849, of whom twelve voted with the government and fifteen against.[46] However much the Russell administration and its supporters might seek to portray the reduction of protection for shipping as the logical extension of the principles established by the repeal of the Corn Laws, there were those who refused to allow themselves to be persuaded.

Among the seaport MPs only a minority voted against repeal on the second or third reading. All of these were men whose position on the issue was well established, most of them representatives for east-coast constituencies. Among London members, John Masterman was the only protectionist. Liverpool's Cardwell and Birch favoured repeal. So also did the two Newcastle MPs, together with Hutt, the member for Gateshead, and Grey, member for Tynemouth. But the member for South Shields voted against, as did the members for Sunderland, Scarborough, Whitby and Hull. Bristol's two representatives were divided on the issue. The patronage factor ensured that dockyard representatives supported the government. All Scotland's seaport members supported repeal and among Irish members only Belfast's Lord Chichester voted against. In contrast to the voting behaviour of some Peelites, no seaport member who had supported the government on the Herries amendment subsequently reversed his vote. Nor is there any sign of deliberate abstentions by free traders anxious not to offend local interests. If constituency pressure had any impact, it had been exercised earlier – when they were selected as candidates or elected as MPs.[47]

With the bill through the Commons, all parties were now free to turn their full attention to the business of rallying their supporters in the Lords. The Protectionists began with a certain tactical advantage. The instinctive disposition of the Upper House was against change, and arguments as to national interest and defence were guaranteed a sympathetic hearing. By the same token, however, Russell's stated determination to resign if defeated, with the threat of political instability to follow, was a consideration which had to be taken into account by any vacillating peers. Initially the balance between these two evils probably favoured Stanley. But neither government nor opposition could take anything for granted, as Mahon's interpretation of the situation for the benefit of his father makes clear:

Opinions are much divided as to the probable fate of the Bill in the House of Lords. The real truth I believe to be that nothing like an accurate calculation can be formed at present since a great many peers have not yet decided their own course.[48]

In consequence, the two weeks run up to the Lords second reading, was marked by, in Greville's words, 'the greatest whipping up made on both sides that ever was known'.[49]

Political allegiances in the Lords might be uncertain, but personal attachments could count for much. In the 1840s the peer with the greatest following, and also entrusted with the largest number of proxy votes, was the Duke of Wellington. By now eighty years old, a revered figure, he was still a considerable presence in public life. Though retired from active party politics, he had been called on to advise on the response to the Chartist troubles and took a lively interest in military questions. His critical views on the quality of national defence, made public eighteen months before, had attracted considerable attention, causing the government some embarrassment.[50] It may have been this, as well as his past reputation, which led the Whigs to assume that unless persuaded otherwise he would vote against the Navigation Bill. This was an alarming prospect, for, as Greville put it, 'though he would probably not carry many votes with him if he went with the government, he would carry a good many if he went against them'.[51]

In fact, it must be doubted whether it was ever Wellington's intention to vote with the Protectionists. He was more Peelite than Tory – significantly Gladstone listed him among those of this group who would support the government – and he shared Peel's belief in the value of political stability. The Duke was no lover of liberals, as Colchester's account of a chance meeting on 27 April makes clear, but neither was he prepared to commit his vote to Stanley:

I overtook the Duke of Wellington riding down to the House, and venturing to say that I hoped we (the opponents) should have the advantage of his vote, he replied, with strong symptoms of disgust, that it was too bad their giving way to Bright and such fellows, but that he could not tell which way he should vote till he had seen the Bill.[52]

Wellington may have hinted to the government that his support could not be taken for granted; if this was the case, the hint achieved its objective. First Ellesmere and then Prince Albert communicated their concern to the Duke. In his reply to the latter, Wellington was somewhat guarded, telling the Prince that much depended on what was proposed. But he affirmed his conviction that a political contest should be avoided and his desire that 'Her Majesty may not be exposed to or feel any inconvenience'.[53]

In this letter of 4 April Wellington expressly denied that he had had any conversation with Stanley on the subject and in fact there is no evidence to suggest that Wellington was ever directly approached from that quarter, though the Duke did not disguise his regret that he could not vote with the opposition side. The only known protectionist attempt to lobby Wellington came from outside Parliament, in the form of a cogent memorial from the Committee of the General Shipowners' Society, setting out the argument in terms designed to appeal to the Duke. This could be, it stated, 'reduced to this single issue, will or will not repeal diminish the number of British sailors employed in the merchant service and therebye endanger the nursery for seamen which that service affords'.[54]

The Protectionist leadership was itself not averse to applying pressure where possible. Stanley warned Aberdeen that he could not be included in the projected Ministry if he voted with the free traders.[55] But both the urgent necessity and the means to rally support were greater on the government side. Peers who were Ambassadors to foreign courts were recalled and on 4–5 May Russell wrote directly to a number of waverers, drawing their attention to the risk that the government might fall. Carrington was one of those persuaded by this argument. 'I am not satisfied as to the extensive alteration proposed in the Navigation Laws, which I have always regarded as of the highest importance to this country', he replied to Russell, but nevertheless he intended to 'yield my own opinion on the point rather than to run the risk of endangering your government.'[56] Meanwhile both Prince Albert and Peel (who was in close touch with Russell through Wood) were using their personal influence. As Stanley recorded in his diary, expediency, not principle, characterised the Crown's appeal:

The arguments used are that the rejection of the bill would lead to a dissolution, that Parliament could not meet again till late, and that the Queen would be seriously inconvenienced by being prevented from going to Scotland. Others are threatened with a renewal of the Corn Law battle; and as a consequence, with an agitation of free traders for an extension of the suffrage.[57]

By the time of the Lords second reading on 7 May the Protectionist managers knew that the numbers on both sides were very close. Disraeli's instinct told him that the bill would pass, but Stanley was still hopeful that some peers might still be swayed. 'Contrary to the general rule', he wrote to Lord Brougham on 4 May, 'I believe there is a floating balance to be worked on in the course of the debate, sufficient to turn the nicely balanced scale.'[58] Part of that 'floating balance' which Stanley had to take into account was Brougham himself. Brougham, the veteran of reform, had become in his old age increasingly unpredictable in his political allegiance, and now not only unexpectedly declared himself against repeal but also wanted to lead the Protectionist attack in the Lords. His motives were perhaps not entirely disinterested. In the judgement of Russell, Brougham's support for Stanley owed much to an ambition to be Lord Chancellor once more. It was not surprising, Russell told his friends in a somewhat laboured joke, to find Brougham now talking about 'seal fisheries' because he was 'fishing for seals' in a future administration.[59] The task of moving the amendment should have fallen to Colchester, who was by now something of an expert on the navigation question, but he was persuaded to stand aside. As Colchester wrote later: 'Lord Brougham was always a powerful advocate of any course which he took up, was a consistent free trader and also a dangerous person to offend politically.'[60] The Protectionists could not afford to deny Brougham a leading role and so risk losing his support, and perhaps that of other nominal free traders. Hence it was Brougham who spoke first for the Protectionists in response to Lansdowne, who opened the debate on behalf of the government.

The central theme of Lansdowne's speech was the proposition that, far from being 'clothed in a cloak of impenetrable armour' under the system of protection which remained, British commerce wore 'a garment of shreds and patches'. Britain had not suffered from past piecemeal relaxation, on the contrary it had maintained its ground. But, Lansdowne went on, it could not be assumed that foreign powers or the colonies would be satisfied with matters as they stood and if the bill were not to be passed much that had been gained would be lost. He therefore called upon the Lords 'to rely upon the energy of this country and the means at its disposal' and support the measure.

Lansdowne's was a deliberately low key, typically urbane, perform- ance designed to portray the Navigation Bill as the natural consequence of past developments and present needs. The most pointed part of his contribution came at its end, when he told the House that he and his colleagues were 'prepared for the consequences of a hostile vote', so leaving no doubt that the government would resign.[61] In contrast, Brougham's lengthy speech was a conscious *tour de force*, in which he defended himself against the charge of inconsistency by referring to a pamphlet he had written in the early 1800s, reiterating his view there of colonial monopoly as the recompense for the dear purchase and current cost of these possessions. Citing the retention of the coasting trade and the manning clauses as evidence of the government's lack of confidence that no damage would result from what was proposed, Brougham dwelt particularly on the defence implications and the inadvisability of making 'such a fearful change' at this of all times.[62] The Protectionists had perhaps been wise to rely on Brougham for the major exposition of their case. The worthy Colchester had, by his own account, 'taken much pains in preparing my speech for the second reading, having consulted works on the subject in the British Museum, as well as those more easily accessible'. But faced with a House 'weary of long speeches' and speaking against a 'constant hubbub from the numerous persons below the bar', he spoke poorly and whatever quality there was in his material evaporated under the nervous strain.[63]

Winding up for the opposition, Stanley appealed to the Duke of Wellington. As he watched from the gallery, the Younger Stanley noted the Duke's reaction to what he described as a 'beautiful peroration' (but which Greville interpreted as an attack): 'The old man appeared moved, turned restlessly in his seat, and covered his face with his hands.'[64] Finally, at 4.30 in the morning of 9 May 1849 the House of Lords divided on the second reading. Both sides mustered their supporters to the fullest extent possible. According to the Younger Stanley, 'two insane peers were brought in and made to vote, the keeper of one being in attendance in the lobby'. But all did not go entirely to plan: 'One vote was lost by the holder giving his vote from the Woolsack, which is not within the House.'[65] Nevertheless, of those counted as present, 105 voted in favour of the measure and 119 against. But this majority for the Protectionists was reversed by the effect of proxy votes. These were cast 68 in favour and 44 against, giving an total majority for the government of just ten. 'To Free Trade is now added Free Navigation', rejoiced a triumphant, and relieved, *Times*.[66]

The bill's opponents were not slow to remark on the role of absent peers in this result. The *Morning Herald* wrote of a 'pocket majority . . . chiefly made up of Ambassadors, Governors and other *employés* of the ministry – whose proxies are naturally at the command of the government for the time being'.[67] But the greatest wound was that inflicted by the Duke of Wellington, who was reponsible for most proxy votes, and had used them in support of the bill. There was no small irony in this. No one could be more associated in the public mind with the defence of the realm than was the Duke. Yet much of the responsibility for ending a system whose justification was precisely this had come to rest with him. The *Shipping Gazette* took refuge in the explanation that the Duke of Wellington was now an old man, while the Stanleyites drew comfort from the perception that he had acted against his true judgement.[68] But nothing could reverse the political impact of what he had done. Wellington had sacrificed the Navigation Laws to save the government.

It seems probable that some of the peers who voted with the government were prompted to do so by the same consideration as that which prompted Wellington – a fear of political instability and consequent social unrest. Personal attachment to the Duke, and also to Peel, may have played a part. But one of their Lordships, at least, felt unable to act freely in support of the bill. On 11 May Londonderry, who had voted with Stanley, wrote in guilty expiation to Peel:

I never was a Deserter, under all the changes of the chequered parties of the day – above all it is not likely that I should be one *à mon age*.
But Seaham pledged himself in the County Durham against the Repeal of the Navigation Laws and so voted. Circumstanced as I am at the head of the coal trade and with such a commercial community at my back with whom the carrying trade and the mercantile marine are so intimately connected, I dared not venture in as a father to take a different line from the son who owes his seat to the position I hold and the interest I wield. If I had opposed the Shipping Interests in their views (whether right or wrong I have no ability to answer) my own individual enterprise of Seaham Harbour (on which I have staked my life upon a throw) might have been seriously mutilated and injured by the secret if not the open revenge of the shipowners trading with my port and serious misfortune might have arisen to me.[69]

In the immediate aftermath of this defeat, the Protectionists felt by no means discouraged. The margin had been narrow and proxy votes could not be used at the committee stage, so Stanley was hopeful of introducing major amendments prior to the third reading.[70] Some supporters of the government assumed that he would be successful; as Charles Wood noted: 'There is a good deal of leeway to be made up – with such a majority of presents against us.' But in the event Palmerston's judgement, that 'we shall probably improve in our majority as we go on', proved to be substantially correct.[71]

Having always taken the view that opposition to the Navigation Bill should focus on the central principle of the need for protection, the Protectionists now found themselves at something at a loss in deciding what changes might be proposed which would not clash with the central principle of the bill. With the aid of Herries and also G. F. Young, as well as a small group of his fellow peers which included the Peelite Ellenborough, Stanley hurriedly drew up a set of amendments, which he set before the House on 21 May.[72] In the knowledge that it had commanded no majority on the floor of the Lords on the second reading, and with several Irish peers absent, the government whips were fearful.[73]

But what Stanley had to offer proved singularly unenticing, if not unfamiliar. At this late stage, Stanley became in effect a convert to treaty reciprocity as far as third party carriers were concerned and also proposed to open the Canadian trade to United States shipping.[74] If Stanley thought that these amendments would attract Peelite peers, he was mistaken. Gladstone advised Aberdeen that the Canada clause was 'open to many objections of which each one would be fatal'. It was Gladstone's view that conditionality would be at variance with existing treaties, there were no equivalent concessions which anyone could offer, it would pave the way for 'perpetual future agitation' from other countries and, finally, by confining the trade to United States ships it would deprive Canada of the much greater benefit of Baltic vessels.[75] Furthermore, in making this free trade concession, Stanley had alienated some of his own supporters. As Campbell commented:

Stanley cut a wretched figure in committee, having attempted to show his destructive amendments harnessed with the principle of the bill. They were not only inconsistent with it, but distasteful to his adherents.[76]

With the defeat of Stanley's amendments by a majority of thirteen, the struggle to defend the Navigation Laws was effectively brought to an end. On 13 June, as the *Shipping Gazette* put it, 'the bill for the destruction of the shipping interests of Great Britain passed the House of Lords'. There was no division.[77]

For the shipping industry the repeal of the Navigation Laws marked the conclusion of a 200-year-long era of protection by the state. After 1 January 1850 foreign vessels were free to do business in Britain's colonial trades and to carry goods from anywhere in the world into British ports. The impact of that considerable change is the subject of the chapter which follows, but the aftermath of repeal was not only an economic question. There was a political aftermath also. Outside Parliament the protectionist revival continued to exert a force, drawing into it some of those who had fought for the survival of the Navigation Laws. But within the parliamentary sphere protection for shipping could not be considered a closed question on either side, and for this the Act itself was largely responsible. Viewed as a measure for liberalisation, the Whig measure fell short. The Act left untouched the coasting trade and it continued to subject shipowners to restrictions as to how they manned their vessels; both omissions bound to attract the attention of free traders and, in the case of the latter, the shipping interests. It was also incomplete in another central respect. Retaliation against countries which failed to respond was not mandatory, but the Act allowed for such a possibility. In this sense it was not a final measure; Navigation Laws might be reimposed. Critics of repeal were not slow to recognise the opportunity this offered.

Notes

1 LCL, Derby Papers, 290 Der(14) 178/1, Derby to Granby, 14 December 1848.
2 Jennings, *Croker Papers*, Bentinck to Croker, 5 October 1847, p. 145.
3 LCL, Derby Papers, 290 Der(14) 152/3, 5 January 1849; 178/3 13 January 1849.
4 *Shipping Gazette*, 28 March 1848, 1 April 1848, 25 January 1849, 27 January 1849.
5 *Shipping Gazette*, 10 January 1849; W. S. Lindsay, *Letters on the Navigation Laws addressed to Lord John Russell containing a review of the measures of Mr Labouchere*, London, 1849; G. F. Young, *Letters on the Navigation Laws originally published in the Standard Newspaper*, London, 1848; NMM, Lindsay Papers, Journal, II, pp. 93–4, 101–2; *Shipping Gazette*, 8 February 1849. Lindsay subsequently saw himself as mistaken in his opposition to repeal. See his letter to Russell, 9 November 1868, quoted Spencer Walpole, *The Life of Lord John Russell*, 2 vols, London, 1891, n.100. Nevertheless, Lindsays's account of the protectionist campaign in his major history is not unsympathetic. See W. S. Lindsay, *History of Merchant Shipping and Ancient Commerce in Four Volumes*, III, London, 1976.
6 GSS, *Annual Report for 1847–48*, 2 March 1849.
7 *The Times*, 17 June 1848. See J. T. Ward, 'Derby and Disraeli', in Donald Southgate (ed.), *The Conservative Leadership 1832–1932*, London, 1974, pp. 61–2.
8 LCL, Derby Papers, 290 Der(14) 178/3, 13 January 1849.
9 PRO, Granville Papers, PRO 30/29/23/1, Granville to Grey, draft, 6 February 1849.
10 *Correspondence with Foreign States relative to the proposed relaxation of the Navigation Laws*, PP 1849 [1029] [1030] [1038] [1041] [1048], LI, pp. 179, 223, 243, 247, 263; *Reply of the United States Government respecting the proposed relaxation of the British Navigation Laws*, PP 1849 [1036] LI, p. 235; PD, Third Series, CIII, 9 March 1849, c. 472.
11 PD, Third Series, CII, 14 February 1849, c. 682–99.
12 PD, Third Series, CIII, 23 March 1849, c. 1196–8; PRO Customs 30/6, Fremantle to Labouchere, 27 February 1849. While Labouchere may have been quick to use the reservation expressed by the Customs as an excuse, Fremantle's explanation makes clear that the objection itself was quite genuine: 'I must take my share of blame for not having more forcibly

stated my objections to you before you brought forward your motion in the House of Commons, as I was unwilling to propose difficulties of a technical character in the consideration of a large question of state policy.'

13 PRO, FO 5/508, f. 216.
14 The complicated history of this Anglo-American misunderstanding can be traced through PRO FO5/501 f. 158, f. 168; FO 5/506 f. 42, f. 45; FO 5/500.
15 L. Strachey and R. Fulford, *The Greville Memoirs*, VI, London, 1938, p. 168.
16 BL, Gladstone Papers, Add. MS. 44777 ff. 283–4, Memorandum, 6 March 1849.
17 PD Third Series, CIII, 12 March 1849, c. 540–63.
18 BL Gladstone Papers, Add. MS. 44777, f. 281.
19 Earl of Malmesbury, *Memoirs of an Ex-Minister*, 2 vols, London, 1884, p. 241.
20 However, John Prest, *Lord John Russell*, London, 1972 p. 299, argues that the government had 'decided against' reciprocity the previous autumn.
21 BL Gladstone Papers, Add. MS. 44777 f. 285.
22 *The Times*, 23 March 1849.
23 Matthew, *Gladstone Diaries*, p. xxxviii, n.6; *The Times*, 10 March 1849.
24 BL Gladstone Papers, Add. Ms. 44777 ff. 286–93; 44368 f. 127.
25 *The Times*, 12 March 1849.
26 PD, Third Series, CIII, 9 March 1849, c. 464-85.
27 *Shipping Gazette*, 12 March 1849.
28 *The Times*, 24 March 1849.
29 PD, Third Series, CIII, 23 March 1849, c. 1203, c. 1225.
30 *Ibid.*, c. 1199-203.
31 PD, Third Series, CIV, 23 April 1849, c. 690; J. R. Vincent, *Disraeli, Derby and the Conservative Party: the Political Journals of Lord Stanley 1849–1869*, Hassocks, 1978, pp. 1–2.
32 Admiral Charles Lord Colchester, *Memoranda of My Life from 1798 to 1859 Inclusive*, London, 1869.
33 *Shipping Gazette*, 24 March 1849.
34 PD, Third Series, CIII, 23 March 1849, c. 1206–47; CIV (19 April 1849), 462–6. See also Anderson's explanation in his letter to *The Times*, 21 April 1849.
35 Jones, *Lord Derby*, p. 136; Moneypenny and Buckle, *Disraeli*, II, London, 1929, p. 1020.
36 *Stanley Journals*, p. 3.
37 PRO, Russell Papers, 30/22 7F f181, Palmerston to Russell, 14 April 1849; SUL, Broadlands Papers, GC/RU/267 (258–277), Russell to Palmerston, 16 April 1849.
38 *Ibid.*
39 PD, Third Series, CIV, 23 April 1849, c. 622–32.
40 *Ibid.: Stanley Journals*, 23 April 1849, p. 5.
41 PD, Third Series, CIV, 23 April 1849, c. 658–76.
42 NMM, Lindsay Papers, *Journal*, II, pp. 99–100.
43 *The Times*, 24 April 1849.

44 PD, Third Series, CIV, 23 April 1849, c. 702–5.
45 Gladstone raised the issue of Baines's position in the House of Commons. PD Third Series, CII, 14 February 1849, c. 681-2. The Younger Stanley reported that a parliamentary agent had offered a shipowner ten free trade abstentions for £1,000. The offer had been refused. *Stanley Journals*, 7 May 1849, pp. 7–8.
46 Conacher, *Peelites and the Party System*, p. 189 n.100.
47 *Divisions of the House of Commons*, 1847–48, 1849.
48 KAO, Stanhope Papers, U1580 317/16, Mahon to Stanhope, 27 April 1849.
49 *Greville Memoirs*, VI, 10/11 May 1849, p. 176.
50 See M. S. Partridge, 'The Russell cabinet and national defence', *History*, LXXII, 1987, p. 235.
51 *Greville Memoirs*, VI, 1 April 1849, p. 172.
52 Colchester, *My Life*, p. 165.
53 SUL, Wellington Papers, 2/162/7, 4 April 1849.
54 Wellington Papers, 2/191/26.
55 *Stanley Diaries*, 2 May 1849, 5 May 1849, pp. 6–7; Muriel E. Chamberlain, *Lord Aberdeen: A Political Biography*, London, 1983, p. 419.
56 PRO, Russell Papers, 30/22 7F f224.
57 Peel Papers, Add. MS. 40601 ff. 277–8, Wood to Peel; *Stanley Diaries*, 5 May 1849, p. 6.
58 *Ibid.*, 2 May 1849, p. 6.; LRO, Derby Papers, 290 Der(14) 178/1, 4 May 1849.
59 Lord Broughton (John Cam Hobhouse), *Recollections of a Long Life*, VI, 1841–52, London, 1911, p. 237.
60 LCL, Derby Papers, 290 Der(14) 178/1, Derby to Brougham, 5 May 1849; Colchester, *My Life*, p. 165.
61 PD, Third Series, CIV, 5 May 1849, c. 1316–28.
62 *Ibid.*, c. 1328-57.
63 Colchester, *My Life*, p. 167.
64 *Stanley Diaries*, 6 May 1849, p. 7; *Greville Memoirs*, VI, 10/11 May 1849, p. 176.
65 *Stanley Diaries*, 6 May 1849, p. 7.
66 *The Times*, 9 May 1849.
67 Quoted in *Shipping Gazette*, 10 May 1849.
68 *Shipping Gazette*, 9 May 1849; *Stanley Diaries*, p. 7.
69 BL, Peel Papers, Add. MS. 40406 f. 351, Londonderry to Peel, 11 May 1849.
70 Colchester, *My Life*, p. 166.
71 *Greville Memoirs*, 11/10 May 1849, p. 176; SUA, Broadlands Papers, GC/TE/326, Palmerston to Temple, 11 May 1849; BL, Peel Papers, Add. MS. 40601 f. 290, Wood to Peel, 16 May 1849.
72 LCL, Derby Papers, 290 Der(14) 178/1, 12 May 1849, Derby to Ellenborough, Derby to Lyndhurst, Derby to Brougham, Derby to Walpole; 290 Der(14) 152/1, Undated, Herries to Derby.
73 Hon. Mrs Hardcastle (ed.), *Life of John, Lord Campbell, Lord Chancellor of Great Britain*, II, London, 1881, p. 253.

74 PD Third Series, CV. 21 May 1849, c. 687–703; 24 May 1849, c. 896–8.
75 BL, Gladstone Papers, Add. MS. 44777, f. 301.
76 Hardcastle, *Life of Lord Campbell*, p. 253.
77 PD, Third Series, CVI, 12 June 1849, c. 11–48 (Stanley recorded his protest in the *Journals of the House of Lords*); *Shipping Gazette*, 13 June 1849.

Chapter Nine

Aftermath

The bill was passed, and the political crisis averted; but the free trade victory ensured no respite for the Board of Trade or the Foreign Office. The Whigs had always seen unilateral liberalisation by Britain as the means by which other countries might be persuaded in a similar policy direction. In the debates on repeal Labouchere had made much of the reciprocal benefits that might be expected as the result of Britain's initiative. Now those claims had to be substantiated and, to this end, British envoys were instructed to enter into immediate negotiations. In the short term there were also more urgent problems. The Act was due to become law on 1 January 1850, and shipowners were anxious to establish the concessions which might be expected from other powers. Indirect trade – freedom to act as third party carriers – was one area of concern. Another was whether foreign-built vessels operating under the British flag would be treated as British in foreign ports. The Liverpool Shipowners' Association, some of whose members were trying to decide whether to invest in American vessels, was particularly anxious for firm answers and wrote to the Board requesting information no fewer than four times in November and December 1849.[1] But despite the long genesis of repeal, officials were singularly ill-prepared to provide advice. 'Great inconvenience may arise from giving *opinions* on such matters', commented Porter in October, on a query from one shipping partnership on trading from the Canaries to the United States. 'At the same time', he continued in the manner of the true public servant, 'it is difficult to avoid giving a *reply*. Would it not be proper to say that the arrangements called for by the act repealing the Navigation Laws not having been completed as regards foreign governments, their Lordships cannot at present give any precise answer to the question.'[2]

Such dependence on the response of other countries was the crux of the matter. Relatively minor questions were generally resolved by January 1850, but the optimism that there would by then be signs of clear progress towards wider objectives was misplaced. Predictably, those maritime powers with least to offer the British shipowner, but who stood to gain most from repeal, proved the most willing to end any discrimination against British vessels. As the British Consul in Sweden had told Palmerston prior to repeal:

the prospect of being debarred from partaking in the struggle that must inevitably arise from the profitable office of serving as carriers for Great Britain and her colonies would ensure the determination on the part of this country that scarce any concession should be considered too great in order to secure such advantages to Swedish and Norwegian shipbuilders as well as shipowners.[3]

In contrast to the Scandinavians, the United States of America, which as the power which gained most from the opening of the colonial trades was the prime target for British commercial diplomacy, continued to prove embarrassingly unresponsive to the government's overtures. The American coasting trade proper having been ruled out, Britain now concentrated on negotiating access for its nationals to the trade from the east coast to California and for the admission of British-built ships to United States registry. But neither the Russell administration nor its successors had any impact on the maritime policy of the United States of America, which remained resolutely protectionist.[4]

Such unwillingness to dispense with flag preference was not confined to the United States of America. Neither was it a short-term phenomenon. Ten years after the repeal of the Navigation Laws, the report of the Select Committee on Merchant Shipping noted that 'having thus opened our ports to the unrestricted competition of all nations, it appears that although many countries have in return thrown open their ports to English shipping, there are others which have hitherto refused to reciprocate'. France, Spain, Portugal, Belgium and Holland all continued to discriminate against British-registered vessels. France imposed higher charges on British vessels than on the vessels of some other nations, even in the cross-Channel trade, as well as virtually excluding them from the indirect and colonial trades. Goods carried in British vessels to Spain paid a punitive 20 per cent duty. Portugal would allow British ships to carry only national or colonial produce, even in the direct trade. The Dutch East Indies were effectively closed to British carriers, and Belgium imposed a differential duty on salt when carried in British ships.[5]

The repeal legislation had offered a means of redress for such discrimination:

it shall be lawful for Her Majesty (if she think fit), by Order in Council, to impose such prohibitions or restrictions upon the ships of such foreign country, either as to the voyages in which they may engage, or as to the articles which they may import into or export from any part of the United Kingdom, or of any British possession in any part of the world, as Her Majesty may think fit, so as to place the ships of such country on as nearly as possible the same footing in British ports, as that on which British ships are placed in the ports of such country.[6]

But as the 1860 Select Committee on the State of Merchant Shipping noted: 'No administration, whether Conservative or Liberal, has ventured to suggest that the retaliatory clauses in the Act of 1849, which have remained dormant and inoperative, should be put in force.'[7] It was not because this was not urged in some quarters, though with diminishing conviction as time went on, but because retaliation carried with it considerable risk. To levy additional duties on the ships or goods of an offending foreign power might provoke still further discrimination against British operators. To deny foreign vessels access to trade with the colonies would prove unacceptable to colonial interests, which were anxious for the maximum supply of cargo space, and wary of imperial monopoly. Faced with the determination of other maritime powers to continue to support their national merchant fleets, there was little Britain could do.

All this was evident at the time of repeal – hence Gladstone's insistence on conditional reciprocity – and indeed it had been predicted by all parliamentary groupings, irrespective of political viewpoint, except the Whigs. If the retaliatory clause is taken at face value, rather than as a cynical parliamentary ploy to convince the doubtful, it would seem that its main justification was as a threat which would induce other powers to enter into negotiation with Britain. As such it succeeded. What could not be guaranteed was the outcome of such talks – not least because the repeal of the Navigation Laws left untouched the types of issue dealt with under reciprocity treaties. As a Board of Trade note for the benefit of the Foreign Office explained:

The object was to remove the restrictions which which previously existed on foreign vessels being *employed at all* in certain classes of voyages, so as to enable the ships of foreign countries to operate in the indirect trade with this country from which they were previously rigorously excluded, and not to regulate the duties to which vessels employed in such voyages were liable.[8]

Negotiations for a new treaty with France to replace that of 1826 floundered partly because of the French insistence on equalisation of local charges. With annual reciprocity compensation running at £34,000 a year, the Customs judged that the additional burden on the revenue which would result was 'so serious as to operate as a complete bar to such a proceeding'.[9] Negotiations with Belgium were similarly hampered by an initial unwillingness on the part of the Board of Trade to add the reduction of duties or tolls on Belgian vessels to what had already been conceded by abolition of the Navigation Laws.[10] In the face of Protectionist criticism, the Whigs were also fearful of seeming ingenuous and open-handed. 'It will probably not be difficult so to word the treaty', Palmerston was assured in an anonymous memorandum on the Belgian negotiations, 'as to make it appear that we obtain advantages by it corresponding to those we give.'[11] In such an atmosphere of grudging liberality, it is small wonder that the weaker European maritime powers, who had derived little direct benefit from repeal, were generally less impressed by British generosity than were the British themselves. And the failure of such nations to respond in kind to Britain's initiative becomes more explicable when it is recognised not only that national fleets had much to lose from the unhampered admission of British vessels to their trades but also that even after 1849 their vessels were by no means guaranteed equality of treatment in British ports. The abolition of the Navigation Laws was not quite the triumph for free navigation that is usually assumed.

The Board of Trade was busy with international maritime negotiations in the year or so immediately following repeal, but its main concern was with an unprecedentedly ambitious programme of merchant shipping legislation, four Acts in all, promoted by Labouchere between 1850 and 1851. Of these by far the most important was the Mercantile Marine Act of 1850.[12] This was a major measure which defined a regulatory function for the Board of Trade in relation to the British merchant fleet which has lasted to the present day. The Act created a Marine Department of the Board, established shipping offices where crews were to be engaged and discharged under official supervision, imposed more stringent penalties for desertion, and set up a system of examination for masters and mates. It also empowered the Board to investigate the causes of shipwreck, and to cancel or suspend masters' and mates' certificates for misconduct.

The Mercantile Marine Act, as also the consolidating Merchant Shipping Act of 1854, with its 504 clauses, is evidence that repeal of the

Navigation Laws did not mark the beginning of a new non-interventionist phase of government policy towards shipping generally. There was no victory for *laissez-faire* here. On the contrary, the scale of state interference in the British shipping industry increased. Indeed, it can be argued that no other group of nineteenth-century capitalists was so confined within a legal framework as were shipowners, and no section of the labour force found itself in so much routine contact with officialdom as the men who went to sea after 1850. Following so closely on the exposure of the merchant fleet to greater foreign competition, it might seem that such legislation was a direct response – an attempt to make the industry fitter to meet that challenge. In fact, repeal was not responsible for these developments. They had a quite separate genesis, with the report of the 1836 Select Committee on the Causes of Shipwreck and the series of consular reports on British seamen published in 1848 probably the greatest influences.[14] But the quality of British seafarers had been one aspect of British competitiveness which had engaged the attention of both the Select Committees on the Navigation Laws, and repeal reinforced arguments for improving standards of training and for regularising conditions of employment. As Wellington wrote to Granville on 2 June 1849:

The observations of witnesses before the Committees of Parliament and the recent decision on the Navigation Laws repeal bill both convince me of the necessity that some effectual measure should be adopted under the control of government to improve the mercantile marine.[15]

Yet any connection between the end of protection for shipping and interventionist legislation was general rather than specific. Labouchere made no mention of Navigation Laws when introducing his Mercantile Marine Bill to the Commons.[16]

Politically the greatest impact of repeal was on the Protectionists. For sections of the Tory leadership, the failure to bring down the government on so clear an issue of principle confirmed what they had already begun to suspect: that protectionism was not a bridge to power but a barrier. Attachment to this creed had to be recognised as a matter of sentiment, not political sense. From now on, Disraeli was to seize every opportunity to disassociate the party from protection. Stanley, though slower to relinquish the general principle, in time came to recognise the same practical realities. In June 1851, although shipowners claimed that repeal was responsible for a sharp decline in freight rates, when presenting a petition to the House of Lords from the Liverpool Shipowners' Association which urged the removal of the remaining burdens of shipping, Stanley did not go beyond pressing the government to exercise the retaliatory powers reserved to the Crown.[17]

While, in the wake of repeal, Disraeli urged Stanley to accept that protection was dead as a political cause, there were those who tried to resurrect it through a public campaign, and indeed succeeded in attracting considerable attention in the press. 'Meetings were held, angry speeches delivered, and in some case riots ensued, which did us no good in the opinion of thinking'persons', commented the Younger Stanley.[18] The most active member of this group of militant protectionists was G. F. Young. Immediately prior to consideration of the repeal bill by the Lords, Young had formed a new protectionist association, the National Association for the Protection of British Industry and Capital. Its aim was to extend the scope of the Society for the Protection of Agriculture and British Industry, with which the Duke of Richmond and Earl Stanhope were particularly associated, to embrace 'agricultural, colonial, commercial, manufacturing and shipping interests'.[19] Despite Stanhope's suspicions that any support from the shipowners would evaporate once the Laws were repealed – 'it must not be forgotten that many of them supported free trade in corn and other commodities' – Young took the Protectionist defeat as an indication that a more broadly based campaign was needed, and threw himself into organising and addressing meetings with characteristic enthusiasm.[20] Already by November 1849 his efforts had earned a well-publicised rebuke from Disraeli, though Stanley judged that Young did little harm and, indeed, he was still at this stage prepared to concede that the National Association was 'useful in keeping alive the spirit of the party'.[21] Disagreement between Disraeli and Stanley on the extra-parliamentary movement continued until March 1851, when a protectionist delegation was led to understand by Stanley, now Earl of Derby, that he could no longer give them his support.[22]

The National Association in no way represented a continuation of the struggle of the General Shipowners' Society against repeal. Despite Young's leading role, other members of the society gave little support. In 1851 he told a meeting in Framlington, Suffolk that he felt ashamed of his fellow shipowners, who were 'recreants, deluded and blind to the destruction impending upon them'.[23] This campaign for the re-imposition of protectionism owed everything to Young's personal commitment, as Disraeli's hostile recollection indicates:

He [Stanley] was in the hands of the Protection Society worked by this George Frederick Young, who was not an agriculturalist, but a commercial and mainly colonial interest man, ignorant of the tenor and situation of the farmers; a man of great energy and of equal vanity, but of ordinary abilities and no cultivation and who was piqued by the success of Cobden and Bright, men of his own class, in agitating England and thought he would show himself as good and powerful as they.[24]

As a Tory organisation, the National Association was unusual in attempting to attract working-class support. The inspiration for this was the aristocratic Stanhope, not Young the anti-union employer of labour, who was sceptical of the value of such overtures. Nevertheless, despite his view that, with the exception of the shipwrights, 'the masses, in the metropolitan districts, at least are bigoted to free trade, apathetic and subject to many sinister influences', Young was persuaded to hold a joint meeting in January 1850 at a Stepney public house with delegates of the London Trades.[25] This particular meeting, which attracted the novel press headline 'The Chartists and the Protectionists', broke up in disarray, having been invaded by 'financial reform' Cobdenite free traders.[26] Such initiatives achieved nothing despite the fact that Young was wrong to assume that London working men supported free trade; bitter experience of the consequences of foreign competition had taught many artisans the value of protectionism.[27] But, equally, their experience as a class meant that any alliance with those who ran the National Association was out of the question. As a result, the only product of its populist efforts was the antagonism of the Protectionist leadership in Parliament, which in turn was to ensure that the campaign would fizzle out. With Derby in office for much of 1852, presiding over a minority administration which offered no challenge to free trade, Young (who had been elected MP for Scarborough in 1851) had to choose between loyalty to party or faction. Young, who was close enough to the Prime Minister to have been offered the Vice-Presidency of the Board of Trade (a post he declined for health reasons), opted for the former. He broke with his colleagues in the National Association by declaring his full support for Derby and for a less than complete re-imposition of the Navigation Laws.[28] His reward from the Scarborough electors in the General Election held in July 1852 was the loss of his seat.[29]

While Young was fighting his rearguard action in support of protection, for others the main issue was 'the practical working of the great experiment of the repeal of the Navigation Laws'. When repeal was still a threat, the extreme protectionists had been able to dominate

the policy of the General Shipowners' Society, but once repeal was a
reality the purists lost control. On 22 January 1850 a special meeting of
the Committee voted nine to five in favour of making representations
to the government for alteration of the 1849 Act to 'allow British ships
to be navigated by foreign seamen'. If shipowners were no longer to
enjoy the benefits of protection, the pragmatists argued, they should
not be restricted as to whom they should employ. An objection that
they should 'abstain from seeking redress by any attempt to weaken the
British sailor or weaken the national defences' was overruled.[30]

At the time when this resolution was adopted, the shipowners
obviously had no direct experience of the effect of repeal. What they
feared was that its impact on the supply of seamen would be that
described in the verse which appeared the following year:

> The seamen, once our country's boast
> Dismissed, neglected, spurned,
> Hath sail'd forever from our coast
> And foreign wages earned.[31]

Their sense of restriction, and grievance, was heightened by the terms
of Labouchere's Mercantile Marine Act. Here they found themselves
united with the seamen in opposition. A memorial sent to the Board of
Trade by shipowners, master mariners and seamen in South Shields
referred to the new system of engagement and discharge of crews as
'servile degradation, vigorous coercion and oppressive taxation'.[32] But
when hostility spilled over into unrest, as at Hull, where it was reported
in February 1851 the sailors had 'a regular committee and committee
room who issue placards' and would do 'their utmost to prevent any
men signing articles at their shipping office to go to sea', labour
agitation was not directed solely at the government.[33] As freight rates
first recovered and then began to show a rise above previous levels, the
shipowners came under pressure from the seamen for better wages,
with some success – a distinct upward trend was apparent by 1853.[34]
Although, as some observers noted, the industry was still nowhere near
employing even the permitted quota of non-nationals (a quarter of the
crew of foreign-going vessels), the shipowners increasingly saw the
restrictions on the employment of foreigners as the unnecessary
blunting of a useful tactical weapon in labour disputes. From at first
seeking only to open the foreign trades, when faced with growing
labour militancy in the coasting trades, the shipowners demanded the
right to take on foreigners even there.

The shipowners had no success in persuading the Whigs to delete the manning clause. To amend so recent a piece of its own legislation would have exposed the government to political ridicule and, in any case, Labouchere had a genuine commitment to its preservation. Nor was the obstruction he had encountered from shipowners over his maritime legislation an encouragement to respond favourably to requests from that source. Once the Derbyites were in office the prospects altered. For all the emphasis the Protectionists had in the past placed upon defence, as the party which had the closest contacts with the shipping interest they were more open to suggestions from this source. There were, though, contervailing influences. In 1852 an Admiralty Committee was in the process of investigating the vexed question of naval manning. Its appointment owed nothing to the repeal of the Navigation Laws. It had long been recognised that there was a need to address the problem of providing adequate trained manpower for the navy in time of war, and its recommendations for the creation of a force of Royal Naval Coast Volunteers and for the introduction of continuous service were very much solutions for the long term.[35] The Manning Committee took it for granted that the merchant fleet would continue to play its historic role in supplying seamen to the navy. Its only anxiety about the impact of repeal related to the decline in the number of boys being taken on as apprentices now that this was no longer compulsory. But consultations with the shipowners in the major ports left the Committee not only in no doubt as to their resistance to any reintroduction of apprenticeship but also very aware of the industry's determination to throw off the restrictions that remained:

The shipowners appear to be disconcerted by recent legislative enactments and inclined to seek for relief in measures we cannot but regard as prejudicial viz. the permission to navigate their ships without any restriction as to the proportion of British and foreign seamen.

Despite the judgement of the 1852 Admiralty Manning Committee that such a course of action would prove 'highly injurious', driving British seamen into serving on United States vessels and weakening the merchant service as the nursery, the shipowners won the argument as far as the government was concerned.[36] Disraeli's Budget of December 1852, which he failed to carry through the House, contained proposals to give 'relief to the shipping interest' which included removing restrictions on employment of foreign seamen.[37] With the fall of the

Derby Ministry, the proposal was adopted by the Aberdeen coalition (from which Labouchere was excluded); and Cardwell's wide-ranging Merchant Shipping Law Amendment Bill, which went before Parliament in July 1853, included a clause which repealed the relevant sections of the 1849 Act.

Ending protection for British seamen produced some parliamentary groupings which would have seemed improbable only a few years before. Hudson, true as ever to his Sunderland shipowning constituents, and Liddell, now an MP for Liverpool where the Shipowners' Association was equally in favour, were to be found on the same side as Sir James Graham, now once again First Lord of the Admiralty. Graham's speech echoed his argument in the repeal debate:

If they added to the commerce of the country, they infallibly added to the number of ships; and if they added to the number of ships, they must infallibly add to the number of merchant seamen, and they thereby also increased the supply to the Queen's service from that nursery for seamen which he was anxious to see preserved.[38]

Those who were against the measure included not only Henley, who thought 'that the public safety ought to override even that strong claim which he admitted the British shipowners to have upon the government' but also Labouchere – on the grounds that 'it would have the effect of wounding the sensibilities of British sailors, and that it would involve us in a difficulty as to the national character of our ships'.[39] Some opponents assumed that shipowners would take on foreign seamen at lower wages, others that it would encourage British sailors to look for employment outside the national fleet, but few failed to draw attention to the self-interested nature of the shipowners' campaign. 'It might be true', Captain Scovell, MP for Bath, told the House, 'that at times the English sailor would ask a higher rate of wages than a shipowner felt disposed to pay him; but that was no reason for a wholesale introduction of foreign sailors into our mercantile Navy.' He pointed out that 47,000 seamen had petitioned against the change.[40] In the Lords, Ellenborough noted that this was a step 'which would increase the profits of the shipowner by the reduction of the already small wages of the sailors'. He particularly objected to allowing foreigners to be employed on coasting vessels, as also did Hardwicke, who told his fellow peers that he had been prepared to accept the previous government's proposal but he never for a single moment contemplated that the coasting trade would be included in that provision. If the principles of free trade were to be carried out in the way proposed by this Bill, they would be compelled not only to keep a standing Navy but to educate their seamen for it.[41]

The passing of the Merchant Shipping Amendment Bill left only one last vestige of the protective system in place – the reservation of the coasting trade to British-registered vessels.[42] There was little to inhibit the government from tackling this provision. Even former supporters of maritime protection acknowledged that, once foreigners were allowed to work on coastal vessels, the traditional argument that coasting particularly deserved preferential treatment because of its role as the main training ground for British seamen was barely appropriate. Indeed, the seamen themselves argued that, in equity, they should not now be denied an opportunity to be employed on foreign-registered vessels. The only reason for retaining the national coasting trade was that other countries did so, but the Board of Trade was still hopeful of gaining access to the United States seaboard for British shipping and, against all experience, saw this final concession from Britain as likely to expedite this. In March 1854 Cardwell brought forward the Coasting Trade Bill. It attracted only brief debate and neither House divided, but with its passage into law the repeal of the Navigation Laws was complete.[43]

Although the opening of the coasting trade – the end of protection for British shipping – was not opposed by the shipping interest, this final step should not be taken as an indication that the policy of repeal was itself regarded as vindicated. The first two years following repeal were difficult for the British industry. Its immediate effect, according to W. S. Lindsay, was to create a mood of 'sullen, sulky, stubborn gloom' among shipowners, which discouraged orders for new vessels.[44] Among the yards which laid off men was that on the Clyde owned by Alexander Scott, who wrote in April 1850 of the 'ruinous effect' which repeal had had on his business.[45] But while the end of shipping protection produced a crisis of confidence among British shipowners, it had quite the opposite effect on their foreign counterparts, who responded by sending vessels into the newly opened trades in the hope of picking up cargoes. The result of this divergence of expectations was that in 1850 tonnage entries (cargo and ballast) into British ports by national vessels actually fell below the level of 1849, whereas those by foreign vessels rose. The following year saw a recovery in the number of voyages undertaken by British vessels, but the share of foreign shipping continued to grow.[46] This was the economic context which provided a stimulus to the campaign for the removal of the remaining manning restrictions, and for invoking the retaliatory provisions of the repeal legislation. Writing in 1852, Lindsay saw in the immediate aftermath of repeal a confirmation of his previous stance on the issue. The effect of abandoning so much of the old system at once, instead of proceeding in stages, had, he argued, produced a system, 'liberal in extreme to strangers and aliens' but 'oppressive in the extreme to one most important body of its own subjects'. He deplored the way the matter had been handled: 'Unfortunately the whole question was made one of party; neither the minister nor the opposition were inclined to meet each other and calmly discuss the various clauses of our then Navigation Laws.'[47]

In fact, already by this time shipowners were becoming less anxious about foreign competition and more concerned with making the most of new opportunities for profit which had begun to present themselves. Gold discoveries in California and Australia increased emigrant traffic, the need for shipping space grew, and freight rates rose.[48] Some reaction had begun to set in, when in 1854 the outbreak of war with Russia in the Crimea brought demand from the government for transports and gave a fresh boost to shipping. 'We got upon good times', was Duncan Dunbar's verdict on the war years, which produced full order books in the shipyards and for some shipowners what the 1860 Select Committee on Merchant Shipping described as 'fabulous' profits.[49] The end of hostilities in 1856 ushered in a period of depression, as peacetime levels of demand failed to provide sufficient employment for the amount of tonnage, British and foreign, now available. It was a predictable outcome, though as ever it appeared to take the shipping industry by surprise. Indeed, even without the post-war reaction, past experience of the working of the shipbuilding cycle should have suggested that some check to expansion was overdue; the war merely served to postpone and accentuate the inevitable downturn. But, anticipated or not, the depression of the later 1850s certainly demonstrated that the ending of protection had in no way diminished the predilection of the shipping interest for seeking its salvation through Parliament. The two earlier depressions resulted in the Select Committees of 1833 and 1844. This, the third major depression of the century to affect shipping, was also the subject of examination by a Select Committee. As with the two previous Select Committees, the terms of appointment of the 1860 Select Committee on Merchant

Shipping – to investigate 'burdens and restrictions' – was not quite what the shipping interest wanted. But again, as in the past, its witnesses ensured that the evidence pointed in the desired direction. 'The policy of the repeal of the Navigation Laws, and of the expediency of reconsidering that much-contested measure, had been prominently brought under notice of Your Committee', noted the Select Committee report.[50]

Ten years after abolition of the Navigation Laws, the question of maritime protection, at least as far as sections of the shipping industry were concerned, was by no means altogether settled. Part of the explanation for this was undoubtedly the desire to find remedies for the immediate crisis of oversupply of tonnage which British shipowners faced, but this re-opening of the issue was only possible because from the standpoint of the late 1850s repeal could not automatically be judged a benign or even neutral factor in the fortunes of British shipping. In December 1858 representatives of shipowners in thirty-seven seaports signed an Address to the Queen which deplored 'the ruinous state of depression into which the British shipping interest is plunged'. The Address referred to 'evils and perils anticipated from a policy which was believed by shipowners generally to be fraught with danger to the supremacy of British navigation', and asked Her Majesty to implement the retaliatory provisions of the 1849 Act on the grounds that their 'apprehensions have been in great measure justified by the result'. This 'result' was the growth in the share of British trade carried by foreign shipping.[51]

Where they were in the position to do so, foreign shipowners had responded very positively to the opportunities which Britain's new maritime policy offered. 'It will be an odd thing', the editor of the *Sydney Morning Herald* commented when news of repeal reached Australia, 'to see a French or American ship taking off your wool to the English market.'[52] But within a year or so of repeal foreign vessels became a familiar presence in trades from which they were formerly excluded. In 1850 83,000 tons of foreign-owned shipping carried cargoes from the North American colonies to Britain. Two years later such vessels already accounted for 11 per cent of all entries from this region. Norwegian owners were particularly attracted by the much enlarged scope which repeal offered to indirect traders, not only in Europe but elsewhere. In the 1840s, when limited by the Navigation Laws to carrying only national produce from home ports, although Norwegian vessels dominated the trade with Britain, their entries (cargo and ballast) into British ports averaged only 119,000 tons annually or just over 2 per cent of all entries, British and foreign. Within a few years of repeal Norwegian entries had risen to five times that tonnage. Even in 1858, a depression year, they amounted to 564,000 tons of shipping – 5 per cent of all voyages to British ports.[53]

Such increases in the amount of business being undertaken by foreign vessels were not achieved at the direct expense of British shipping, since, as Figure 1 shows, the demand for additional cargo space was sufficient to ensure that the tonnage entries of British vessels also showed an upward trend. Nevertheless, repeal was decisive in

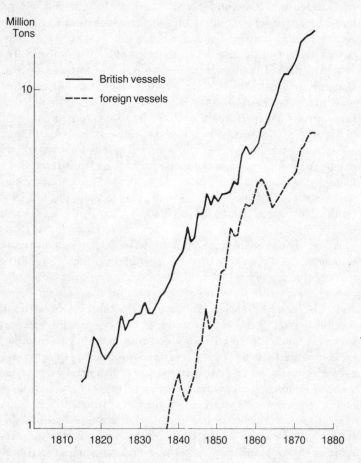

Figure 1 *Tonnage of British and foreign shipping entering United Kingdom ports 1815–75*

giving other national merchant fleets access to cargoes which would otherwise have been denied them and vessels were built to serve the new trades. 'A few years ago', the British Consul commented in 1860, 'the Norwegian flag was scarcely ever seen beyond the confines of Europe and [now] it waves in every part of the globe'.[54] Indeed, in contrast to the tendency of British historians to see the repeal of the Navigation Laws as of little practical significance, historians of the Baltic seafaring nations have long regarded this change in policy by the world's greatest trading nation as a significant economic turning point in their nineteenth-century maritime development.[55] If one of the justifications for the original introduction of Navigation Laws was the desire to stunt the growth of the Dutch merchant navy, it would seem that, by limiting the size of the international market for their services, the Laws continued in the first half of the nineteenth century to be effective in retarding the development of other nations' merchant fleets.

Table 11. *Tonnage and percentage share of British and foreign entrances into United Kingdom Ports 1845/49–1865/69 (five-yearly averages, '000 tons)*

	British		Foreign	
Years	Tons	% Share	Tons	% Share
1845/49	9,181	69.5	4,035	30.5
1850/54	10,052	60.1	6,682	39.9
1855/59	13,858	60.8	8,941	39.2
1860/64	15,546	60.3	10,250	39.7
1865/69	21,887	67.75	10,415	32.25

Source: William Page (ed.), *Commerce and Industry, Tables of Statistics for the British Empire from 1815*, London, 1919, p. 162.

Despite the fact that even before repeal foreign vessels constituted a sizeable presence on some routes, the overall impact of the opening of the British carrying trade was still marked. In 1848 foreign-owned vessels accounted for just under 29 per cent of the total tonnage entering and clearing British ports with cargo. In 1850, the first year when they were allowed access to colonial and indirect trades, their share was 33 per cent and by the late 1850s it was averaging almost 40 per cent (see Table 11) Such growing dependence on other national merchant fleets to service Britain's trade reflected the failure of British shipping to match the expansion of business. As the Select Committee on Merchant Shipping noted:

Although within the last 10 years British shipping has increased absolutely to a much greater extent than during any corresponding antecedent period, its comparative increase has not kept pace with that of the foreign shipping employed in our home trade and in that of our Colonies and possessions, and some remarkable instances are adduced of the great augmentation of foreign shipping frequenting our ports.[56]

'Home trade' in this context meant all overseas trade with Britain. The coasting trade, opened in 1854, remained very firmly the province of British shipowners. In 1857 total entries and clearances of non-national vessels with cargo totalled only 103,000 tons – a minute proportion of total domestic shipping movements.[57]

The voyages made by British vessels to and from British ports did not represent the full extent of their employment. In the same way as many of the foreign vessels trading with Britain were acting as third party carriers, British vessels also found work in indirect trades. As Derby told G. F. Young in January 1852:

We must always remember there is a large addition to our trade, which does not appear in our imports or exports, or entries inward or clearances outward, in the neutral trade which we have obtained under the reciprocity system, so far as other countries have allowed it to work.[58]

This is a useful reminder that the ending of protection meant some compensatory liberty for British vessels, though no consistent statistical series exist to enable us to measure the extent of this business, either before or after repeal. Access to indirect trades, which made 'making up' cargoes easier because of the greater variety of destinations permitted, was also reponsible for a sharp decline in British clearances in ballast, which fell by two-thirds between 1848 and 1858.[59] However, not every foreign power was keen to allow British ships unhampered access to its trade. The central objection of the shipping interest to the practical working of the repeal legislation, as expressed in the 1858 Address – that 'the universal admission of foreign ships to all the privileges of British ships has not induced the governments of many foreign states to admit British shipping to equality of privileges with their own ships' – applied particularly to indirect trade. But, as the Board of Trade argued in reply, given the countries concerned – France, Spain and Portugal – and the fact that despite discriminatory treatment British vessels were to be seen acting for them as third party traders, the amount of additional business available for transfer to the British flag was comparatively small.[60] That France, Spain and Portugal also denied British vessels access to their colonies, while their vessels freely entered British colonial ports, was another cause of complaint. With both the British and home markets open to such vessels, they were able to secure higher freights. As one shipowner told the 1860 Select Committee: 'It is very galling, indeed, and is enough to break one's heart, to see my ship lying in Calcutta, getting 15s a ton, and a French ship lying alongside, getting 60s, 70s and 80s a ton'.[61] But it was the continued refusal of the United States of America to offer any compensation for the opening of Britain's trade with her overseas possessions that particularly rankled. None of the shipowners who gave evidence to the 1860 Select Committee argued for a return to the Navigation Laws in their entirety, but several were prepared to urge on government the exclusion of United States vessels from colonial carriage.[62] However, given colonial sensitivities, to revert to the pre-1850 situation was clearly impractical and the idea received little support in political circles. In the event, it was not any action on the part of the British but rather the Civil War which dealt the looked-for blow to American competition.[63]

In June 1862 the statistician John Glover reviewed the tonnage statistics of ten years following repeal for the benefit of a meeting of the Royal Statistical Society. 'Now that the question has at large emerged from the stormy atmosphere of prediction into the calmer region of fact', he told his listeners, it was possible to evaluate a decade which was 'perhaps the most remarkable in the trading history of any country.' However, as Glover himself conceded, 'the calmer region of fact' did not exclude the possibility of continued disagreement about the consequences of repeal:

In the greatly increased tonnage supply the advocates of the measure find their justification, seeing how largely it was required by the trade of the decade; while on the other hand the opponents find their justification in the unprecedented increase of foreign tonnage in the trade of the United Kingdom.[64]

Certainly, neither side in the debates which preceded repeal could be said to have been proved right by what had happened in the ten years under the new policy. Far from being ruined, the British shipowner had enjoyed considerable prosperity for much of this period, but there was nothing to suggest that this prosperity was in any way connected with the abolition of the Navigation Laws and, significantly, free traders did not claim that it was. For them, the justification of freer navigation was that it had allowed the supply of shipping more readily to keep pace with demand. But had restrictions remained, it could not be assumed that British shipowners would have been unable to respond by investing in even more tonnage and redirecting their efforts from third party to national carriage. The protectionist prediction that foreign shipping would take a greater share of business had proved correct, but its corollary – that this would mean a smaller British merchant fleet – had not. The nation's registered tonnage amounted to 4.6 million tons in 1860, almost a third more than in 1850. As far as manning was concerned, again the direst prophesies had proved unfounded. Encouraged by circumstances associated with the Crimean War the number of foreign seamen serving on British ships had jumped spectacularly from 7,321 men in 1853 to 13,200 the following year – almost 8 per cent of the manpower of the merchant fleet. But thereafter the proportion remained fairly stable for the rest of the decade.[65]

As far as British shipbuilding was concerned repeal had only a limited effect. Ending the compulsion on British shipowners to buy British-built vessels did not result in any significant loss of business for the shipyards. Between 1855 and 1859 111,000 tons of foreign-built vessels came on to the British register, as against 1.2 million tons built in Britain. British yards, in particular those specialising in steam shipping, also produced ships for foreign owners. In 1859 30,000 tons of shipping was sold overseas, although not all of this would have been new tonnage.[66] It can safely be concluded that British shipbuilding lost nothing from the ending of its protected status. Rather it gained export markets, although not to the fullest extent possible because of the refusal of some countries, including the United States of America, to admit foreign-built vessels to national registry. What is less clear is how far the increasing competition faced by British shipowners after 1850 was responsible for improvements in the design of British-built vessels.

Contemporaries judged that mid-century investment by foreign owners in ships of above-average tonnage for use in former British colonial trades was imitated by some British shipowners, but they attributed improvements in hull design to the new, 'Moorsom', system of tonnage measurement introduced in 1855.[67] This reform, which originated in a tonnage commission of 1849, can itself be traced to the ending of protection since its implementation was particularly urged on the Board of Trade by the influential shipbuilder Money Wigram, who argued that some change was essential if British yards were to compete.[68] Nevertheless, while the development of sailing ships such as those capable of beating American clippers on the Foochow–London passage necessarily owed everything to repeal (without this there would have been no United States presence in the trade), for most shipowners the stimulus to investment in new vessels was not the fear of losing an existing trade to foreign rivals, or the expensive joy of a contest, but the guarantee of a good return which buoyant trade offered between 1852 and 1856. It was this, not any stimulus from repeal (apart from that possibly offered by any improved access to indirect trades) which in the words of the 1860 Select Committee report 'imparted a new excitement to shipping enterprise', and encouraged 'the construction of larger ships of a greatly improved character'.[69]

As far as steam shipping was concerned, the fact that by 1870 investment in the newer technology enabled the British merchant fleet to regain its pre-repeal share of British trade has sometimes led to the erroneous impression that this was a conscious response to the new policy. There is nothing to connect the pace of adoption of steam in the 1850s with the ending of protection. The transition to steam power depended, as in the past, largely on progress in achieving greater fuel economy and the availability of appropriate trades. With steam-shipping in 1860 less than 10 per cent of total British registered tonnage, the Age of Steam still lay some years in the future.[70]

This scrutiny of shipping in the 1850s shows that controversy over ending maritime protection did not cease in 1849. The question remains as to the significance of that decision. The longer perspective allowed to the historian may promise a firmer verdict than that possible for contemporaries even after ten years of the new system, but it is not one easily couched in such terms as the 'success' or 'failure' of free trade or protectionism.[71] One reason for this is that aspects of the impact of protection on the performance of the British shipping industry in the early nineteenth century remain elusive, though perhaps susceptible of a more quantitative methodology than that employed here. Because of the competition from his fellow nationals, no individual British shipowner was a monopolist as the result of the Navigation Laws, but this is not to say that Britain as an economy did not enjoy a monopoly in the supply of shipping services to some parts of the world. It clearly did. But putting a value on this presents problems both of a practical and conceptual nature. Contrasting freight rates before and after repeal would permit an evaluation of the additional earnings accruing to British shipowners as a result of protection, as also of the additional costs imposed on British commerce by the regulations which confined carriage in some trades to the national fleet. However, given the variety of short-term upward influences on freight rates in the early 1850s, it is difficult to distinguish any countervailing downward pressure for which the opening of trades to foreign vessels might have been responsible. But in any case the history of the Navigation Laws, as also recent work on the theory of flag preference, should warn of the danger of evaluating maritime policy in narrow sectoral terms.[72] In 1860 it was by no means certain that the share of British shipping in national carriage might not continue to fall, but whether this outcome could be regarded as a damaging consequence of repeal depended on the value placed on maintaining a national fleet (with consequent savings to the balance of payments), as against the benefit to commerce from a free market in shipping services. In the first half of the nineteenth century the criteria of success in protective policy were overtly non-economic – the maintenance of a sufficiently large merchant marine to provide a source of manpower for the navy.

No attention has been paid to developments after 1860, when 'British shipping got its second wind'.[73] Aided by increased investment in steam shipping, by the end of this period the national fleet had regained the share of British trade it had had before repeal. However, while it is fair to conclude that this shows that free competition and maritime dominance were not incompatible, it should not be taken as evidence that protection for shipping should be equated with failure, or that repeal was a precondition for Britain's later maritime success. The ending of protection for British shipping, by encouraging the development of other national fleets, made the transfer to steam *necessary* if Britain was to hold its own; other factors made it *possible*.

Notes

1 PRO, BT 1/474/2124.
2 *Ibid.*, 12 October 1849.
3 PRO, FO 73/233, 8 January 1849.
4 See PRO, BT 3/38, 5/497; FO 5/511-2, 97/28. For US maritime policy see John G. B. Hutchins, *The American Maritime Industries and Public Policy, 1789–1914*, Cambridge, Mass., 1941.
5 *Report from the Select Committee appointed to inquire into the State of Merchant Shipping*, PP 1860 XIII, p. vi.
6 16 & 17 Vict. c. 107, s. 11.
7 *S. C. Merchant Shipping*, PP 1860 XIII, p. xi.

8 PRO, BT 3/41, 9 November 1850.
9 PRO, BT 1/477/901/50, 20–22 March 1850.
10 PRO, BT 3/38, 2 August 1849.
11 SUL, Broadlands Papers, GC/LA/1-31/17.
12 13 & 14 Vict. c. 93; Roger Prouty, *The Transformation of the Board of Trade 1830–1855: a Study of Adminstrative Reorganisation in the Heyday of Laissez Faire*, London, 1957, pp. 87–98.
13 17 & 18 Vict. c. 104.
14 *Report from the Select Committee on the Causes of Shipwrecks*, PP 1836 (567) XVII, p. 373; *Papers relating to the Commercial Marine*, PP 1847–48 [93] LIX, p. 141.
15 SUL, Wellington Papers, 2/162/99.
16 PD, Third Series, CXII, 20 June 1850, c. 108–14.
17 PD, Third Series, CXVII, 17 June 1851, c. 847–57. On the politics of the early 1850s, see Stewart, *Politics of Protection*; Jones, *Derby*; J. B. Conacher, *The Aberdeen Coalition 1852–1855: a Study in Mid-Nineteenth-Century Party Politics*, Cambridge, 1968.
18 Stanley Diaries, p. 13; Robert Blake, *Disraeli*, London, 1966, pp. 289–90.
19 *Shipping Gazette*, 1 May 1849. See Stewart, Policy of Protection, pp. 148–50.
20 KAO, Stanhope Papers, U1590 C201/2, Stanhope to Foskett, 11 May 1849.
21 Moneypenny and Buckle, *Disraeli*, III, p. 231; Hughenden Papers (Microfilm), BIII/55, Stanley to Disraeli, 13 November 1849.
22 *Stanley Diaries*, p. 52.
23 Young, *Speeches*, London, 1851, p. 35.
24 Moneypenny and Buckle, *Disraeli*, II, p. 1030.
25 KAO, Stanhope Papers, U1590 C201/1, Young to Stanhope 28 May 1849, 6 June 1849.
26 *Ibid.*, Pike to Stanhope, 10 January 1850; *Illustrated London*, News 12 January 1850.
27 See John Belchem, 'Chartism and the trades 1848–1850', *English Historical Review*, XCVII, 1983, pp. 558–87.
28 KAO, Stanhope Papers, U1590 C122, Young to Stanhope, 7 May 1852; Stanhope to Young, 8 May 1852, 12 May 1852; Maccoby, *Radicalism*, pp. 302–3.
29 Stewart, *Policy of Protection*, p. 192.
30 GSS, Minutes, V, 22 January 1850.
31 KAO, Stanhope Papers, C198/9–11.
32 *Return of Memorials to the Committee of the Privy Council against the operation of the Mercantile Marine Act*, PP 1851 (334) LII, p. 307.
33 PRO, HO 45.
34 Jon Press, 'Wages in the mercantile marine 1815–1854', *Journal of Transport History*, 3rd ser., 2, 1981, pp. 38–9. There was a precedent for lifting manning restrictions in response to labour unrest. In response to disturbances in 1824–25, the 1825 Ships Registry Bill suspended the Navigation Laws for two years to allow employment of foreigners. See Rowe, 'North east coast seamen', p. 81, n. 2.

35 Bartlett, *Great Britain and Sea Power*, pp. 307–309.

36 *Report from the Admiralty Manning Committee*, PP 1852–3 (LX).

37 PD. Third Series, CXXIII, 3 December 1852, c. 845–6.

38 PD, Third Series, CXXIX, 12 July 1853, c. 111, c. 121–2, c. 107. For a hostile protectionist analysis of Disraeli's shipping proposals see 'The Budget', *Quarterly Review*, XCII, 1853, pp. 241–70.

39 *Ibid.*, CXXVIII, 5 July 1853, c. 1227–9.

40 *Ibid.*, CXXIX, 12 August 1853, c. 1671–2.

41 PD, Third Series, CXXIX, 12 July 1853, c. 104.

42 16 & 17 Vict. c. 131.

43 17 & 18 Vict. c. 5; PD. Third Series, CXXXI, c. 462–6, c. 850–5.

44 NMM, Lindsay Papers, Journal, p. 109.

45 GUA, Scott Papers, GD 319 11/I/18, Scott to Beattie, 13 April 1850.

46 Page, *Commerce and Industry*, p. 157.

47 W. S. Lindsay, *Our Navigation and Commercial Marine Laws Considered with a view to their general revision and consolidation, also an inquiry into the principal maritime insitutions*, London, 1852, pp. 9, 16.

48 Lindsay, *History of Merchant Shipping*, III, pp. 93–109.

49 *S. C. Merchant Shipping*, PP 1860 XIII, Q. 418; p. ix.

50 The General Shipowners' Society regarded W. S. Lindsay, the Select Committee's proposer and Chairman, as hostile to their interests. Certainly he did not accept that protection was the solution to its difficulties. See GSS, *Minutes*, V, 10 February 1859; *S. C. Merchant Shipping*, PP 1860 XIII, p. ix.; W. S. Lindsay, *Our Merchant Shipping: its Present State Considered*, London, 1860.

51 *An Address to the Queen from the Owners of British Ships and others interested in the Prosperity of British Navigation and of the subsequent correspondence in reference thereto*, PP 1859, XXV.

52 *Sydney Morning Herald*, 10 September 1849.

53 *Accounts of Navigation*; PRO, FO 73/251.

54 *S. C. Merchant Shipping*, PP 1860 XIII, Q. 3309.

55 See, for example, Simon Liebermann, *The Industrialisation of Norway 1800–1920*, Oslo, 1970, pp. 116–17; Helge W. Nordvik, 'The shipping industries of the Scandinavian countries, 1850–1914', in Fischer and Panting (eds), *North Atlantic Fleets*, pp. 120–1.

56 *S. C. Merchant Shipping*, PP 1860 XIII, p. ix.

57 *Address*, 1859 XXV, p. 9.

58 BL, Young Papers, Add. MS. 46712, 13 January 1852.

59 Imlah, *Pax Britannica*, p. 172.

60 *Address*, PP 1859, XXV, p. 7.

61 *S. C. Merchant Shipping*, PP 1860 XIII, Q. 371.

62 *Ibid.*, Q. 1858, Q. 1900; Report, p. ix.

63 Hutchins, *American Maritime Industries*, pp. 304–14.

64 John Glover, 'On the statistics of the tonnage during the first decade under the navigation law of 1846', *Journal of the Statistical Society*, XXVI, 1863, p. 2. Glover's understanding of the statistics was better than his understanding of the 1849 Act, which he described as 'the law which repealed sundry Customs' regulations'.

65 Glover, 'Statistics', pp. 6, 9. He points out that the new mode of tonnage measurement introduced in 1855 has the effect of understating the increase between 1850 and 1860; *Statistical Tables and Charts Relating to British and Foreign Trade and Industry 1854–1908*, PP 1909 [4854], p. 695.

66 *Ibid.*

67 See Graham, 'Sailing ship', pp. 78–9.

68 PRO, BT 167/24.

69 *S. C. Merchant Shipping*, PP 1860 XIII, p. viii.

70 See Robin Craig, *The Ship: Steam Tramps and Cargo Liners 1850–1950*, London, 1980; Graham, 'Sailing ship'; Harley 'Shift from sailing ships'.

71 But see Imlah, *Pax Britannica*, pp. 171–2.

72 See, for example, the discussion by A. H. Vanags, 'Flag discrimination: an economic analysis', *Maritime Studies and Management*, 1983. For an overview of recent work, see Ernst G. Frankel, *The World Shipping Industry*, London, 1987, pp. 46–8.

73 Imlah, *Pax Britannica*, p. 173. See Sarah Palmer, 'The British shipping industry 1850–1914', in Fischer and Panting (eds), *North Atlantic Fleets*, pp. 87–114.

Bibliography

This bibliography contains only those sources cited in footnotes.

Manuscript sources

Broadland Papers, Southampton University Library
Colyer Fergusson Papers, Kent Archives Office
Derby Papers, Liverpool City Libraries
Gladstone Papers, British Library
Graham Papers, Microfilm, Institute of Historical Research
Granville Papers, Public Record Office
Hughenden Papers, Microfilm, London School of Economics and Political Science
Huskisson Papers, British Library
Lindsay Papers, National Maritime Museum
General Shipowners' Society Records, London General Shipowners' Society
Manchester Chamber of Commerce Records, Manchester Chamber of Commerce
Peel Papers, British Library
Russell Papers, Public Record Office
Scott Papers, Glasgow University Archives
Stanhope Papers, Kent Archives Office
Wilson Papers, Manchester Record Office
Wellington Papers, Southampton University Library
Young Papers, British Library

Official publications

Divisions of the House of Commons
Hansards Parliamentary Debates
Public General Statutes

Parliamentary Papers: Reports of Select Committees

Report from the Select Committee on the Means of Improving and Maintaining the Foreign Trade of the Country, 1820 (300) II, p. 365.

First Report from the Select Committee of the House of Lords on the Means of Extending and Securing Foreign Trade (Timber Trade), PP 1820 (488) III, p. 381.

Report from the Select Committee of the House of Lords on the State of the Coal Trade of the United Kingdom, 1830 (653) VIII, p. 1.

Report from the Select Committee on the present state of Manufactures, Commerce and Shipping in the United Kingdom, 1833 (690) VI, p. 1.

Report from the Select Committee on the Causes of Shipwrecks, PP 1836 (567) XVII, p. 373.

Report from the Select Committee appointed to inquire into the state and condition of the Commercial Marine of the Country, and to take into consideration and report on the best mode of encouraging and extending the employment of British Shipping, 1844 (545) VIII, p. 1.

Report from the Select Committee on the Dartmouth Election Petition, PP 1845 (164) XII, p. 39.

Reports from the Select Committee of the House of Commons to inquire into the Operation and Policy of the Navigation Laws, 1847 (232) (246) (392) (556) (678) X, p. 1.

Reports from the Select Committee of the House of Lords on the Policy and Operation of the Navigation Laws, 1847–48 (340) (431) (754) XX Pt. II, p. 1.

Reports of the Select Committee of the House of Commons on Public Petitions, 1847–48, 1849, Unpublished, House of Lords Record Office.

Report from the Select Committee on the Plymouth Election Petitions, 1852–53 (497) XVIII, pp. 9, 67.

Report from the Select Committee appointed to inquire into the State of Merchant Shipping, PP 1860 (530) XIII, p. 1.

Parliamentary Papers: Accounts and Returns

Annual Statements of Navigation

Correspondence relative to Petitions of the Ship Owners of London, PP 1826–27 (28) XVIII, p. 446.

Return of all Tolls, Dues, Fees and other charges . . ., PP 1844 (366) XLV, p. 317.

Account of the Sums paid out of the Consolidated Duties of Customs, PP 1844 (551) XLV, p. 367.

Returns of the number and tonnage of vessels that entered and cleared at each of the ports of each colony, coastwise, to and from the United Kingdom and to and from foreign ports December 1842–December 1843, PP 1844 (36) XLV, p. 337.

Letter from the Secretary of the North American Colonial Association and Reply from the Chairman of the General Shipowners' Society, PP 1846 (83) (97) XLV, pp. 347, 351.

Return of the Number of Colonial Built Ships registered at each port of the United Kingdom, PP 1847 (309) LX, p. 309.

Return and Further Return of the Number of Foreign Ships admitted into the United Kingdom under suspension of the Navigation Laws to June 1847, PP 1847 (557) (670) LX, pp. 333, 335.

Report of an Admiralty Committee to Inquire into the Supply of Seamen for the Merchant Service, PP. 1847–48, XLI (233), p. 439.

Papers relating to the Commercial Marine, PP 1847–48 [913] LIX, p. 141.

Return and further return of Articles Seized, Ships Detained and Penalties Imposed in the United Kingdom for contravention of the Navigation Laws 1841–1846, PP 1847 (286) LX, p. 327.

Correspondence with the Colonies relative to the proposed relaxation of the Navigation Laws, PP 1849 [1016] [1032] [1035], pp. 149, 163, 169.

Correspondence with Foreign States relative to the proposed relaxation of the Navigation Laws, PP 1849 [1029] [1030] [1038] [1041] [1048], LI, pp. 179, 223, 243, 247, 263.

Reply of the United States Government respecting the proposed relaxation of the British Navigation Laws, PP 1849 [1036] LI, p. 235.

Return of Memorials to the Committee of the Privy Council against the operation of the Mercantile Marine Act, PP 1851 (334) LII, p. 307

Accounts Relating to Shipping, PP 1852 (376) XLIX, p. 17.

Correspondence between the Board of Treasury and the Board of Admiralty on the Subject of the Manning of the Royal Navy, together with copies of a Report of a Committee of Naval Officers, PP 1852–53 [1628], p. 11.

Extracts of Report and Appendix of Committee of 1852 on Manning the Navy, PP 1859 Session 2, (45) XVII Pt. II, p. 237.

Correspondence on an Address to the Queen from the Owners of British Ships and others interested in the Prosperity of British Navigation, PP 1859 Session I, [2494] XXV, p. 407.

Supplementary Correspondence between the General Shipowners' Society and the Secretary of State for the Home Department on the Address, PP 1859 Session 2 (86) XXVII, p. 549.

Return of the Number of Apprentices 1835–1860, PP 1861 (849) LVIII, p. 23.

Return of Compensation for Differential Dues on Foreign Ships under Reciprocity Treaties 1820–1860, PP 1861 (123), LVIII, p. 71.

Comparative Trade Statistics, PP 1903 [C. 176] LXVII, p. 253.

Statistical Tables and Charts Relating to British and Foreign Trade and Industry 1854–1908, PP 1909 [4854], p. 695.

Works of reference

Bean, W. W., *Parliamentary Representation of the Six Northern Counties of England*, Hull, 1890.

Boase, Frederic, *Modern English Biography*, 1892–1921, reprinted 1965.

Dictionary of National Biography, Oxford, 1885–1900.

Dictionary of American Biography, New York, 1928–36.

Dod, Charles R., *Electoral Facts from 1832–1853, Impartially Stated*, 2nd edition 1852, reprinted with an introduction by H. J. Hanham, Brighton, 1972.

Mitchell, B. R., *British Historical Statistics*, Cambridge, 1988.

Page, William (ed.), *Commerce and Industry: Tables of Statistics for the British Empire from 1815*, London, 1919.

Newspapers and periodicals

Liverpool Times
North British Railway and Shipping Journal
Newcastle Guardian
Shipping Gazette
Sunderland and Durham County Herald
Hull Advertiser
Economist
The Times

Printed primary sources

Anon., *Annals of Lloyd's Register: Being a Sketch of the Origin, Constitution and Progress of Lloyd's Register of British and Foreign Shipping*, London, 1884.

Anon., 'Mr Huskisson's speech on the shipping interest', *Blackwood's Edinburgh Magazine*, XXII, July 1827.

Anon., 'The Budget', *Quarterly Review*, XCII, 1953.

A. Barrister, *Mr Ricardo's Anatomy of the Navigation Laws Dissected*, London, 1848.

Allen, J., *The Navigation Laws of Great Britain, Historically and Practically Considered*, London, 1848.

Bright, John and Thorold Rogers, J. E. (eds), *Speeches on Questions of Public Policy by Richard Cobden M. P.*, I, London, 1870.

Bristol Poll Book, Bristol, 1847.

Browne, Houston, *The Navigation Laws – their History and Operation*, London, 1847.

Brooke, John and Sorensen, Mary (eds), *The Prime Minister's Papers: W. E. Gladstone, I Autobiographica*, London, 1971.

Broughton, Lord (John Cam Hobhouse), *Recollections of a Long Life, VI, 1841–52*, London, 1911.

Colchester, Admiral Charles Lord, *Memoranda of My Life from 1798 to 1859 Inclusive*, London, 1869.

Corporation of the City of London, *Report of an Inquiry into the Port of London*, London, 1833.

Dibs, J., *The Navigation Laws: Three Letters to Lord John Russell M. P. showing the Justice, Necessity and Economy of Protection to British Shipping*, London, 1849

Dunn, James, *A View of the Navigation Laws*, Sunderland, 1847.

Foot, M. R. D. and Matthew, H. C. G. (eds), *The Gladstone Diaries III, 1840–47*, Oxford, 1974.

Glover, John, 'On the statistics of the tonnage during the first decade under the Navigation Law of 1846', *Journal of the Statistical Society*, XXVI, 1863.

Gooch, G. P. (ed.), *The Later Correspondence of Lord John Russell 1840 –1878*, 2 vols, London, 1925.

Hardcastle, Hon. Mrs (ed.), *Life of John, Lord Campbell, Lord Chancellor of Great Britain*, II, London, 1881.

Jennings, L. J. (ed.), *The Croker Papers*, 3 vols, London, 1884.

Levenson Gower, F., *Bygone Years: Recollections*, London, 1905.

Lindsay, W. S., *Letters on the Navigation Laws addressed to Lord John Russell containing a review of the measures of Mr Labouchere*, London, 1849.

Lindsay, W. S., *Our Merchant Shipping: its Present State Considered*, London, 1860.

Lindsay, W. S., *History of Merchant Shipping and Ancient Commerce in Four Volumes*, London, 1876.

Malmesbury, Earl of, *Memoirs of an Ex-Minister*, 2 vols, London, 1884.

Manchester Chamber of Commerce, *Report of the Directors . . . on the Injurious Effects of Restrictions on Trade*, Manchester, 1841.

Mather, James, *An Address to the Electors of the Seaports of the United Kingdom on the Navigation Laws: and their Duties at this Critical Juncture*, South Shields, 1847.

McCulloch, J. R., 'Navigation Laws', *Edinburgh Review*, XXXVIII, 1823.

McCulloch, J. R., 'The complaints of the shipowners', *Edinburgh Review*, XC, 1827.

McCulloch, J. R., *A Dictionary of Commerce*, London, 1844 edition.

Mill, John Stuart, *Principles of Political Economy with some of their Applications for Social Philosophy. Collected Works of J. S. Mill*, edited by E. C. G. Gregory, Toronto, 1965.

Moore, John B. (ed.), *The Works of James Buchanan*, VII, Philadelphia, 1909.

Morley, John, *The Life of Cobden*, 2 vols, London, 1881.

Mosse, R. B., *The Parliamentary Guide: a Concise History of the Members of Both Houses of Parliament, their Connexions, Pursuits etc.*, London, 1836.

Political Economy Club, *Minutes of Proceedings 1899–1920. Roll of Members and Questions Discussed 1821–1920 with documents bearing on the History of the Club*, VI, London, 1921.

Revans, J., *England's Navigation Laws, No Protection to Shipping*, London, 1849.

Ricardo, David, *The Works and Correspondence of David Ricardo*, IX, edited by Piero Sraffa, with the collaboration of M. H. Dobb, Cambridge, 1965.

Ricardo, J. Lewis, *Anatomy of the Navigation Laws*, London, 1847.

Senior, Nassau, 'Free trade and retaliation', *Edinburgh Review*, LXXVIII, 1843.

Sheahan, James, *History of Hull*, Hull, 1866.

Smith, Adam, *An Inquiry into the Nature and Causes of the Wealth of Nations*, edited by R. H. Campbell and A. S. Skinner, 2 vols, Oxford, 1976.

Strachey, L. and Fulford, R., *The Greville Memoirs*, VI, London, 1938.

Tooke, Thomas, *Free Trade: Some Account of the Free Trade Movement as it Originated with the Petition of the Merchants of London*, London, 1853.

Vincent, J. R., *Disraeli, Derby and the Conservative Party: The Political Journals of Lord Stanley 1849–1869*, Hassocks, 1978.

Walpole, Spencer, *The Life of Lord John Russell*, 2 vols, London, 1891.

Young, G. F., *Letters on the Navigation Laws Originally Published in the Standard Newspaper*, London, 1848.

Young, G. F. *Speeches*, London, 1851.

Published secondary sources

Albion, R. G., *Forests and Seapower*, Harvard, 1926

Alderman, Geoffrey, *The Railway Interest*, Leicester, 1973.

Allison, K. J. (ed.), *A History of the County of Yorkshire, East Riding: I, The City of Kingston-upon-Hull, Victoria History of the Counties of England*, Oxford, 1969.

Armstrong, J., 'Coastal shipping' in Freeman, Michael J. and Aldcroft, Derek H. (eds), *Transport in Victorian Britain*, Manchester, 1988.

Bagwell, P., 'The Post Office Steam Packets 1821–1836 and the development of shipping on the Irish Sea', *Maritime History*, I, 1971.

Bartlett, C. J., *Great Britain and Sea Power 1815–1853*, Oxford, 1963.

Belchem, John, 'Chartism and the trades 1848–1850', *English Historical Review*, XCVII, 1983.

Blake, Robert, *Disraeli*, London, 1966.

Blaug, Mark, *Ricardian Economics: a Historical Study*, New Haven, Conn., 1958.

Brady, Alexander, *William Huskisson and Liberal Reform: an Essay on the Changes in Economic Policy in the Twenties of the Nineteenth Century*, London, 1928.

Brock, Michael, *The Great Reform Act*, London, 1973.

Bromley, J. S. (ed.), *The Manning of the Royal Navy: Selected Public Pamphlets 1693–1873*, Navy Records Society, London, 1974.

Brown, Lucy, *The Board of Trade and the Free Trade Movement 1830–1842*, Oxford, 1958.

Burton, V. C., 'Counting seafarers: the published records of the registry of merchant seamen', *Mariner's Mirror*, 71, 1985.

Burton, V. C., 'Apprenticeship regulation and maritime labour in the nineteenth century merchant marine', *International Journal of Maritime History*, I, 1989.

Cain, P. J. and Hopkins, A. G., 'The political economy of British expansion overseas, 1750–1914', *Economic History Review*, 2nd Ser., XXXIII, 1980.

Chamberlain, Muriel E., *Lord Aberdeen: a Political Biography*, London, 1983.

Checkland, S. G., *The Gladstones: a Family Biography 1764–1851*, Cambridge, 1971.

Clapham, J. H., 'The last years of the Navigation Acts', *English Historical Review*, XXV, 1910, reprinted in Carus-Wilson, E. M., *Essays in Economic History*, III, London, 1962.

Conacher, J. B., *The Peelites and the Party System 1846–52*, Newton Abbot, 1972.

Conacher, J. B., *The Aberdeen Coalition 1852–1855: a Study in Mid-Nineteenth-Century Party Politics*, Cambridge, 1968.

Cookson, J. E., *Lord Liverpool's Administration: the Crucial Years 1815–1822*, Edinburgh, 1975.

Cottrell, P. L., 'The steamship on the Mersey 1815–1880: investment and ownership', in Cottrell, P. L. and Aldcroft, D. H. (eds), *Shipping, Trade and Commerce: Essays in Memory of Ralph Davis*, Leicester, 1981.

Craig, R. S., 'British shipping and British North American shipbuilding', in Fisher, H. E. S. (ed.), *The South West and the Sea, Exeter Papers in Economic History*, 1, Exeter, 1968.

Craig, R. S., 'The ports and shipping, c.1750–1914', in John, Arthur and Williams, G. (eds.), *Glamorgan County History, V: Industrial Glamorgan 1700–1970*, Cardiff, 1980.

Craig, R. S., 'Capital formation in shipping', in Higgins, J. P. P. and Pollard, Sidney (eds), *Aspects of Capital Investment in Great Britain 1750–1850: a Preliminary Survey*, London, 1971.

Craig, Robin, *The Ship: Steam Tramps and Cargo Liners 1850–1950*, London, 1980.

Davies, P. N., 'The development of the liner trades', in Matthews, Keith and Panting, Gerald, *Ships and Shipbuilding in the North Atlantic Region*, St John's, Newfoundland, 1978.

Davis, Ralph, 'Maritime history: progress and problems', in Marriner, S. (ed.), *Business and Businessmen*, Liverpool, 1978.

Edsall, N. C., *Richard Cobden – Independent Political Radical*, Cambridge, Mass., 1986.

Feinstein, C. H., 'Capital formation in Great Britain', in Mathias, P. and Postan, M. M. (eds), *Cambridge Economic History of Europe*, VII, Part I, Cambridge, 1977.

Fetter, Frank Whitson, *The Economist in Parliament: 1780–1868*, Durham, NC, 1980.

Forster, Ben, *A Conjunction of Interests: Business, Politics and the Tariffs 1825–1879*, Toronto, 1986.

Foster, John, *Class Struggle and the Industrial Revolution: Early Industrial Capitalism in Three English Towns*, London, 1974.

Frankel, Ernst G., *The World Shipping Industry*, London, 1987.

Fraser, Derek, *Urban Politics in Victorian England: the Structure of Politics in Victorian Cities*, Leicester, 1976.

Gash, Norman, *Lord Liverpool: the Life and Political Career of Robert Banks Jenkinson, Second Earl of Liverpool*, London, 1984.

Gomes, Leonard, *Foreign Trade and the National Economy: Mercantilist and Classical Perspectives*, London, 1987.

Gordon, Barry, *Political Economy in Parliament 1819–23*, London, 1976.

Gordon, Barry, *Economic Doctrine and Tory Liberalism 1824–30*, London, 1979.

Graham, Gerald S., 'The ascendancy of the sailing ship 1855–1885', *Economic History Review*, 2nd ser., IX, 1956.

Grampp, W. D., *The Manchester School of Economics*, Stamford, 1960.

Greenhill, Basil, *The Ship: the Life and Death of the Merchant Sailing Ship 1815–1965*, London, 1980.

Hendlin, Lilian, *George Bancroft: the Intellectual as Democrat*, New York, 1984.

Harcourt, Freda, 'British oceanic mail contracts in the age of steam 1838–1914', *Journal of Transport History*, 3rd ser., IX, 1988.

Harley, Charles K., 'The shift from sailing ships to steamships 1850–1890', in McCloskey, Donald N. (ed.), *Essays on a Mature Economy: Britain after 1840*, Harvard, 1971.

Harper, Lawrence A., *The English Navigation Laws: a Seventeenth-Century Experiment in Social Engineering*, New York, 1939.

Harris, Leonard, *London General Shipowners' Society, 1811–1961*, London, 1961.

Hausman, William J., 'The English coastal coal trade, 1691–1910: how rapid was productivity growth ?', *Economic History Review*, 2nd ser., XL, 1987.

Hilton, R., *Corn Cash and Commerce: the Economic Policies of the Tory Governments 1815–1830*, Oxford, 1977.

Hollander, Samuel, *The Economics of Adam Smith*, London, 1973.

Hollis, Patricia, *Pressure from Without in Early Victorian England*, London, 1974.

Hutchins, John G. B., *The American Maritime Industries and Public Policy, 1789–1914*, Cambridge, Mass., 1941.

Hutchison, I. C. G., *A Political History of Scotland 1832–1924: Parties, Elections and Issues*, Edinburgh, 1986.

Hyde, F. E., *Mr Gladstone at the Board of Trade*, London, 1934.

Imlah, Albert H., *Economic Elements in the Pax Britannica*, Cambridge, Mass., 1958.

Jackson, Gordon, *The British Whaling Trade*, London, 1978.

Jackson, Gordon, 'The ports' and 'The shipping industry', in Freeman, Michael J. and Aldcroft, Derek H., *Transport in Victorian Britain*, Manchester, 1988.

Jarvis, R. C., 'Fractional shareholding in British merchant shipping', *Mariner's Mirror*, XVL, 1959.

Jones, Stephanie, 'Shipowning in Boston, Lincs.', *Mariner's Mirror*, LXV, 1979.

Jones, Stephen, 'Community and organisation: early seamen's trade unionism on the north east coast, 1764–1844', *Maritime History*, III, 1973.

Jones, William Devereux and Erickson, Arvel B., *The Peelites*, Ohio, 1972.

Jones, William Devereux, *Lord Derby and Victorian Conservatism*, Oxford, 1956.

Lee, C. H., 'Some aspects of the coastal shipping trade: the Aberdeen Steam Navigation Company, 1835–1880', *Journal of Transport History*, new ser., VIII, 1975.

Lee, C. H., *British Regional Employment Statistics*, Cambridge, 1979.

Liebermann, Simon, *The Industrialisation of Norway 1800–1920*, Oslo, 1970.

Lower, Arthur R. M., *Great Britain's Woodyard: British America and the Timber Trade, 1763–1867*, Toronto, 1973.

Maccoby, S., *English Radicalism 1832–1852*, London, 1934.

Matthews, R. C. O., *A Study in Trade Cycle History*, Cambridge, 1954.

McCord, N. and Carrick, A. E., 'Northumberland in the General Election of 1852', *Northern History*, I, 1966.

McCord, N., 'Gateshead politics in the age of reform', *Northern History*, IV, 1969.

McCord, N., *The Anti-Corn Law League, 1838–1846*, London, 1975.

McGowan, Alan, *The Ship: the Century Before Steam: the Development of the Sailing Ship 1700–1820*, 1980.

Moneypenny, W. F. and Buckle, G. E., *The Life of Benjamin Disraeli, Earl of Beaconsfield*, 2 vols, London, 1929.

Moore, D. C., 'The other face of reform', *Victorian Studies*, V, 1961–62.

Moore, D. C., *The Politics of Deference*, London, 1976.

Morrell, W. P., *British Colonial Policy in the Age of Peel and Russell*, Oxford, 1930.

Neal, F., 'Liverpool shipping in the early nineteenth century', in Harris, J. R. (ed.), *Liverpool and Merseyside: Essays in the Economic and Social History of the Port and its Hinterland*, Manchester, 1969.

Nordvik, Helge W., 'The shipping industries of the Scandinavian countries, 1850–1914', in Fischer, Lewis R. and Panting, Gerald E. (eds), *Change and Adaptation in Maritime History: the North Atlantic Fleets in the Nineteenth Century*, St John's, Newfoundland, 1984.

Nossiter, T. J., *Influence, Opinion and Political Idioms in Reformed England: Case Studies from the North East 1832–1874*, Brighton, 1975.

O' Brien, D. P., *James Ramsay McCulloch: a Study in Classical Economics*, London, 1970.

O'Neil, C. F., 'The contest for dominion: political conflict and the decline of the Lowther interest in Whitehaven, 1820–1900', *Northern History*, XVII, 1981.

Palmer, Sarah, 'Investors in London shipping 1820–1850', *Maritime History*, II, 1972.

Palmer, Sarah, 'Experiment, experience and economics: some factors in the development of the early merchant steamship', in Matthews, Keith and Panting, Gerald (eds), *Ships and Shipbuilding in the North Atlantic Region*, St John's, Newfoundland, 1977.

Palmer, Sarah, 'The most indefatigable activity – The General Steam Navigation Company 1824–1850', *Journal of Transport History*, 3rd ser., III, 1982.

Palmer, Sarah, 'The British shipping industry 1850–1914', in Fischer, Lewis R. and Panting, Gerald E. (eds), *Change and Adaptation in Maritime History: the North Atlantic Fleets in the Nineteenth Century*, St John's, Newfoundland, 1984.

Palmer, Sarah, 'John Long: a London shipowner', *Mariner's Mirror*, LXXII, 1986.

Partridge, M. S., 'The Russell cabinet and national defence, 1846–1852', *History*, LXXII, 1987.

Pollard, Sydney and Robertson, Paul, *The British Shipbuilding Industry 1870–1914*, Cambridge, Mass., 1979.

Potter, J., 'The British timber duties, 1815–1860', *Economica*, new ser., XXIII.

Press, Jon, 'Wages in the mercantile marine 1815–1854', *Journal of Transport History*, 3rd ser., II, 1981.

Prest, John, *Lord John Russell*, London, 1972.

Prouty, Roger, *The Transformation of the Board of Trade 1830–1855: a Study of Administrative Reorganisation in the Heyday of Laissez Faire*, London, 1957.

Redford, A., *Manchester Merchants and Foreign Trade*, 2 vols, Manchester, 1934–56.

Reed, Donald, *Cobden and Bright: a Victorian Political Partnership*, London, 1967.

Rowe, D. J., 'A trade union of the north east coast seamen in 1825', *Economic History Review*, 2nd ser., XXV, 1972.

Rowland, K. T., *Steam at Sea : A History of Steam Navigation*, Newton Abbott, 1970.

Rubinstein, W. D., 'British millionaires – 1809–1949', *Bulletin of the Institute of Historical Research*, XLVII, 1974.

Rubinstein, W. D., *Men of Property: the Very Wealthy in Britain Since the Industrial Revolution*, London, 1981.

Sager, Eric W. and Panting, G., 'Staple economies and the rise and decline of the shipping industry in Atlantic Canada, 1820–1914', in Fischer, Lewis R. and Panting, Gerald E. (eds), *Change and Adaptation in Maritime History: the North Atlantic Fleets in the Nineteenth Century*, St John's, Newfoundland, 1984.

Sayer, Arthur D., Rostow, W. W. and Schwartz, Anna Jacobson, *The Growth and Fluctuation of the British Economy 1790–1850*, 2 vols, Oxford, 1953.

Semmel, Bernard, *The Rise of Free Trade Imperialism 1750–1850*, Cambridge, 1970.

Schuyler, Robert Livingstone, *The Fall of the Old Colonial System: a Study in British Free Trade 1770–1870*, Oxford, 1945.

Shannon, Richard, *Gladstone: I 1809–1865*, London, 1982.

Slaven, A., 'The shipbuilding industry', in Church, Roy (ed.), *The Dynamics of Victorian Business: Problems and Perspectives to the 1870s*, London, 1980.

Slaven, A., 'Shipbuilding', in Langton, John and Morris, R. J. (eds), *Atlas of Industrialising Britain 1780–1914*, London, 1986.

Smart, William, *Economic Annals of the Nineteenth Century*, London, 1910–17.

Southgate, Donald, *The Passing of the Whigs 1832–1836*, London, 1962.

Stewart, Robert, *The Politics of Protection: Lord Derby and the Protectionist Party 1841–1852*, Cambridge, 1971,

Taylor, R., 'Manning the Royal Navy: the reform of the recruiting system, 1852–1862: first part', *Mariner's Mirror*, XLIV, 1958; 'second part', XLV, 1959.

Thomas, E. G., 'The Old Poor Law and maritime apprenticeship', *Mariner's Mirror*, LXIII, 1977.

Thomas, J. A., *The House of Commons 1832–1901: a Study of its Economic and Functional Character*, Cardiff, 1939.

Vanags, A. H., 'Flag discrimination: an economic analysis', *Maritime Studies and Management*, 1983.

Ville, Simon P., 'Total factor productivity in the English shipping industry: the north east coal trade, 1700–1850', *Economic History Review*, 2nd ser., XXXIX, 1986.

Ville, Simon P., *English Shipowning during the Industrial Revolution, Michael Henley and Son, London Shipowners 1770–1830*, Manchester, 1987.

Ville, Simon P., 'Rise to pre-eminence: the development and growth of the Sunderland shipbuilding industry, 1800–50', *International Journal of Maritime History*, I, 1989.

Vincent, J. R., *Poll Books: How the Victorians Voted*, Cambridge, 1968.

Ward, J. T., 'Derby and Disraeli', in Southgate, Donald (ed.), *The Conservative Leadership 1832–1932*, London, 1974.

Williams, David M., 'Customs evasion, colonial preference and the British tariff 1829–42', in Cottrell, P. L. and Aldcroft, D. H. (eds), *Shipping, Trade and Commerce, Essays in Memory of Ralph Davis*, Leicester, 1981.

Williams, David M., 'The rise of United States merchant shipping on the North Atlantic, 1800–1850: the British perception and response', in Reynolds, Clark G. (ed.), *Global Crossroads and the American Seas*, Missoula, Mont., 1988.

Wright, H. R. C., *Free Trade and Protection in the Netherlands 1816–1830: a Study of the First Benelux*, Cambridge, 1955.

Unpublished secondary sources

House of Lords Record Office, B. J. Enright, 'Public Petitions in the House of Commons', unpublished typescript, 1960.

Jones, Stephanie, 'A Maritime History of the Port of Whitby 1700–1914', unpublished Ph.D. thesis, University of London, 1982.

Palmer, Sarah Rosalind, 'The Character and Organisation of the Shipping Industry of the Port of London, 1815–1849', unpublished Ph.D. thesis, University of London, 1979.

Index